Differentiation and diversity
in the primary school

Differentiation and diversity in the primary school

Edited by Eve Bearne

London and New York

First published 1996
by Routledge
11 New Fetter Lane, London EC4P 4EE

Simultaneously published in the USA and Canada
by Routledge
29 West 35th Street, New York, NY 10001

Selections and editorial matter © 1996 Eve Bearne;
individual chapters © their writers

Typeset in Palatino by
Florencetype Ltd, Stoodleigh, Devon

Printed and bound in Great Britain by
Biddles Ltd, Guildford and King's Lynn

British Library Cataloguing in Publication Data
A catalogue record for this book is available from the
British Library

Library of Congress Cataloguing in Publication Data
A catalogue record for this book has been requested

ISBN 0–415–13198–7

Contents

Contributors

Eve Bearne has taught English, drama and education in schools and colleges for thirty years. She was a project officer for the National Writing Project and editor of a number of their publications. She is co-editor of a series of books about children's literature and has written and edited several books about language and literacy. She is a part-time senior lecturer at Homerton College, Cambridge and spends the rest of her time writing and researching in education.

Avril Dawson has experience of working with the whole age-range, from nursery to adult education. At the moment she is a special needs teacher in a middle school in Suffolk working individually with children who have statements of special education needs and in classrooms supporting children across a range of subjects. Recent work has concentrated on children's development of their perception of themselves through storytelling and writing.

Christine Doddington is Director of Primary Postgraduate Studies at Homerton College, Cambridge. She is a senior lecturer in education, teaching drama and philosophy of education within the Primary/Postgraduate course. She is a professional tutor for the initial teacher education course. Her current area of interest is the place of the arts in education.

Ian Eyres was a primary class teacher and language specialist for 13 years. His particular areas of interest are drama, writing and bilingualism. He is currently a peripatetic language and curriculum development teacher with Cambridgeshire's Multicultural Education Service.

Peter Fifield qualified as an archaeologist before deciding to train as a teacher. He has worked in comprehensive schools and special education for some years. His work is mainly concerned with the humanities and he is currently developing ways of extending access to the curriculum for children who experience a range of medical, physical and learning difficulties.

Ian Frowe is a lecturer in education at Homerton College, Cambridge. Prior to that he worked in the Wirral.

Noelle Hunt started her teaching career in Papua New Guinea working with primary age children of several nationalities. More recently she has worked in Hertfordshire for the Dacorum Language and Curriculum Support Centre as a peripatetic language support teacher. In addition to teaching she has a shared responsibility for developing resources in the Centre's library.

Ruth Kershner works as a lecturer at Homerton College, Cambridge. She is a professional tutor for primary postgraduate students and contributes to courses in special educational needs and the psychology of education. She previously worked as a child care worker, a Key Stage 1 class teacher and learning support teacher, developing a particular interest in the education of children who experience difficulties with learning.

Frances Lockwood is a Year 2 teacher at a primary school in Stockport. After graduating from Homerton College, Cambridge in 1993 she spent a year as a postgraduate student at Exeter University completing her MA in Engish Literature. As her teaching experience develops, Frances hopes to extend her understanding of the range of 'special needs' brought to the primary classroom, with particular interest in the development of language learning.

Patricia Maude is head of the physical education department at Homerton College, Cambridge. She has taught PE extensively over many years to children, students and teachers and has contributed to conferences on physical education in this country and overseas.

Sheila Miles is a senior lecturer in education and at the time of writing was a key researcher at Homerton College, Cambridge. She is a joint director of an ESRC funded project on teacher professionalism and has written widely in the field of initial teacher education and equity issues.

Katy Pearson teaches in a junior school in Kentish Town, London. She has worked for some years in primary education and is particularly interested in the ways in which young children use information books in the classroom for research and the varying levels of confidence shown by children who have special educational needs when they approach curriculum tasks independently.

Jennifer Reynolds taught in Liverpool and Oxfordshire after qualifying from I. M. Marsh, Liverpool Polytechnic in 1990. She then took a year off to travel in Asia and now teaches in a junior school in Cambridgeshire. She is currently researching children's gendered interests in reading and has developed a database to help young readers select and review books which she hopes will soon be commercially available

Ros Smith has taught science in both primary and secondary schools. At present she is involved in research with the Open University into gendered discourse in science education. She is particularly interested in how collaborative talk can enhance children's scientific understanding.

Gavin Thompson studied drama at Homerton College, Cambridge, but was also interested in media studies and philosophy. As part of a thesis on literacy he has carried out surveys into children's perceptions of visual texts. He now works in advertising in London.

Tatiana Wilson has been teaching in London for five years. She is currently the humanities postholder at Lark Hall Junior School and Autisic Unit and is a member of the Lambeth Schools Advisory Committee for Religious Education (SACRE) group.

Isobel Urquhart works as a teacher at Homerton College, Cambridge, contributing to courses in language and the psychology of education. She was previously a learning support co-ordinator in a secondary comprehensive school, and subseqently special educational needs projects teacher for Essex LEA.

Alison Wood is a senior lecturer in the mathematics department at Homerton College, Cambridge. She has worked there for many years teaching mathematics both to B. Ed specialist students and to primary postgraduate students who follow a generalist course. Latterly she has been working mainly with students teaching children at Key Stage 2 and has developed a particular interest in the difficulties experienced by teachers in providing suitable work for the most mathematically able pupils between the ages of 7 and 11.

Introduction

While there is currently much emphasis on differentiation in schools, there is no clear consensus about what the term means or implies. It is linked in many teachers' minds with 'mixed ability teaching' but there is nevertheless considerable debate about just what differentiation might look like in the classroom. So – what is differentiation? And how is it done? The term was confirmed in the National Curriculum through the Education Reform Act of 1988 which formally welcomed the idea of differentiation. This Act legislated for every pupil's entitlement to a curriculum which is broad, balanced, relevant and 'subtly' differentiated. Many teachers who for some time had been striving to provide equal opportunities for a range of learners in their classrooms might have been forgiven for thinking that politicians who make decisions about the curriculum had come to understand something of the value and importance of diversity in the experiences, knowledge, languages and cultures which children bring to school. After all, the National Curriculum Council defined differentiation as a process where curriculum objectives, teaching methods, resources and learning activities are planned to cater for the needs of individual pupils (NCC 1991).

All well and good, but what are the assumptions underlying the apparently welcome concept of differentiation as outlined in government documents? And what criteria might be used to make decisions about differentiation in schools? If 'differentiation' means 'seeking to find differences between pupils' then the curriculum will be managed in a way which will make it easy to assess those differences. If, on the other hand, differentiation means looking at classroom approaches to learning and trying to provide access, then the success criteria will include considering the effectiveness of the learning experience and the provision of a varied and flexible environment for learning. It will also include the teacher's capacity to allow for the success of the class as a whole as well as looking at individual achievement. Does differentiation imply an attempt to identify and widen differences between

individual pupils or does it carry with it the notion of welcoming difference while providing equitable access to education for all?

Some clues might be found in the inclusion of 'differentiation' in the
key terms and concepts of one of the early documents sent out to all
teachers. It was defined as:

> Planning of pupils' work to take account of differences in the abili-
> ties, aptitudes and needs of individual pupils. Also used in the context
> of assessment where differentiation by task and outcome are used to
> assess what pupils know, understand and can do.
>
> (NCC 1992: 67)

There were no guidelines about how this might be carried out, however,
and this gap is evident in much of the statutory and non-statutory material which has been produced by the National Curriculum Council and
the School Curriculum and Assessment Authority.

The review of the National Curriculum (1994), otherwise known as
the Dearing Report, confirmed the lack of clarity of the concept, reporting
that:

> many teachers were unclear about how the proposed end of key stage
> statements should be used in art, music and physical education,
> particularly to help differentiate pupils' attainment.
>
> (SCAA 1994: 10)

Where differentiation is used explicitly in the revised National
Curriculum documents it is in relation to 'exceptional performance'. The
use of differentiation in official government documentation seems to be
in terms of assessing individual performance. The OFSTED guidelines
for inspection of schools, however, refer to the need for teachers to
'match' work to pupils' attainments and abilities. The guidelines
note that:

> it is a central part of the inspection process to come to the difficult
> judgement of whether the standards achieved are as high as can
> reasonably be expected, taking into account the capabilities, circum-
> stances and previous attainments of pupils.
>
> (OFSTED 1993: part 4, para 3.1B)

In terms of Department of Education thinking, then, there seems to
be no explicit – or even agreed – definition of differentiation. Where
some parts of the National Curriculum documentation seem to suggest
that teachers should be differentiating *pupils*, other sections – and inspection documentation – seem equally clear that teachers should be
differentiating curriculum *content*. Of course, this is not as confused as
it appears; if you sort the sheep from the goats the implication is,
perhaps, that you also give them a different daily diet and keep them

in different environments; while the pasturage might look similar, there are significant differences in its nutritive content. You also consider one category as more valuable than the other.

So it is perhaps the implications of a requirement for differentiation which need to be examined carefully, particularly in terms of entitlement and access to a full curriculum. That is why the link between differentiation and diversity is critical and why it is the title of this book. Using both terms together captures the sense that while pupils may have differing abilities, aptitudes and interests, the pupils themselves are, nevertheless, of equal value. The book examines some of the critical issues related to the complex matter of differentiation. It is not geared towards a how-to-do-it view of differentiation, although it is rich in examples of how teachers have managed to provide for diversity in offering a differentiated approach to learning. A variety of perspectives is reflected in the different chapters; the book itself is diverse in the kinds of views represented and in the ways in which the contributors write about either principles of diversity or practices for differentiation. There are no easy answers here, rather a textured set of contributions towards an important area of educational debate. This is a book which can be approached in different ways. The five parts are arranged to cover some general areas of the debate surrounding differentiation; within each part there are reflective overviews as well as accounts of classroom practice and the final part offers a framework for review of school and classroom practice.

Any attempt to unpick the notion of differentiation immediately stumbles into a set of contradictions and tensions. The general areas for debate seem to settle round issues of equal opportunities and access and the related concerns of holding a view of provision for individual learning which can be articulated within wider curriculum considerations. Accompanying these areas of debate are the tricky matters of achievement and ability. There would be no disagreement amongst those concerned with education about providing a curriculum and learning environment which will encourage the most satisfying achievements for all pupils. Nor would there be any significant dispute about the usefulness of monitoring progress. The ways in which monitoring may be carried out, however, is an area for some debate. That it is possible to achieve fully informative monitoring through differentiated assessments (like the restricted access of Key Stage 3 test papers) seems ludicrous, yet the practice is all too real and damaging. Expediency and 'cost-effectiveness' seem to have tinged the debate about how best to describe and assess progress in learning.

The whole area of assessing progression and describing 'ability' deserves a hard critical examination in the context of what differentiation seems to mean for some and what it might come to mean. Issues of principle are matched by equally pressing matters of school and class-room management. Professionalism becomes an issue when teachers are faced with tensions between preparing their pupils for assessments which are predicated on partial and divisive methods and their embedded desire to promote the learning of all pupils as effectively as possible. A critical approach to the whole area of differentiation and an explicit link with principles of welcoming and working with diversity might help resolve some of the tensions both in principle and in practice. There is certainly room for discussion and debate in order to clarify some of the key issues. Part I, 'Definitions and scope of differentiation', opens up the debate and leads into an account of research which deliberately sets out to capture the voices of teachers as they outline and reflect on the assumptions they hold about what differentiation means and implies. It then goes on to consider the principles underpinning decisions made about a curriculum for diversity.

In general, recognised sites for differentiation are seen in terms of the management of learning: by input, task, content, resources, grouping, support, response and outcome. This book does not simply attach chapters to areas like these but addresses some of the underlying issues, for example just what teachers might mean when they identify learners as 'struggling', 'special needs children' or 'high fliers'. Any analysis of the implications of differentiation uncovers some complex – and even muddled – assumptions about the notion of ability. These assumptions are represented by some of the easy, everyday vocabularies of education, describing children in general terms as 'less able' or 'more able'. Such descriptions may mask other kinds of judgements, but one of the most commonly held views about ability seems to be that literacy (or sometimes numeracy) is equated with general learning ability. While it is true that any pupil's confidence or insecurity with literacy is bound to have an impact on learning and equally true that literacy is undoubtedly of critical importance, it is essential to be clear about what is intended by any description of ability. It is also important to attempt to disentangle the strands of assumptions which lead to classroom practices which hamper the intellectual development of children who are perfectly capable of complex concept formation, but who lack fluency or experience in literacy. Part II, 'Differentiation and literacy', looks in detail at some of the issues related to definitions of literacy ability and pushes the debate further by considering a wider view of literacy and what this might offer to a curriculum geared towards diversity.

Many of the contributors to this book point out that too ready an acceptance of blanket definitions of ability can result in restrictive and exclusive practices. Exclusion through differentiation seems to have been tackled most thoroughly by those who are involved in education for children who are defined as having special educational needs. Analysis and critique on the exclusive potential of certain conceptions of differentiation owes much to the work done by educators in this field. (e.g. Ainscow; Booth *et al.*) This book, however, is intended to consider differentiation within mainstream education – specifically in the primary school. Recent OFSTED reports have given attention to the importance of challenging pupils who are already achieving well, particularly at Key Stage 2 and the introduction to Part III 'The range of learners', addresses the debate about 'high achievers', opening up discussions about what might constitute 'the range'. It is easy to concentrate on those children whose learning needs most obviously claim our attention as teachers and to neglect others. Many of the chapters in this book deal with the complexities of providing for – and extending the learning of – the whole range of learners and this part examines the factors involved in providing a curriculum and classroom experiences for inclusion rather than exclusion. It tackles some of the tricky matters of classroom organisation and examines the cultural implications involved in catering for diversity.

Management of the curriculum is a central area for considering differentiation; at the same time, differentiation is very much a classroom issue. Several chapters in the book examine the principles which might feed whole-school decisions, while others describe management arrangements for making classrooms hospitable to diversity. Part IV 'Issues of assessment', traces the whole process of planning for and assessing learning to take account of diversity. Part V takes this further by offering a framework for 'Constructing a policy for differentiation' – a model for establishing or reviewing whole-school policy and practice for differentiation and diversity. It explores four key questions: How do we identify the needs of a diverse range of learners? How do we provide differentiated contexts for learning? How do we provide differentiated approaches to learning? How do we assess differentiated learning? Readers who are looking for practicality and suggestions for monitoring the operation of differentiation might want to start with this final section before reading about some of the more critical issues.

One of the threads running throughout this book is the assumption that diversity and difference are welcome in classrooms. Another related thread is the view that a curriculum which addresses equal opportunities and entitlement is necessarily one which allows for differentiation in provision for a range of learners. Rather than seeing differentiation as a means of grading pupils, different chapters propose the view that this is necessarily restrictive and more likely to lead to depressed attainment than improvement in standards. Managing a differentiated curriculum is seen as the positive means of promoting the progress of all learners. Each chapter represents a strand in the complex weave of arguments about diversity and differentiation, describing and analysing a range of ways designed to ensure entitlement to as full a curriculum as possible for the full range of pupils. The curriculum has to satisfy two requirements which can create tensions – it has to reflect those broad educational aims which are good for all children, whatever their capabilities, whilst allowing for differences in the abilities, aptitudes and needs of those children. The contributors to this book hope to enlarge the debate about how best to cope with these competing demands. Since diversity is a central concern, the chapters themselves represent a diversity of approach. The book not only reflects different subject areas, age groups of children, types of school and points of view, but also provides a balance between analysis and reflective description of classroom practice. Some of the material outlines approaches which teachers have developed to respond to the demands of their pupils' diversity and which attempt to provide for different but equal access to the curriculum whilst meeting government requirements. Other contributions deal with wider, less classroom-focused issues. The variation in approach is intended to signal that this is an attempt to put into practice for readers some of the points made in the chapters themselves. If in classrooms we need to cater for a range of ways in to learning, then as far as possible a book about diversity ought to offer similar variety. Although the chapters represent different perspectives, however, all offer thoughtful approaches to the whole matter of how best to provide for mixed ability and differentiation in schools.

One of the teachers who was interviewed in the research for Chapter 1, commented: 'we seem to be looking for a global definition of differentiation; I don't think we can have one.' Neither do we. While offering no hard and fast definition of terms, the contributors to this book hope that the varying chapters will reflect their principles of inclusion and difference and offer readers diverse opportunities to think critically about differentiation.

REFERENCES

Ainscow, M. (1990) 'Responding to Individual Needs', *British Journal of Special Education* ,17, 2 : 74–77

Booth, T., Swann, W., Masterton, M. and Potts, P. (1992) *Curricula for Diversity in Education* and *Policies for Diversity in Education*, London, Routledge

School Curriculum and Assessment Authority (1994) *The Review of the National Curriculum*, London, SCAA

National Curriculum Council (1991) *Science and Pupils with Special Educational Needs*, York, NCC

National Curriculum Council (1992) *Starting out with the National Curriculum*, York, NCC

Department for Education Office for Standards in Education (1993) *Handbook for the Inspection of Schools London*, London, HMSO

Part I

Definitions and scope of differentiation

Introduction to Part I

Some of the most egregious sins against equity of access are committed in the name of providing for individual differences.

(Coombs 1994: 3)

The jargon smooths over the messiness of real classroom life.

(Thomas 1993: 14)

These two comments suggest the complexity of attempting to get to grips with the implications of differentiation – let alone trying to define the term. In taking a critical view, the oppositions and tensions surrounding differentiation become even more tricky. While for some the emphasis is on the difficulties of supporting individual learning needs, for others the constraints are most obvious when trying to make ideals into everyday classroom reality. There seem to be tensions between attempts to provide both for individual and communal educational entitlements. There are also obvious dangers in trying to pin down a necessarily complex and unstable concept with a few slick words. Trying to find a definition for differentiation runs the risk of either being so general as to be meaningless, or sacrificing detail and richness for the sake of a smart answer.

This section will try to avoid both of these pitfalls by first of all suggesting in this introduction a range of characteristics which might be included in a description of what differentiation involves and implies. The first chapter examines how teachers describe what they would include as elements of differentiation. Finally, these observations are related to the values and principles which might underpin views of differentiation. In this way the contributors hope to offer detail, precision and clarity without sacrificing complexity.

Opinions and definitions of differentiation vary considerably in emphasis, but one recurrent feature identified by commentators is a contrast in viewpoint between those who highlight differentiation between groups and those who focus on differentiation between individuals (Stradling and Saunders 1991). Crudely put, this might be seen as a distinction between a sorting exercise where all the 'high fliers' or 'low attainers' are put into (apparently) homogeneous groups, or a view which attempts to diagnose individual strengths – or more likely weaknesses – in order to provide for progression. Each of these perspectives tends towards seeing the *learner* as pivotal, rather than looking at the curriculum. This emphasis on the pupil as a central focus for differentiation has led on the one hand towards ways of encouraging greater pupil participation in learning (group work and collaboration between pupils of like abilities) and the evaluation of learning (setting targets for learning), and on the other hand towards a formulation which all too easily topples into a deficit view of the pupil. Either of these views of differentiation can lead to labelling the individual as 'failing' rather than identifying gaps in curriculum planning or the organisation of work as contributory factors to low attainment. A related feature of both views is that they almost inevitably veer towards looking at failure and low attainment rather than opportunities for satisfaction and success in learning.

There are grounds for criticism of too inflexible an approach to 'ability' grouping. While acknowledging, of course, that grouping pupils is a perfectly acceptable classroom practice to promote learning, it is important to recognise that even if learners can be grouped according to common qualities, they are nevertheless not likely to form genuinely homogeneous groups. As outlined in the Introduction, it is by no means a simple matter to group according to 'ability'. Such groupings beg the question: 'ability in what?' Every teacher is aware that pupils who show a high level of confidence and competence in one area of the curriculum may well experience difficulties in another area. Also, while some pupils do indeed fail in their schooling, a view of differentiation which focuses mainly on individual performance can lead to an exclusive approach to teaching and learning. Rather than open up opportunities, it can close them down. It is all too easy to blame the learner than to look critically at the arrangements for learning.

In order to redress the balance there needs to be some coherent view of the curriculum and the learning environment in relation to the diversity of what each individual brings to the classroom. If education is to be inclusive rather than exclusive, 'pupils and teachers will need a wide range of strategies and flexibility of timing and approach if they are to achieve the common goals set out in the National Curriculum targets' (Weston 1992). Recognition of diversity will also allow both teachers and pupils to go beyond those common targets!

Differentiation which genuinely allows for diversity of learning style or approach may need to take the following factors into account:

- variations in fluency of English, which may not be the first language;
- those who read visual, iconic or numerical material more readily than verbal texts;
- gender differences;
- physical differences;
- those who learn better by ear than by eye;
- those who learn through practical experience;
- the range of previous experiences brought to the classroom;

as well as the fact that any learner might use a range of approaches to learning according to the task, the context, the time of day, the learner's perceived needs, etc. This implies the need to plan for a variety of ways in to learning, flexibility in grouping arrangements as well as a clear idea of how, when, why and by whom learning is going to be evaluated and assessed. In other words, differentiation needs to be perceived in terms of entitlement to as full and flexible a curriculum as possible and to be thought of in terms of how the curriculum might cater for and build on diversity.

Teachers themselves can provide a fruitful resource for examining just how this might be achieved. Chapter 1 'Thinking and talking about differentiation', begins by identifying the ways in which teachers perceive and reflect on what they do about differentiation – and what they see as workable classroom approaches. As their comments reveal, the external demands made by the National Curriculum and OFSTED are not necessarily in conflict with most teachers' everyday practice. In the same way that pupils do not represent homogenous groups of thinkers, neither do teachers, and it is as well to take this into account when examining their views of the scope and implications of differentiation. Added to the personal and diverse experiences which teachers represent, is the fact that sometimes professional ways of speaking can obscure rather than clarify ideas. Ruth Kershner and Sheila Miles used an inventive method for probing just what might lie behind and beneath teachers' descriptions of what differentiation meant to them and so were able to examine the 'competing imperatives' which teachers feel themselves subject to.

In many of the discussions about differentiation, teachers appeared to be using an organising principle based on their perceptions of the differences between activities and subject areas, as well as their perceptions of the differences between children. One headteacher aptly summarised the position, identifying differentiation as a slippery concept: 'you try and grasp it and suddenly it shoots out of your hand.' In opening up the area for debate, the writers of Chapter 1 point out:

What appears to be most significant is the variation of ways in which teachers understand the meaning of differentiation, and the breadth and depth with which they employ it.

They go on to stress the importance of finding out what teachers think in order to 'engage with them and develop ideas together'. This chimes well with one of the central elements of the book as a whole: theoretical issues about the curriculum relate to methods of teaching and learning and about management and policy as they are reflected through descriptions of teachers' and pupils' personal and classroom experience.

Chapter 2 'Grounds for differentiation', picks up the theme of 'competing imperatives' by considering some of the values and principles of the primary curriculum and their relationships to the development of both personal and communal knowledge. This chapter examines, first, the notion that differentiation for development of knowledge involves at one and the same time a view of the individual as a learner and a theory of 'common structures of content' within the curriculum on offer. It is not just a matter of providing an appropriate curriculum in terms of content, however, since views of what is seen as 'publicly agreed knowledge' can be characterised in different ways and give rise to differing practices according to the values and priorities of those who define the curriculum and its content.

In arguing for a flexible view of the curriculum, Christine Doddington points out that 'the urge to reduce human understanding to the "fixed" and "agreed" is strong within educational debate.' Rather than settling for a definition of differentiation which favours either an individual formulation or a sense of the implications of commonly agreed knowledge, she relates these to classroom practice. Careful analysis of just what a curriculum for diversity implies and involves leads to precise location of these ideas in a classroom example which shows that 'thinking and genuine understanding can only occur through active engagement and processes of interpretation'. The chapter, and Part I, ends with the suggestion that 'differentiation might help set out a description of classroom activity which illustrates how a teacher values both communal and personal knowledge'. This goes some way towards meeting the competing demands implied by the need to provide an accessible curriculum for a diversity of learners. It also enlarges the scope of possible definitions of what differentiation might involve.

REFERENCES

Coombs, J. R. (1994) 'Equal Access to Education', *Journal of Curriculum Studies*, 26, 3 (May/June)
Stradling, R. and Saunders, L. with Weston, P. (1991) *Differentiation in Action:*

A whole school approach for raising attainment, London, HMSO

Thomas, G. (1993) 'Good Behaviour' a review in *The Times Educational Supplement*, 11 June

Weston, P. (1992) 'A Decade for Differentiation', *British Journal of Special Education*, 19, 1 (March)

Chapter 1

Thinking and talking about differentiation

'It's like a bar of soap . . . you try and grasp it and suddenly it shoots out of your hand'

Ruth Kershner and Sheila Miles

A deputy headteacher of a primary school is discussing the staff's recently written policy on differentiation:

> . . . we do now have the statement [on differentiation] which will need to be reviewed. I don't believe things are finished just because it's now on a piece of paper. . . . I think during the next year we will need to plan a staff meeting where we discuss how we've moved forward and how we feel about it now.

Interviewer: Can you think of any resistances in the school or difficulties which might occur?

> I don't think so . . . our staff are much too caring for that . . . they all see it as very important . . . there really wasn't a great deal of dissent when we were discussing it. The only slight concern from a management point of view is whether some of the staff have really fully understood what we were talking about. I don't think there would be resistance, but clarity of understanding may be the problem. I think you have to differentiate with the teachers too.

This conversation illustrates some of the complex issues associated with differentiation in primary schools. The deputy headteacher suggests that a school policy on differentiation needs as much thought and discussion after the writing of it as before. She implies that teachers who care about children are likely to want to differentiate effectively. Yet problems may arise when individual teachers construe the meaning of differentiation in their own terms. As she hints above, there may not be a common understanding within a staff team; teachers, like the pupils in their classes, respond in many different ways, and good school management will have to take account of these differences in trying to establish a common set of principles and practices.

This chapter is concerned not only with what teachers think about differentiation in the current educational climate, but also with how to find out about their knowledge, beliefs and feelings. We recently explored this topic in interviews with teachers and headteachers in three primary schools. Unsurprisingly, this research confirmed that teachers have their individual views about the policy and practice of differentiation and that they express their ideas in diverse ways. Before reporting some of our findings and considering the significance of what individual teachers said to us, we will discuss in more general terms why it is important to take account of what teachers think about their roles in relation both to educational policies and to the children to whom the policies apply.

It has been a feature of recent years that teachers have been faced with numerous changes in educational policy, not least the continuing development of the National Curriculum since the late 1980s. Fullan (1982) points out that we need to understand the 'meaning of change' for all the people involved if policy developments at any level are not to fail. This understanding of the significance of teachers' thinking has informed recent debates about how to help teachers to implement the educational changes that have been imposed throughout the last two decades in Britain. For example, in their discussion of the impact on teachers' practice and thinking of recent changes in policy for children with special educational needs, Brown and Riddell (1994: 222) observe that

> the preaching of well-meaning policy-makers or educational theorists is unlikely to bring about change in teachers' thinking unless it takes as its *starting* point the ways in which teachers already perceive and think about what they do . . . and what they see as practical in their own classrooms.

Initiatives in in-service training, staff development and support systems for teachers have shown that there are a number of ways to tap into teachers' professional knowledge and expertise, using carefully planned methods of collaboration and consultation in relation to actual, current experience in school (Upton 1991). These initiatives assume that it matters what teachers think, and that it is important to find ways to draw on teachers' understanding and experience in order to implement educational changes effectively.

As becomes clear in the chapter, the external demands on schools regarding differentiation are not .fundamentally opposed to most teachers' current practice, but there are significant differences in the way that individual teachers interpret their day-to-day responsibilities in this area. Teachers' views and opinions can sometimes be taken for granted as representative of a 'group mind'. However, teachers are not all the same; they have different levels of knowledge and experience, and they work in different settings. Like everyone else, they have personal and individual ways of thinking about children and education, and they have their private language and images as well as the more public and shared communications that are developed in the informal and formal dialogues of training, teamwork and appraisal in schools.

Teachers' private thoughts and feelings are particularly salient in their work with individual children and their families which can sometimes be frustrating and troubling (Greenhalgh 1994). Anyone familiar with primary classrooms will know that individual children can make their needs and feelings evident in many ways. It can be demanding and stressful for teachers to attempt to respond to the immediate concerns of all of their pupils in an open-minded, flexible and fair way. As Pollard (1987) discusses, both teachers and pupils have to develop coping strategies in the classroom setting, and the final 'working consensus' may unexpectedly serve to crystallize classroom processes and expectations in a way that limits the opportunities for certain pupils to learn.

In any discussion of differentiation it is important to remember that children are sensitive to the implications of teachers' actions in the classroom, and a high proportion of children respond to their perceptions of what the teacher seems to expect of them. There has been a long tradition of research into 'teacher expectations' about children and the concept of the 'self-fulfilling prophecy', much of which has seemed to confirm the view that teachers' views about children are highly significant and influential on the children's learning (Dusek 1985). Many researchers have focused on mediating factors like classroom communication, organisation and curriculum planning, and some, like Pollard above, have paid particular attention to children's active involvement in the social processes through which teachers' views may have their effect on pupils' behaviour and attainments in school. The process of expectancy is not simple, however, not least because peers, families and social influences beyond the classroom have their effects on children, as do the children's own beliefs about why they are successful or not (Rogers 1992). There are also, of course, differences between teachers in what they expect of children, and Brophy (1991: 357) comments that reviews of the research indicate that

> self-fulfilling prophecy effects of teachers' expectations are minor or non-existent in most teachers' classrooms, but play a significant role in the classrooms of the minority of teachers whose expectations are both inaccurate and rigidly held, and who thus do a poor job of meeting the needs of many of their students.

This distinction may be particularly important in relation to teachers who hold strongly to the view that the causes of children's lack of progress tend to lie 'within the child' (e.g. 'low intelligence', 'lack of effort' or 'problems at home') rather than in school factors and processes, and there has indeed been evidence in recent years that many teachers

who are faced with the challenge of teaching children with learning difficulties will tend to identify the cause of the problem in that way (e.g.
Croll and Moses 1985; Weedon 1994).

Teachers' professional decisions are likely to be influenced not only
by their perceptions of educational policies and of the children in their
classes, but also by other beliefs about what 'good practice' involves.
Alexander (1992: 186) discusses the 'competing imperatives' that must
be reconciled in teaching. There are matters of values, of political
expediency, of knowledge, understanding and perceived practicality. All
of these must be balanced by professional judgement, although as
Alexander notes, teachers may believe as a matter of principle that some
considerations should take precedence over others.

The preceding discussion suggests that teachers' reasons for imple-
menting a policy of differentiation may relate not only to imperatives
like 'ought to', 'have to' or 'want to', but also to the knowledge that
they 'already do' differentiate in some way between pupils. This is an
inevitable human response as well as a matter of professional judgement. Questions remain about how individual teachers understand
differentiation, and how they respond in practice to the perceived challenges of this aspect of teaching.

PERCEPTIONS OF DIFFERENTIATION

The term 'differentiation' can have many layers of meaning for different
people, and it is currently underpinned for many teachers by the frustration and occasional cynicism often associated with terms that are in
vogue. It is not easy to make any one meaning explicit in a way that
indicates its central role in teaching and also succeeds in separating it
from other aspects of teaching. As one headteacher said to us:

> I think that's one of the problems with jargon and with the profes-
> sion as a whole. . . . We seem to be looking for a global definition of
> differentiation. I don't think we can have one. I think it's a term that,
> I suppose like a bar of soap really, you try and grasp it and suddenly
> it shoots out of your hand.

In her editorial introduction to the 1992 *British Journal of Special
Education* special issue on the topic of differentiation, Margaret Peter
says that the shared assumption of the range of contributors to the issue
is that 'differentiation is about meeting every child's learning needs so
that each can share in the same curriculum, usually in the same schools'
(Peter 1992). She goes on to point out that there can, however, be
different principles and values underlying the promotion of differentiation as a worthwhile aim in education. For some, the ideology of equal
opportunities takes precedence, while others may be more concerned

with the incorporation of differentiation into the repertoire of professional teaching skills and 'good practice' in education. Some people may see differentiation as a cost-effective means of avoiding 'wastage' of pupils' talents, while others may focus entirely on pragmatic political expediency in carrying out a policy that has been imposed on teachers and schools by the National Curriculum and OFSTED (see Editor's introduction). Teachers, of course, may find competing views of this type between colleagues in their staff team, and even within their own individual, multi-faceted sets of beliefs about the meaning of differentiation in the current educational context.

THE RESEARCH

At the time of our research study, January 1995, the primary teachers we interviewed had barely had time to absorb the changes, the new slimmed-down version of the National Curriculum Orders having just landed in their post-boxes after the Christmas break. We decided that this would be a good time to find out how teachers describe differentiation and the part it plays in their professional decision making. We were interested to explore teachers' understandings about it, to tap their 'knowledge-base' to find out whether they were able to make explicit the foundations of their professional practice. One way of doing this would be to analyse the language used and the images they construct when discussing differentiation.

Research was conducted in three large primary schools. One is a school in Cambridgeshire fed by a 1960s housing estate built as a London overspill. It is an area of high unemployment and the headteacher described it as having one of the highest crime rates in the county. The second school is a primary school in inner-city London with a large ethnic minority population. Again, it is an area of high unemployment with very few amenities. The third school is in a New Town which has recently experienced increased unemployment. The closure of many of the large firms was having a 'knock-on' effect on small businesses. This school and the Cambridgeshire school had both recently carried out staff development work on the topic of differentiation.

The research was prompted by the responses of the postgraduate student teachers we work with who were trying to apply the concept of differentiation in their school placements. Differentiation appeared to mean so many different things to them. There were at one extreme the rather bland statements in official documentation (see Editor's introduction) and at the other, the lengthy debates in the special needs literature (e.g. Hart 1992). In the Autumn term of 1994, primary postgraduate students were asked to produce diagrammatic and written descriptions to show some of their responses to the concept of differentiation that they had been discussing in school and college. We selected ten different examples which exemplified a range of understanding about differentiation. These were then made into a set of illustrative cards which were used in the interviews as a device to extend and probe teachers' own understandings of the term.[1] The cards were used early in the interviews by asking the teachers and headteachers to identify any of the ten cards that interested them for any reason – perhaps because they found that the image resembled their own ideas, or because it surprised, puzzled or even annoyed them. They were then invited to talk about their selections.

We interviewed four teachers in each school trying to get a balance of the following characteristics: length of experience, special responsibilities for equal opportunities or special needs, phase of teaching (Key Stages 1 and 2), and membership of senior management including headteachers. We were interested in a range of issues which we felt would help us to analyse how teachers define and use the concept of differentiation. We explored how they would apply it to different children, whether they felt that factors like depth of subject knowledge improved their ability to differentiate, whether they had received any in-service training on this aspect of their work and, at a school level, management decisions and policy provision.[2]

THE FINDINGS

In talking about differentiation, we found that teachers used a wide range of definitions which primarily focused on individualised teaching. More importantly, however, many also stressed the pedagogical implications of teaching style (including using a variety and multiplicity of styles), as well as certain pastoral and socio-cultural aspects that needed to be addressed. Defining the word and operationalising it was something new, although the actual practices were old, something which was part of experienced teachers' professional expertise and craft knowledge. One teacher, when asked whether she saw 'differentiation' as an important part of her teaching, said 'I think I do it unconsciously, until I actually stop and think "why did I do that?". . . I do a lot of things by instinct after so long.'

The use of the cards in the interviews proved to be helpful in developing our discussions about differentiation. They allowed the teachers to respond to their perceptions of other people's ideas. No-one seemed to have any difficulty in understanding the purpose of the card activity and, indeed, many seemed to find it intriguing. The activity supported the value of looking at *how* people think and express their ideas as well as *what* they think. We found individual differences between the teachers in both respects.

When, at the start of the interviews, the teachers were asked to try to put down on paper their own ideas about differentiation in words, pictures or diagrams, it became clear that some were immediately comfortable with either words or diagrams, while others very definitely preferred to talk in that setting. One teacher, after having glanced at some of the cards, was very fluent in producing a diagrammatic view of differentiation, explaining her ideas as she did it. In contrast, a teacher with many years of experience was attracted to Card 10, which includes a number of ideas about differentiation in one 'topic-web'-type diagram, (see p. 27) because she thinks the ideas are 'very honest, very true . . . very clear, with lots of meanings', but she felt that she would not be able to think about them as quickly and get them down on paper. Clearly, differentiation for her is a complex concept, not easily and quickly expressed in simple terms in the context of an interview during the school day. It is only when she has to explain her ideas to students or interviewers, for example, that she makes her thoughts and principles explicit. In contrast to this experienced teacher, students in initial training become used to responding very quickly to the many requests to express their ideas in a range of ways while they are studying intensively. As careers develop, however, there is not as much need to respond at such pace.

PUTTING THE CARDS ON THE TABLE

Examples of the teachers' responses to the different cards are given below, highlighting some of the ways in which teachers think about differentiation. We then go on to discuss some of the issues emerging from the interviews as a whole.

Card 1

This is the most 'pictorial' in depicting a classroom setting, and it was rarely chosen for comment during the interviews. We can only speculate that it is uncontroversial in content and that the image itself may not communicate an underlying principle or belief as immediately as the other nine cards.

Card 2

This was chosen by a number of teachers with a generally positive response, but for different reasons. For example, when asked why she had chosen it, one teacher said

> Well, I suppose I agree with it. Everyone is at a different level and they need activities that they can cope with and yet will lead them

Card 1

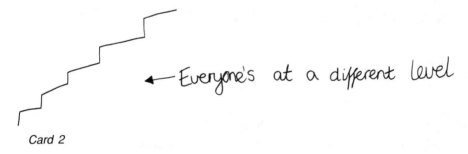

Card 2

onto the next stage. You've got to start from something that a child can do to be able to make any progress and so they feel some sort of satisfaction in being able to accomplish something.

(Experienced teacher; KS1, with responsibility for SEN)

This card also struck a chord with another teacher in the same school, but she was prompted to think about the distinctions between children rather than the process of an individual child's progress up the educational escalator. Sometimes, in the responses, there are several ideas operating at once. Whilst acknowledging that 'everyone's on a different step and they need to be perhaps treated differently', one teacher went on to recognise that as a teacher 'it does help to sort them, put them in a range of levels' (Experienced teacher; KS2).

Card 3

Card 3

This image was interesting to one teacher because on first impression she found it to be similar to her own ideas about differentiation. She went on to note, however, that there was a significant contrast with the image that she had produced at the start of the interview.

> I think somebody's thought rather well here, because they're saying three groups of children, but there's not a particular hierarchy or order in these groups. They are just three different groups. Which is rather nice, whereas my picture clearly shows some little people and some big people, and a hierarchy if you like.
>
> (Newly qualified teacher; KS1)

This example shows how the different illustrations enabled her to reflect on her own ideas and refine them in the course of the interview.

Card 4

This card had a mixed response from the teachers. One teacher responded directly:

> top, middle and bottom. I think you can generally group as I said. I've got eight in my top group, four in my bottom group and the rest

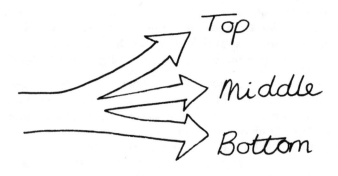

Card 4

are in the middle . . . if you have to put them in a group I could put them in a top, middle and bottom group.

(Recently qualified teacher; KS1)

In contrast, another teacher seemed to be alerted by this image to her concerns about labelling children at an early age. She rejected it because:

it's a bit hard to categorise children or groups, particularly when they're young, as top, middle and bottom. Because even if you do have children in rough ability groups, which I tend to do in my class, there are still children who are good at some things and not so good at other things. And you could in fact mix the groups in different ways, really if you wanted to, even the children who find, say, reading difficult, might be good at maths.

(Experienced teacher; KS1, with responsibility for SEN)

Ultimately there could be little difference between the views and practice of these two teachers, including their awareness of children's individuality. The image, however, evoked differing responses, relating more to day-to-day practice for one teacher, and more to complex issues and longer term strategies for the second, more experienced teacher.

Card 5

This proved interesting in that different teachers found different aspects of the image relevant to them. One experienced teacher (KS2) was

Card 5

prompted to reflect on the degree to which differentiation can be extended to take account of individual children in the primary classroom. She said, 'I know that is relevant but when you've got a wide variety of ability in the class it's a luxury. You just really can't . . . you'd be differentiating yourself to death!'

The same image on Card 5 evoked different thoughts in another experienced teacher with responsibility for SEN. She said it reminded her of a five-year-old child in her class who arrived that year with an attitude of 'Oh, I can't do it'. She told him that he could and the staff gave him a lot of encouragement. He stopped saying it, and 'he's made great strides which has given him a real sense of achievement'. She went on to say 'I think it's very sad if a child does say that, especially when they're only five.'

These two responses to Card 5 highlight the competing demands on teachers in relation to differentiation: to understand and help individual children while finding practical solutions to managing the class as a whole.

Card 6

This card made one teacher think immediately of the range of children's ability in any classroom. She observed, 'I think everyone's got children in their class that write like that. Both ends of the spectrum' (Experienced teacher; KS1).

The same image caught one teacher's eye because of the particular subject matter: 'I was very impressed with doing emergent writing in nursery school, and it's really generated a lot of interest in children's writing. ' On seeing the card she thought

Differentiaton is   --

My nme is Saly sad the dog

The dog came into the room and saw his friend - Hello he said My name is Fred .

Card 6

I'd like to read that one properly ... this shows very clearly two different levels. Somebody who's finding writing quite difficult, but has certainly written something rather nice, and then a child who is actually far more able in writing.

(Newly qualified teacher; KS1)

This second comment suggests that some teachers may respond particularly well to discussion of abstract topics like 'differentiation' when they are set in the context of personal subject interests.

Card 7

This was noticeably the one illustration where the image itself provoked strong feelings. Several teachers rejected it as confusing or difficult to understand. Some, however, quite liked it, as is shown by this comment from one teacher who had himself produced quite a similar version at the start of his interview:

That one looks to me like a busy and interactive classroom with a whole range of activities and obviously some highlighting going on here and some specific interactions. I feel that these bold arrows show some very definite tasks going on and these smaller minor ones may be some spark off points which take us on from there ... and these little wavy lines are the richness and the contextual work that's coming out of that.

(Deputy headteacher; KS2)

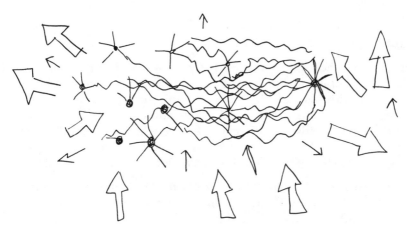

Card 7

Card 8

Card 8 received some simple affirmations from teachers who recognised their own planning strategies in the image given. Others elaborated on the meaning of the image:

> although you might be able to set work like that there might be times when there might be interaction between one and two, and two and three, for various other reasons, for behavioural reasons. A child might be put with group one if that group's the top group (for) peer tutoring and leading by good example.
>
> (Experienced teacher; KS1, co-ordinator
for PSHE and behaviour)

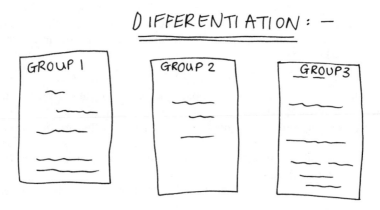

Card 8

Card 9

One headteacher linked this with Cards 4 and 8 under the general heading of 'differentiation by task', one of the terms that he had recently discussed with his staff. He discussed this strategy in general, rather critical terms, pointing out that that this approach may lead to an attitude of 'we will only set different tasks. We will not extend them in any other way ... .We will simply set worksheets or tasks that they can complete.' He sees this as too limited a view of differentiation:

> I would never condemn it outright. I use it, or the members of staff use it and it has to be done, But I don't think it's the only way in which differentiation can and should be used.

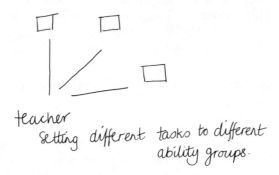

teacher
Setting different tasks to different
ability groups.

Card 9

Card 10

This card was welcomed by a number of people since it offered a number of different ideas about differentiation, expressed in an accessible way. One headteacher said 'it implies that differentiation is not one thing and can go off in different ways, and that's what interests me.'

As noted earlier, this image is one that a number of the teachers aspired to if they had the time:

> I think if I had to write something down, it's probably number 10. If I was asked, given a few minutes, that looks like the sort of thing I desperately try and write down to cover everything.
>
> (Experienced teacher ; KS1)

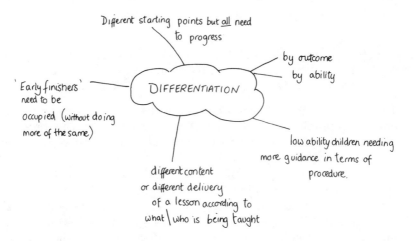

Card 10

As the teachers' responses to all ten cards indicate, the concept of differentiation includes a number of distinct ideas which can link with specific aspects of practice. It also comprises a complex and multi-layered set of principles, which underpin a number of significant issues.

ISSUES EMERGING FROM THE INTERVIEWS

Becoming aware of the term

The teachers we interviewed found it difficult to determine at which point of their professional lives the concept of differentiation actually became inscribed in their consciousness. Several experienced teachers (some teaching for as long as thirty years) said to us that the concept was not new. It was, rather, something which was part of their professional repertoire, and which suddenly had a special term to describe it. As one teacher with responsibility for special needs (who had been teaching in London schools) said, 'My understanding of differentiation is planning for mixed ability. Meeting each child's individual needs. Which in fact I've always done and then, before it became a buzz word.' She gave an example of how a friend of hers who had recently been interviewed in a secondary school for a job was told when discussing differentiation, 'Primary teachers do it all the time. It's just that secondary teachers have just caught on to it.'

Changing usage of the term

As noted above, the familiarity and usage of the term has changed over time. In one school, teachers had only recently become more comfortable with talking about 'differentiation'. One described the staff's earlier feelings:

> I must admit we got a bit hot under the collar about that sort of thing. What is this word? Where is the definition of it?. . . We felt uncomfortable with it because no-one came up with a finite definition.

The reason for the change in attitude had been the focus on differentiation for appraisal as part of an OFSTED inspection. This process had helped the staff to come to a common understanding of the meaning and the associated expectations.

One deputy headteacher (KS2) also found it difficult to locate the exact period when differentiation became a significant concept for her: 'it's something I found I was doing and when I did start talking about differentiation, it's something that was going on in the classroom already.' Nevertheless, when she defined the concept, she did so with complete clarity, producing a complex definition which brought out the importance of factors like the appropriateness of task for children of different abilities; the availability of a range of approaches and teaching strategies to match children's needs; the use of differential teacher input to pupils; and the value of including a range of different activities and outcomes:

> My view of differentiation is to make sure that the work you're doing in the classroom is appropriate to every child in the classroom and if necessary you have to give them a slightly different task, or a very different task, or a similar task but with extra support. I think it's making a task different. It's also making your approach to make sure that you don't always teach in a classroom in exactly the same way. And by doing this everybody has a chance to access at least some of what you are doing. And trying to be aware of individual needs. So you may have to approach something in two different ways to accommodate children . . . So it's very much looking at an individual child's needs and trying to cater for them through the approach and the work that you set.

Teachers' awareness of their professional knowledge

The deputy headteacher above had clearly thought very carefully about the principles of her teaching, and she was quite explicit about her strategies. She described, for example, some of the different teaching styles that she had adopted in order to build in a variety of activities that would cater for children who did not have proficiency in writing skills to be able to show their understanding in a number of different ways such as concept mapping; many children who found writing difficult really enjoyed doing this, 'because they'd got the words and they'd just got to find a few words to join things.' Finding different approaches to recording was an important part of this teacher's strategy.

In contrast, a significant aspect that came out of the research was the way in which some teachers differentiated by drawing on their professional knowledge without acknowledging it as a conscious process. Feiman Nemser and Buchmann (1985) say:

> Since teaching is concerned with learning, it also requires thinking about how to build bridges between one's own understanding and that of one's students. Thus, pedagogical thinking is strategic, imaginative, and grounded in knowledge of self, children, and subject matter.
>
> (cited by Wilson *et al.* in Calderhead 1987: 115)

Teachers in our study illustrated the complex 'mix' of professional knowledge upon which their day-to-day decisions were based and there was a significant difference in the facility to do this as expressed by the experienced and newly qualified teachers.

An experienced teacher described it this way:

> You don't necessarily use the language (of differentiation), but you do it. You know all the children's strong points and where they need help, and so, all the time you're working, you're sort of watching out for a child who's struggling or needs a little bit of extra help, or needs a bit of stretching.
>
> (Experienced teacher; KS2)

This teacher described how she dealt with one child with learning difficulties. She said that during the day, this child was constantly in her mind:

> I'm weighing up whether her being in the group is beneficial to her, the other children, or the activity is beneficial to her or whether she would be better off if she did something else.

She had a professional repertoire of strategies on which she could draw. She felt that her experience had enabled her to build up a 'bank of ideas' whereas new teachers tended to keep to rigid plans in order to survive.

A newly qualified teacher found that even having had lectures on differentiation at college she still felt unprepared to deal with the thirty children in her class. When she started, she was given help with how to differentiate by her school mentor and this enabled her to talk about particular children and gain advice on how to plan work for them.

Equity issues

Another important aspect of differentiation mentioned was one of equity: do certain forms of differentiation enhance or reduce equal opportunities? Pollard makes this crucial observation: 'The question to be asked is whether there are patterns of differentiation which might represent a less than just and fair treatment of the individual attributes and rights of each child and each social group ' (1987: 160). He raises a number of important polarities in his article on social differentiation in primary schools which he says can result from the way teachers use differentiation. These question whether the process of differentiation used opens up horizons or leads to closure; whether it facilitates or stunts children's growth; whether it is abling or disabling; whether it enfranchises or disenfranchises, and whether it increases or decreases social awareness.

These limits on pupils' educational opportunities can arise when, over a period of time, the children's collective responses to teachers' decisions have the effect of maintaining and even magnifying the effects of classroom strategies like the formation of activity groups or sets. For example, Pollard (1984) describes one classroom in which a process of negotiation within a group of children allowed all of them to 'get the right answer', confirming in this way the teacher's original judgement of their 'abilities' in relation to other children in the class.

Teachers in the multi-ethnic London school raised some of these issues. A newly qualified teacher (KS1) commented on the possibility of negative labelling through grouping for differentiation. 'I don't think it's very good if you're always putting the kids, the same kids in the same groups. Or they get the same label ... the kids realise they're in this group.'

Another experienced teacher (KS1) was very aware of the dangers referred to by Pollard, devising conscious strategies to avoid grouping which led to negative self-perceptions and outcomes.

> I try to plan a variety of tasks and a variety of grouping so they don't always sit in ability groups. Children belong to different groups according to different activities ... so that they mix ... it does depend on the task.

Although she hadn't defined her practice as differentiation, she described a variety of techniques used for grouping taking into account ability, gender or cultural background. Sometimes she put those with similar levels of attainment together for an activity like writing a story; at other times she mixed the children for collaborative writing, or deliberately paired children of different levels of attainment. She said she had not regarded such strategies as differentiation, 'but I do plan for it. I suppose I think of it more as group dynamics of classroom management.' Another method she used was to mix boys and girls, but this was problematic in the school which had a high proportion of Muslim children and the teacher acknowledged that this might be a culturally unacceptable practice.

Salient characteristics of children requiring differentiation

Teachers in our sample clearly saw the need for teaching in different ways, using different styles of teaching according to the perceived needs of the children as well as the demands of the curriculum.

We attempted to explore what the teachers saw as the distinctive characteristics of children needing special consideration, and they mentioned aspects such as behaviour, personality, ability to work with other people, children whose first language was not English and children with problems at home as well as levels of attainment in different curriculum areas and special educational needs.

Some teachers saw differentiation as becoming increasingly complex as the children proceed through the school. One teacher, for example, referring to the strategy of 'differentiation by task' said that 'at the top end in the junior school ... the group work and the differentiation has been in action since they were five and so you do end up with a really wide variety of ability ... and knowledge.' She continued,

> differentiation is something that we think about a great deal because we have children who are unable to follow the level of the National Curriculum that would be assumed to be normal for their year group and therefore in order for them to progress they have to have the work pitched at a different level, which I interpret as differentiation.
> (Experienced teacher; KS2)

Teachers were aware that children who cannot be accommodated in this way will need to be taken through the stages of assessment for special educational needs, and many teachers gave examples of children with individual education plans and statements whose work needed special planning.

Other examples of differentiation focused on the need to respond to the children's home situations. One teacher spoke of a child's parents having split up, or illness in the family. 'We obviously accommodate their needs in that sense and I see it as a way of sort of catering for individual needs and supporting them in a pastoral context ' (Recently qualified teacher, KS1).

A newly qualified teacher at Key Stage 1 said she needed to differentiate from the moment children came into school in the morning, responding to their moods and readiness to work.

The children's responses to different curriculum areas was also seen to be an important differentiating factor. A number of teachers saw the danger of keeping children in permanent groups for all subjects based on their attainment in the core subjects. An interesting distinction was made here between what teachers considered to be academic subjects and those 'not so academic' such as art, history and P.E. For the 'less academic subjects' differentiation was more likely to be on the basis of factors such as personal relationships, friendship groups or out-of-school experience.

Teachers stressed the importance of attending to how children get on together in the classroom: 'Sometimes groups have to be manipulated for other reasons because you know, relationships can make or mar a group.' Personality was often mentioned in relation to differentiation and grouping and many teachers felt that planning needed to include a consideration of the social dynamics of grouping. One teacher pointed out that where she had not considered these factors adequately the children's learning was less effective. Sometimes it was felt to be important to keep certain personalities apart; but at other times decisions were made to include a particular child with positive social qualities in a group in order to weld it together.

I suppose I've mixed the groups up as to very outgoing and able children and very quiet shy children, rather more for P.E., I try to build groups like that on a completely different basis.

(Newly qualified teacher; KS1)

This teacher pointed out that age was also a consideration particularly where classes consisted of two year groups. 'Sometimes in my group work I actually put my youngest children, the least able year ones with my most able year twos because I find that works very well.' She felt that there are benefits for the older children as well, as by helping the younger children they are explaining the work and 'it makes them think more about what they're doing.' This type of differentiation usually involved some physical or practical activity.

As shown above, in many of the discussions about differentiation, teachers appeared to be using an organising principle based on their perceptions of the differences between activities and subject areas, as well as their perceptions of differences between children. Nevertheless, a large part of teachers' professional expertise consists of a detailed knowledge about the strengths and weaknesses of all the children they teach, something that comes with experience. A newly qualified Key Stage 1 teacher described the problems of getting to know a class when first becoming a teacher:

When you get a class you take a time getting to know them. You've got to group them for management straight away, but you do take time getting to know them, and as soon as you start to know them, you actually want to regroup them.

This young teacher felt that SATs imposed their own additional pressure and that the planning and organisation for the whole year could be affected by the fact that they were coming up in the summer term.

The majority 'in the middle'

While it can be seen that teachers base their decisions about differentiation on a detailed understanding of the variation in children's needs, even from day to day, there remains the problem of the large group of children who do not stand out as individuals in the primary classroom. Sometimes the most significant aspect for teachers is the pace at which this group of children works:

I have got mainly a large middle . . . so I tend to give [them] what I give the high, but I don't always expect them to finish it. Or if I give them the same sheet with six questions on it, I'll only expect them to do three of them, but they're the same questions as the higher one.

(Recently qualified teacher; KS1)

This teacher had been very explicit in describing her strategies and expectations for children of 'lower ability' and 'higher ability' in different lessons. Her familiarity with the National Curriculum, gained at college, enables her to 'pitch at Level 2' as the baseline for setting work for the majority of children, before going on to adapt activities for the few. There is recognition, however, that the categories are not hard-edged. As one experienced Key Stage 1 teacher said, 'even if you do have children in rough ability groups . . . there are still children who are good at some things, and not so good at other things . . . and you could mix the groups in different ways.' The broad 'middle' group can therefore also be differentiated. As Hart (1992) argues, *all* children will benefit from a wider range of opportunities for learning (including learning through talk, practical experience, and co-operative work), and they may require a specific pedagogy tailored to their needs.

CONCLUSION

It became clear to us during the research that teachers see differentiation as an integral part of their work; it is deeply embedded in their sense of professionalism. From their discussion, it was clear that their use of different strategies to enhance the learning of all their pupils was based on a deep understanding of the individual needs of the children. they teach. Their planning is rooted in this aspect of their professional knowledge and their sense of professional responsibility.

There are a number of issues which would benefit further exploration in order to extend our understanding of how teachers develop their views and practices; these include length of teaching experience and the effects of working in different school settings. In addition, a topic that has recently been receiving much attention from educational researchers as well as politicians is the effect of teachers' subject knowledge on their teaching (Bennett *et al.* 1994; Aubrey 1994; Alexander, Rose and Woodhead 1992). We found in our interviews that while some individual teachers and headteachers recognised the importance of subject knowledge for effective teaching, this factor was not significant in management decisions such as the allocation of teachers to certain classes over the years. However, some teachers acknowledged that where they had specific subject knowledge, they were able to make finer distinctions in their differentiation. This would be a fruitful area to explore further.

What appears to be most significant is the variation of ways in which teachers understand the meaning of differentiation, and the breadth and depth with which they employ it. Some see it purely as differentiation by task and outcome. Others, as the chapter illustrates, have a much wider conception which embraces social, cultural, personality and equity factors, enabling them to draw on pedagogical strategies of a more sophisticated and complex form. During the interviews, teachers were able to talk in depth and detail about the principles underlying their practice and the use of the cards was an important catalyst for extending the discussion. It may be that in addition to traditional forms of discussion, schools could use strategies like our card activity as a collaborative means of establishing a common understanding within the staff team.

A final point, perhaps the most obvious to emphasise, is that the message received is not aways the one that is sent. Teachers not only think and feel different things about their roles and responsibilities, but they use words and images in different ways. Furthermore, it is likely that personal preferences, fluency and ease of communication in different modes of thinking will depend as much on individual experience and the task in hand, as on a global 'style' of using words or images. This point is central to the development of strategies for differentiation in schools. It is important to find ways to gain access to what and how people think, in order to engage with them and develop ideas together. This applies to education for children and adults and it is one of the main concerns of this book. The long-term aim may be, however, to focus on the degree to which growing children and adults can be helped to operate and communicate fluently and flexibly in different modes. This would seem to be the essence of successful, generalisable learning and teaching.

NOTES

1   Research methodology: we were particularly interested in finding ways of interviewing that would attempt to go beyond the sometimes arid and limited methods that have been used in the past to find out about teachers' thinking. As writers like those contributing to the collections by Calderhead (1987) or Brophy (1991) have shown, the complex nature of teachers' practice and thinking needs to be recognised fully in research methodology. Research that simply focuses, for example, on what teachers would do if faced with a certain standard dilemma in 'any school' is likely to result in rather different findings from research which involves teachers' reflecting on their own practice at key decision points in their current working life. There is a danger of collecting one-dimensional findings with little explanatory or predictive value if teachers' views are not explored thoroughly. The interviews with teachers and headteachers involved extended discussion about differentiation, prompted by a range of questions designed to approach the topic in different ways. This was intended to provide us with a rich understanding of the teachers' views and experiences, allowing for inconsistencies to emerge and possibly to be explored and resolved. For example, we would want to find out whether a teacher's practice in relation to one child or a group of children bears out his or her stated understanding of what differentiation means in general terms.

2   Interview schedule for teachers:

A   Language, images and perceptions of differentiation

1. Differentiation has been a word used frequently in the National Curriculum and HMI documentation; what does the word conjure up for you either in words, pictures or diagrams?
2. Is differentiation a word you use or do you use anything else to describe what you mean?
3. (*Show cards and ask them to select the ones that interest, surprise or puzzle them*)
   Why have you selected those particular cards?
4. If you use the term differentiation or some equivalent word, do you use it differently in different subject contexts?

B   The ways teachers differentiate

5. Can you give examples of your teaching which use the idea of differentiation?
6. What special characteristics of children do you think require differentiation?
7. Can you give any examples from your class this year?
8. How have you adapted your teaching to cater for them?
9. How has this affected the curriculum content and planning in your class?
10. Does this fit in with the National Curriculum? Are there any problems?
11. Are there any circumstances in the school which help or hinder you to differentiate well?

C   Documentation, policies and training

12. Is there anything in the school documentation or policy on differentiation? How is it used in the school?
13. Have you or has anyone else in the school received any training on differentiation?
14. Do you think differentiation ought to be part of school policy? If so, what could be done throughout the school to make it more effective?
15. Do you think that differentation ought to be part of your work?

The interview schedule for headteachers was adapted to include questions about management issues, and external demands and expectations about differentiation (e.g. from OFSTED).

REFERENCES

Alexander, R. (1992) *Policy and Practice in Primary Education*, London: Routledge
Alexander, R., Rose, J. and Woodhead, C. (1992) *Curriculum Organisation and Classroom Practice in Primary Schools: a discussion paper*, London: DES
Aubrey, C. (ed.) (1994) *The Role of Subject Knowledge in the Early Years of Schooling*, London: Falmer Press
Bennett, N., Summers, M. and Askew, M. (1994) 'Knowledge for teaching and teaching performance', ch. 3 in A. Pollard (ed.) *Look Before You Leap: Research Evidence for the Curriculum at Key Stage Two*, London: The Tufnell Press
Brophy, J. (ed.) (1991) *Advances in Research on Teaching Vol. 2: Teachers' knowledge*

of subject matter as it relates to their teaching practice, Greenwich, Connecticut: JAI Press Inc.

Brown, S. and Riddell, S. (1994) 'The impact of policy on practice and thinking', in S. Riddell and S. Brown (eds) *Special Educational Needs Policy in the 1990s*, London: Routledge

Calderhead, J. (1987) *Exploring Teachers' Thinking*, London: Cassell

Croll, P. and Moses, D. (1985) *One in Five: The Assessment and Incidence of Special Educational Needs*, London: Routledge and Kegan Paul

Dusek, J.B. (ed.) (1985) *Teacher Expectancies*, Hillsdale, NJ: Lawrence Erlbaum Associates

Feiman Nemser, S. and Buchmann, M. (1985) 'The First Year of Teacher Preparation: transition to pedagogical thinking?', Research Series 156, East Lansing, MSU cited in J. Calderhead (ed.) 1987 op. cit.

Fullan, M. (1982) *The Meaning of Educational Change*, Toronto, Ontario: OISE Press

Greenhalgh, P. (1994) *Emotional Growth and Learning*, London: Routledge

Hart, S. (1992) 'Differentiation. Part of the problem or part of the solution?', *The Curriculum Journal* 3(2): 131–142

Peter, M. (1992) Editorial *British Journal of Special Education*, 19(1)

Pollard, A. (1984) 'Coping strategies and the multiplication of differentiation in infant classrooms', *British Educational Research Journal*, 10(1): 33–48

Pollard, A. (1987) 'Social Differentiation in Primary Schools ', *Cambridge Journal of Education* 17(3) : 158–161

Riddell, S. and Brown, S. (eds) (1994) *Special Educational Needs Policy in the 1990s*, London: Routledge

Rogers, C. (1992) 'Motivation in the primary years', ch. 6 in Rogers C. and Kutnick P. (eds) *The Social Psychology of the Primary School*, London: Routledge

Upton, G. (ed.) (1991) *Staff Training and Special Educational Needs*, London: David Fulton Publishers

Weedon, C. (1994) 'Learning Difficulties and Mathematics', ch. 7 in S. Riddell and S. Brown (eds) *Special Educational Needs Policy in the 1990s*, London: Routledge

Chapter 2

Grounds for differentiation
Some values and principles in primary education considered

Christine Doddington

The idea of differentiation seems to invite a focus on the differences between people rather than what is common. This may seem at first to be a straightforward idea. It is not quite so uncomplicated, however, since the degree to which we consider the human race as comprising individuals with differences, or as a mass of humanity with much in common, can vary. Sensitivity to the extent of 'difference' between people has grown as the idea of the individual has increased in significance. Also, difference between people is discerned not so much by simple identification, but through the values and purposes that are held in mind. For this reason, alerting ourselves to difference is seen as appropriate at some times and irrelevant at others. This means that, depending on the context, any perceived difference, such as race, gender or age, may be acknowledged and influential or deliberately disregarded. Educational contexts are good examples of such contrasting approaches where particular values and priorities can exert pressure to distinguish between people, or alternatively, disregard difference in favour of common provision. Any claim in schools for differentiation or common entitlement then, rests less on empirical evidence, more on values, assumptions and professional judgement. In this chapter I will examine some of the underlying assumptions of commonality and difference in education and explore some of the values and priorities on which those conceptions are based. I then go on to look at ways in which apparently contrasting positions can be drawn together in carefully conceived class-room practice.

There seem to be oppositions in educational thinking between views which concentrate on the individual and those which look at common features or qualities. Many studies of learning encourage teachers to consider awareness of personality, background and experience, cultural influence and the subtle effects of myriad social encounters on people. At the same time there has been a continued debate about what should be seen in education as common provision for all. This apparent tension echoes a wider debate between those who wish to promote individualism and those who search for what connects humanity or particular groups. Despite the controversy, this dichotomy may be misleading when we think about the classroom context. For example, differentiation in the classroom may require us to focus on individuals and difference by making distinctions between children's performance in a particular task. However, it is also related to what should be common, since the principle of entitlement is to provide equal access to what is deemed of value and essential for all. Differentiation may be required precisely to achieve that access. Any structure put forward as the basis for a curriculum will rest in part on judgements made about value and emphasis and in part on individuals and entitlement. The teacher in the primary classroom therefore consciously, or sub-consciously, expresses her values and priorities when she determines what will be common experiences for all and what learning experiences are designed to be different for different children.

I want to explore differentiation by exposing particular values and principles that can lie implicit within characterisations of the primary curriculum. However, discussion of this will inevitably rest on funda-mental ideas about education. The debate of how education should be best conceived is traditionally conducted on the basis of different sets of values about life and versions of what should be seen as 'the good life' for all. Here then, decisions about how we prepare the next gener-ation for adult life are necessarily based on value judgements about what should be regarded as a common entitlement for all as well as what account should be taken of the individual.

KNOWLEDGE

One familiar, well-rehearsed claim for education is that the good life is above all dependent on people being well informed and able to think and reason for themselves. The argument follows that since different well-established forms of knowledge offer models of good reasoning, the best way of achieving this goal for all is to develop in individuals a broad base of knowledge. Any rational construction of a curriculum following this line would need to be based on the kinds of knowledge that are seen as fundamental to developing reason, with teachers respon-sible for initiating children into these publicly agreed ways of reasoning about, and understanding the world.

The claim that everyone should gain knowledge is nevertheless prob-lematic. It is often argued that much of the so-called 'knowledge' we gain in school, particularly primary school, is often discarded and of little direct use in our adult lives. However, the argument for a know-ledge-based curriculum suggests that the knowledge we gain at school is not so much about acquiring facts, but more about entering different ways of thinking. Most of life's personal and communal projects and choices depend on being able to think in a variety of ways in order to arrive at sound judgements. The design of buildings can serve as an illustration of this: thinking scientifically about materials used to design buildings will highlight different issues to aesthetic considerations; also important will be consideration of the function of the building and how people will wish to relate together, living or working in close proximity. It could be argued that all of these areas of reasoning are of equal import- ance. There may be dire safety consequences if aesthetic design is prioritised without due consideration to technology. There might also be serious consequences if people's wishes and aspirations are neglected in favour of economics. All of these different sets of considerations have their roots in the mathematical, social, artistic and scientific thinking that should be enshrined in the familiar subject knowledge of the curriculum. By learning to think scientifically and aesthetically children are entering the world of shared understanding which drives modern life. In school, by encouraging individuals to enter a world of shared understandings, teachers eventually enable children to 'belong' to and participate in society. More specifically, being able to understand and participate in the reasoning behind decisions can be prized for empowering individ- uals within their communities and within their own lives. This line of thinking has developed into claims that knowledge should therefore be seen in education as a liberating force, enabling above all else the exercise of personal autonomy.

The liberal rallying cry of 'knowledge as an entitlement for all' is based on the fundamental notion that areas of human knowledge offer several distinctive ways of enquiry and understanding of human experience within the world. These distinct ways of knowing are characterised by interrelated networks of concepts which constitute a language particular to that way of seeing and understanding. These concepts are based on equally characteristic sets of procedures for making judgements of worth or truth that have evolved over the passage of time. For example, the material world, understood and investigated by what we have come to call science, has evolved sophisticated concepts and refined procedures which have a fundamental connection with the early exploratory play of children. A young child attempting to dismantle a clockwork toy to see how it works or asking questions about where rain comes from is beginning to reason scientifically. In the same way, the sensual plea- sures children gain from patterns in movement and sound form part of the foundations for later understanding found refined within the domain of the arts.

A view based on the centrality of knowledge then would claim that while some learning may occur unintentionally, teachers can plan to develop these early beginnings by attending explicitly to the concepts

and procedures that will eventually allow initiation into the sophisticated vocabularies that comprise different facets of human knowledge
and understanding. The curriculum is seen as a means of scaffolding
the publicly agreed concepts and procedures that constitute these fundamental ways of understanding the world. From this perspective, teaching
becomes a question of mapping access.

'KNOWLEDGE' AND THE CURRICULUM

The language in which the National Curriculum is framed appears to
share the priorities and values of a traditional view of education associated centrally with knowledge. If knowledge is accepted as sets of
constructed vocabularies that stand pre-formed and independent of the
whims and predilections of individuals, this might suggest that initiation into these vocabularies can take a standardised route. There seems
a natural progression from the simple to the complex, particularly when
the complex is seen as a composite of the simple. For example, to begin
to understand the concept of multiplication we first need to have sure
understanding of the principle of addition, since multiplication can be
understood as accumulated addition. However, complex concepts and
ideas do not always break down into simple parts. It is not possible to
prescribe and chart the steps for grasping the meaning of a poem for
instance.

It is easy to see why those involved in constructing the National
Curriculum were drawn to a simplistic model of progression from the
simple to the complex. Heartened by this apparently straightforward
structure they also chose to simplify the idea of knowledge by categorising it under subject headings. After all, here was a familiar and
unchallenging pattern by which knowledge could be organised. This
allowed difficult and complex questions about how knowledge should
best be characterised and any examination of its value in education to
remain comfortingly under wraps. It was another small step to elaborate the model by leaping to the assumption that mapping the acquisition
of, or entry into, the knowledge encapsulated by subject headings was
possible by progression through a series of levels. Teachers who plan
for differentiation with this model implicit in their thinking, seem only
to be required to locate the child on the ladder of conceptual understanding and devise the most effective way that allows/provokes a child
to make the next step.

However, the assumption that knowledge and understanding grow in
pre-specified patterns through levels in subjects is problematic.
Retrospective tracing of how we have arrived at understanding something complex might serve as a concrete example to set against the idea
of fixed routes and 'building blocks' for understanding. Like many

aspects of developed understanding, we learn about sex through a medley of life's experiences, which may include being taught in schools, acquiring information elsewhere and through social encounter (both vicarious and personal). If we were to gather together a group of adults who claim to have some degree of understanding about sex, they would almost certainly have arrived at their understanding through different routes. The extent of common knowledge might include some basic biological facts and these may well have been offered in school in the form of a sequence of lessons, but the points at which each person made sense of what was on offer would have varied. They are likely to have retained what was significant information at the time and discarded much which lacked meaning, re-learning some elements at a later date if or when the need arose. Furthermore, information and 'the facts' would not have been fully grasped in isolation. To be meaningful and relevant they would need to 'fit' for each individual within a conceptual framework and rest within a scientific context rather than 'everyday' understandings. An egg forming into an embryo is then understood within the context of specific scientific concepts such as growth and fertilisation rather than simplistic ideas of something growing in size alone or even resting on the idea that the event can happen through wish fulfilment.

Accumulation of biological facts alone does not comprise sex education, however, and it is frequently argued that facts about human reproduction should be contextualised within the complexities of forming human relationships. If we therefore tie in this realm of knowledge, the potential for different times and depth in individual understanding surely increases. Growth of understanding about relationships seems so personalised as to be unchartable in any detailed common pattern. We might agree that it is important to link the biological facts with a growing understanding of relationships, but a common sequence through levels of understanding cannot be prescribed. This begins to raise doubts about the neatness of subject divisions and levels. Differentiation for developing knowledge seems to point not to common structures of content with differentiated steps, but to ways in which children individually make sense of factual content, acquire concepts and learn how to make judgements so that they are able to increase their understanding in a broader and integrated sense.

Exploring what might constitute knowledge and understanding has already raised implications for teachers who are attempting to differentiate and has revealed inadequacies in the underlying construction of the National Curriculum. The argument that the National Curriculum lacks a thought-through rationale has been well rehearsed by a number of critics. At the same time, despite criticism, it might even be welcomed as advantageous to individual teachers. It is possible that the lack of any coherent basis allows teachers to develop ownership of what they plan by interpreting and choosing what to prioritise. At Key Stage 1 and Key Stage 2, however, this would include being able to approach the National Curriculum quite literally which might suggest a curriculum constructed through subjects, with priority given to the specified factual content. At present a large proportion of primary teachers are responsible for an individual child's whole school-based education for at least one year. This arrangement offers, as an alternative, scope for planning with a broader understanding of knowledge in mind and less fragmentation of the child's learning experiences in the classroom than separate subject headings may imply.

The fact that the National Curriculum has a high level of pre-specified content and is divided into subjects and levels might suggest that gaining knowledge is the same as digesting factual content. If this is emphasised as the main focus of a curriculum for teachers in their planning, there is less need for them to consider how children best develop understanding; they merely have to work at making the 'content' digestible. If the framework of the curriculum reflects this priority, with accumulated facts valued above all, then the speed or ease with which children are able to take in and retain factual content could call for a form of differentiation such as ability setting or streaming. However, I am suggesting that such a view offers an impoverished conception of knowledge. Factual content is an inadequate equation for knowledge; concentration on the acquisition of facts neglects conceptual understanding and the significant procedures of reasoning and judgement that are integral to gaining real knowledge.

An emphasis on factual content also overlooks important distinctions between various ways of reflecting on the world. It could lead to devaluing understanding which appears not to incorporate an obvious body of factual information. Access to the world created through the arts, for instance, is not dependent on factual knowledge. The arts draw on subtleties of perception and judgement which need to be rigorously questioned but which cannot be reduced to explicit formulas for determining correctness or worth. Helping children to understand the meaning of rhythm, or dramatic tension, requires direct connection to personal experience. This is because the meanings of these concepts are not rigidly fixed but have to be contextually explored and interpreted. Evaluation of works of art necessarily draws upon the person as much as any 'neutral' and fixed set of criteria that can be applied. The lens of understanding through which art is revealed to the observer has both a cultural/communal dimension as well as being deeply personal. This is in part why the idea of a canon for literature draws such fierce opposition from many who work within the field of art in all its forms.

The very notion of a canon seems to misunderstand the nature of thinking within the arts by offering a needlessly fixed content for the curriculum. The arts are different, but no more nor less important in ultimately helping children to understand the world than areas of knowledge which appear to have more 'settled' and agreed content. Since I am suggesting that facts and content are incidental to but not central to developing knowledge, I am claiming that a 'facts-focused' or 'content-based' curriculum should not be confused with a 'knowledge-based' curriculum.

If developing knowledge in education is seen as a coherent extension of conceptual understanding together with practice in the procedures of reasoning and judgement related to distinctive concepts, then content becomes less significant. Historical periods or specific places become significant only in as much as they allow children to experience features of different kinds of knowledge. A teacher's judgement comes into play not only in relation to *what* children should encounter next but *how* they should engage with the values and concepts and participate in the procedures that are intrinsic to this particular way of understanding and coming to know the world. The idea is that a child should participate in procedures that are as intrinsic to different ways of understanding as different concepts. For example, to arrive at a mathematical proof, there are steps which show the validity of the original hypothesis. Teachers can express different values and priorities in the way they hope children will engage with this mathematical procedure – should the aim be for children to take on board the formula as a device to practise and use when appropriate, or should teachers be trying to help children engage in and understand the mathematical thinking that underpins the formula?

This dilemma is perhaps sharpened where procedures do not relate to obvious formulae. If understanding is required for judgements about what constitutes an eloquent poem or a moral action, should the teacher see her role as one of helping children become familiar with different sets of commonly agreed criteria (perhaps cross-culturally) or one of engaging children actively in the kind of thinking people have used to arrive at shared criteria? In accepting a 'broader than facts' view of knowledge, we are still left with the job of refining how we should best characterise knowledge in the service of educating children. Whatever we decide about the entitlement for all will determine something of how we differentiate to achieve that entitlement. It is clear that the interrelationship between the individual and what is seen as publicly agreed knowledge and traditional ways of thinking can be characterised in different ways. Furthermore, these different characterisations will suggest quite various practices and are dependent upon different values and priorities.

THE INDIVIDUAL

I would like now to focus on some of the ideas that seem to imply the need to tailor the curriculum to the individual. If we return to our group of adults who have claimed some understanding of sex, discussion is likely to reveal understanding which is to some degree common, but also individual experiences and interpretation for meaning. If we ask what education should contribute to understanding and how best it might be structured, we return to what should be common for all and questions of how best to allow for individuals to make sense of it. One dimension of 'making sense' that seems significant, urges us to focus on each individual's way of finding meaning. The personal narrative that tells how an individual's understanding about sex has evolved, will no doubt reveal an *ongoing, individually charted search for meaning*. Personal concerns and interests and our capacity for understanding lead us to interpret facts and experiences as they appear relevant to us. This would seem to be the dynamic that is necessary for any form of integrated and authentic understanding and is less concerned with sheer accumulation of knowledge, more with the cultivation of an attitude or disposition to all that lies external to ourselves. Michael Bonnett in his book *Children's Thinking* develops ideas related to authentic understanding and characterises this attitude thus:

> The child who has grown confident in asking questions, critically evaluating evidence from her own perspective and reflecting on the significance of what she has learnt, has a very different attitude towards life compared to the child who basically seeks accepted answers.
>
> (Bonnett 1994: 121)

If teachers attach value to this dimension of understanding, there are implications for differentiation. To suggest that teachers need therefore to differentiate for individual patterns of meaning might seem at first to require access to each child's personal view of the world. This would of course be fraught with difficulty. However, if children were to be acknowledged as able to contribute significantly to the making of meaning and their own general understanding in this way, the onus would be on teachers to plan for learning experiences which would allow for and recognise this. Teachers would need to be astute enough to infer and recognise differences between children in the way they approach ideas that are new or challenge what they already think. It would be a mistake to see a child who was reticent to question and passive towards new 'knowledge' as set in that way of living. Teachers who valued this approach to life would wish to encourage and develop this form of critical evaluating in children. They would need to differentiate in the ways they support the timid, and challenge the thinking of individuals already established in an authentic approach to understanding. Bonnett has described the teacher's role here as one of 'empathetic challenging' (Bonnett 1994: 114), and this would seem to require quite specific differentiation in the way teachers relate and respond to children as they express their ideas. Rejecting a tentative suggestion from one child might crush their sense of themselves and their worth, while a teacher's rejection made in the spirit of seeking a 'better' suggestion may provoke another child to greater depth in their thinking and ultimately a surer sense of themselves and the value of their ideas.

One further dimension to consider in terms of differentiation might be to allow the space, time and opportunity for children to determine a degree of depth and direction in which their learning takes them. In other words, where the development of authentic understanding is valued, and within the flexibility of the primary curriculum that has been preserved, it might be that children could be encouraged to differentiate for themselves to some extent, on the basis of extending their own concerns and understanding. This suggestion, however, raises the prospect of over-individualised and perhaps even idiosyncratic understanding at the expense of shared experience. To what extent should standardised understanding be stressed and highly individualised understanding be seen as something to be avoided? For personal meaning to be valued in education, the grip of publicly standardised knowledge as a basis for defining the curriculum would undoubtedly need to be loosened. At the same time, the idea of developing personal concerns *within* understanding which is communal, could be explored. The example of knowing about sex may again help here.

The whole area surrounding relationships associated with human reproduction offers a particularly rich mix of publicly shared and personal knowledge. The public domain is not straightforward, however, because sex is a good example of understanding which is woven with blends of what might be called scientifically verifiable facts and folklore. Above all, it is drenched in cultural mores and ritual and can be offered as understanding developed as a result of 'caught wisdom', not to mention downright fantasy and hearsay. Significantly, all of this can be regarded as within the public domain which may be shared within a given group as 'true' understanding. Given the extent of story and woolly half-truths that this area is prone to, it might seem reasonable to press for the supremacy of objective truth. The first stages of paring away the fictions that linger from erroneous information or the stories of an earlier age might be simple, but before long we would find ourselves in far more complex territory associated with cultural understanding of what it is to be human. If the urge relentlessly to pursue 'verifiable, objective truth' continues, we are likely to be left with a residue of the internal chemistry or mechanics of sex and little else. The process will have reduced a rich and developed area of humanity to an arid template of very little relevance to our sense of living. Although he is specifically referring to the study of education, Dewey has suggested how the process of using the 'scalpel' of scientific method on human behaviour has dangers:

> we must employ science modestly and humbly; there is no subject in which the claim to be strictly scientific is more likely to suffer from pretence, and none in which it is more dangerous to set up a rigid orthodoxy, a standardised set of beliefs to be accepted by all.
>
> (Dewey 1978: 17)

The urge to reduce human understanding to the 'fixed' and 'agreed' is strong within educational debate. However, the assumption that all knowledge should be seen as having fixed foundations explored by a fixed method has been challenged and there have even been calls for a reassessment of what we see as 'true'. The argument put forward is that it is more appropriate to see what is true as collectively constructed, evolving over time and somewhat organic, rather than that which can be revealed as if it is a fixed reality. The support for this argument is complex but if we allow ourselves to play with the idea for our present purposes there are some interesting implications. The great value of this perspective for education is that it allows for no thesis or belief – no matter how fundamental – that is not open to further interpretation and criticism. This presentation of all knowledge and understanding as crucially embedded in culture, time and tradition offers a dynamic and evolving vision of the world in which everyone can genuinely participate at whatever age or ability. The sense of waiting to become independent thinkers until one 'knows enough' is lost and progression is seen as a continual refinement and testing of provisional understandings.

COMMUNITIES FOR DIALOGUE

However, arguments raised against knowledge being seen as fixed can appear to suggest a kind of nihilistic relativism leading ultimately to isolated individualism. The key ideas that have been suggested to help guard against this have been a stress on the importance of 'dialogue' and 'community'. In the example of the group claiming knowledge about sex, there is obvious possibility for idiosyncratic understanding, but this possibility diminishes with shared dialogue. This may be further reduced with a commitment to extend the depth and quality of that shared understanding. If the group is formed with a clear intention to explore and be critical of their shared understandings, to have concern for truth and

to enquire both without and within their shared horizons, being recep-
tive to the different as well as the confirming, then, it is argued, this is
a procedure in which both personal and communal understanding will
be taken forward.

Setting up an active community critically engaged in thinking seems
to echo some of the aspirations behind statements of shared values and
principles in primary schools, often expressed in written form in their
prospectus or statement of school aims. However, if they are to imbue
the life and practice of the school more work is needed. For the teacher
in the classroom, planning for these principles to 'flavour' the experiences of every child will require sensitivity, understanding and
judgement. What is more, differentiation will be crucial. It might help
to set out a description of classroom activity which illustrates how a
teacher valuing both communal and personal understanding might allow
this to influence her practice.

In a topic designed around the theme of Ancient Egypt, a Year 3
teacher has planned for her class to encounter historical and geographical knowledge. The topic is also designed to link together a variety of
language and maths activities, as well as offer experience in the arts.
Studying the Egyptians should also raise some ethical and religious
issues by allowing children to encounter ideas such as weighing of the
heart to determine goodness and preserving the body for an afterlife.
After a few weeks of study during which the teacher has used a variety
of methods and activities to introduce and explain something of the
culture of the Ancient Egyptians, she is aware of differences in the way
children have understood what she has carefully planned for them all
to encounter. Nearly every child is taken by the biological details of
mummification which are gloriously remembered in gruesome descriptions. A few seem to have placed this securely within their scientific and
geographical understanding of location by referring to the effects of heat
and decay. One or two others seem to sense the importance of symbols
and have grasped how belief influenced the practices. However, the
majority seem to relish their knowledge of mummification outside of
any historical or geographical context. Indeed some have located their
understanding more securely within their knowledge of horror films and
stories!

The dilemma faced here is a common one faced by teachers. One
approach might be to locate the children with 'gaps' in their understanding and set different tasks for those who need to revisit aspects of
the topic. However, this teacher, while ever-conscious of the importance
of the individual in making meaning, also sees value in the exchange
and development of knowledge in shared experiences. In her view, a
common experience will never offer standardised understanding, but
can be an effective focus for enhancing individual perceptions and

understanding and she is confident this can be valuable for all the children to extend their thinking in different ways. Rather than individualised tasks designed for children to revisit content, she therefore constructs a fictional framework for further activity with all the children. This is achieved by carefully using a variety of dramatic conventions, including taking a role herself, to build belief in an imaginary context.

As 'experts' on Egypt within a museum, the children are offered the prospect of a special mission to visit Cairo – a British archaeologist is claiming to have located an undiscovered tomb. They plan their trip with reference to maps, and the process of making decisions about what to take with them as a group reminds everyone of features concerning the geographical location and strengthens the purpose of their visit by group decisions made about the equipment they will need. On arrival in Egypt the group is surprisingly refused entry by the teacher in role as an official. Until they can convince the official their interest and knowledge about Ancient Egypt is genuine, they risk being sent back to Britain. In order to persuade the Egyptian official, they need to refer back to their original sources of information (books, resources and previous work) to create a convincing case. Having successfully persuaded the official of their expertise and integrity, the archaeology team enter Egypt and physically move from the banks of the River Nile into the scorching desert to the pile of rubble that is believed to be the tomb, supported in their movement by a careful narrative 'voice-over' from the teacher. They dig down and as they break through the tunnel into the first room they are transported back in time to discover a scribe finishing hieroglyphs along the wall of the tomb. The teacher is able to capitalise on the strength of each child's imagination aroused by this dramatic event and the earnest writing that springs out of this experience shows fluency, vividness and a degree of personal investment that seems worthy of recording for a number of the children. Individual understanding is checked and clarified within groups as the children plan what they wish to find out when they return to the tomb and interview the scribe. Insight and understanding is furthered as the scribe answers the children's questions. As the discussion proceeds the scribe is able to enquire legitimately about his visitors' modern lives. This exchange may be skilfully designed by the teacher to help a number of the 'Egyptologists' see similarities and a relationship between the two cultures and shed light on some of the 'unconnected' pieces of information they have previously acquired.

My intention in setting out this concrete example in some detail has been to give a tangible illustration of classroom activity which might reflect a particular view of knowledge and a commitment to extending individual understanding within an established community of enquiry.

In my example I have tried to show a teacher committed to encouraging children to explore and be critical of their shared understandings. The teacher was trying to support a concern for truth and yet encourage an openness to common understanding both within the children's shared horizons and in the wider context of knowledge constructed external to them. I would suggest that the relationship between the traditions and the individual children was presented in this example as organic and supportive of authentic understanding without the restrictions of pre-ordained steps of learning prescribing both curriculum and differentiation.

I believe that this idea has been worth pursuing because there seems to be such strong resonance with the aspirations of many primary schools. If teachers value helping children to engage with living traditions in the way I have characterised them, then recognition of the individual's concerns and search for meaning has implications for differentiation. Also of value, however, are common experiences and encounters which will support the establishment of a communal sense of contemplation and enquiry.

SUMMARY

I have attempted to show how a restricted view of knowledge as facts will lead to a simplistic form of stepped differentiation which will not serve children's understanding, nor the teacher aspiring to plan for growth of understanding. With a fuller conception of knowledge, teachers will need to provide children with opportunities to engage with networks of concepts through practice in the distinctive procedures of reasoning and making judgements characterised in the fundamental ways we traditionally describe the world and human achievement. Charting progression here is far less straightforward than the notion of subject levels implies and necessarily raises issues about differentiation. I have focused on one significant dimension which is, of necessity, different for individuals. This element is the individualised patterning for meaning on which coherent and authentic understanding crucially depends. While a logical structure for knowledge may stand outside any individual, the suggestion is that thinking and genuine understanding can occur only through active engagement and processes of interpretation.

This path may appear to be leading through individualised meanings to relativistic isolation. However, we have developed traditional practices for coming to know the world that are of value and, more importantly, are inescapable. What is judged as common will need to be continually reappraised. Hans Georges Gadamer (Gadamer 1979) in his extensive work on the dialogic nature of understanding has suggested that we belong to traditions before they belong to, and are appropriated by, us. One further crucial issue for teachers arising from this is the nature of the relationship they wish to establish for children with these traditions. When teachers differentiate for individuals on this view, they are trying to ensure that the encounter between knowledge and the child remains significantly effective for the development of thinking.

Education is undoubtedly a shared journey into a shared world. Primary teachers still have some choice in how they present the curriculum – and I have suggested that where both commonality of experience and individual meaning are valued there may be a case for teachers differentiating by encouraging a community for enquiry. With individuals valued through shared contemplation and open dialogue, children can have a genuine role to play helping to differentiate the curriculum for their own understanding.

REFERENCES

Bonnett, M. (1994) *Children's Thinking: Promoting Understanding in the Primary School* London: Cassell

Dewey, J. (1978) 'Science of Education', in Archambault , R. D. (ed.) *John Dewey on Education*, New York: Modern Library

Gadamer, H. G. (1979) *Truth and Method*, London: Sheen & Ward

Part II
Differentiation and literacy

Introduction to Part II

There is no doubt that literacy is a central factor in education. Much of the curriculum is articulated through reading and writing and literacy holds a critical importance in life generally. Literacy confers power, that is why it matters and why it is important to have a critical approach to the whole area of literacy in education. Being able to read and write successfully means having access to further and higher education. However, being literate means more than simply the ability to decode print, getting hold of the surface message. It means being able to bring experience and knowledge to bear on any text which is presented; being able to 'read the small print'; 'read between the lines'. It does not take much imagination to appreciate the deeply damaging effects of not having access to literacy; lack of confident literacy affects not only learning opportunities but the fundamental human rights of any individual or group. Wayne O'Neil describes the ability to see beneath the surface as 'proper literacy' and the practice of simply tracking words on the page as 'improper' literacy. He puts it like this:

> Proper literacy should extend people's control over their lives and the environment and allow them to continue to deal rationally and in words with their lives and decisions. Improperly it reduces and destroys their control.

> (O'Neil 1977)

The legal requirement for all children to attend school means that it is easy to accept the idea of literacy as an automatic right; from here, it isn't too great a step towards seeing the acquisition of literacy as a kind of duty – either pitying or blaming those individuals in society who are non-literate or not as fully literate as would generally be considered acceptable. In this way, of course, they receive a double blow; not only do they experience the de-powering effects of not being able to handle the reading and writing demands which others tend to take for granted, but they also suffer from stigma because they lack that power. It goes further than that, however. The critical issues about literacy are not just related to individual attitudes towards others who have less success in the formal requirements of schooling. One of the main areas of critical literacy lies in the definition accepted by any group about what it means and involves. It isn't just that those who are more literate have power over those who are less or non-literate. What is critical is that those who have power to define what *counts* as literacy hold the greatest power. Literacy can be exclusive as well as inclusive. Frank Smith points out the significance of 'joining the literacy club' (Smith 1984) and this is important, of course, for any child, but questions arise about who writes the rules for the club and what if they change? Literacy can be used to perpetuate divisions between people as well as offering access to knowledge and power.

Taking a critical view of literacy, then, means taking on the idea that lack of power over the written word isn't just the result of an individual's failure to get the hang of the literacy offered in school. It also means that the ways in which literacy opportunities are presented in schools (and elsewhere) can themselves create divisions and exclude some children from ever having the chance to exercise power over their own literacy, or over the social rights which literacy confers. This is why using literacy as a criterion for differentiation needs careful scrutiny. The texts children read and write are often linked with the values held by society about what counts as valuable and valued literacy. Jenny Cook-Gumpertz describes literacy as 'a socially constructed phenomenon' (Cook-Gumpertz 1986). She goes on to say:

> In early modern times literacy was regarded as a virtue, and some elements of moral virtue still seem to attach to it in that judgements about literacy skills tend to have prescriptive or normative overtones. A literate person was not only seen as a good person, but as someone capable of exercising good and reasonable judgement, for a literate person's taste and judgement depended upon access to a written tradition – a body of texts – reflecting centuries of collective experience.
>
> (Cook-Gumpertz 1986: 1)

Judgements about what counts as valuable literacy, then, seem to be tied up with judgements about an individual's worth or value. The issue of what literacy is all about becomes more and more complex. It isn't just about how we help children to become successful readers and writers, but also about the kinds of texts they read and write and the value placed upon those texts. Further than that, it's also about how professionals involved in 'the literacy business' actually do their jobs. The way literacy is described by teachers, parents and others involved in education, and the kinds of texts which are given value or status are part of a society's theory of literacy. This theory will, in turn, underpin the ways in which literacy is introduced by governments and in schools.

Teachers are becoming more and more aware that the literacy practices of homes vary, as do the ways in which parents and other adults perceive valid and valuable literacy. These perceptions make a difference to children's prospects of taking on school versions of literacy. Teachers' awareness of the diversity of home literacy experiences, especially at Key Stage 1, is an essential ingredient for widening the possibilities of future access to learning for all children.

Shirley Brice Heath has been one of the most influential researchers into the relationship between home and school literacy and the effects on learning (Brice Heath 1983). In her study of three different communities and their literacy, she identified elements of certain 'ways of taking' meaning from texts as critical factors in future success in learning. In families in the middle-class community of her research the print environment and literacy practices of home and of school were very similar. In the poor white and black communities there were significant contrasts between what home and school saw as valid ways to use narrative, for example. In the poorer white community, reading the Bible was a significant literary event. Since to this community Bible truth was literal – what is written is fact – school practices of changing stories or seeing them as imaginary were unfamiliar and often unacceptable ways of treating reading. School practices also differed from social literacy practices in the black community, where reading was very much a public affair so that solitary reading was again unfamiliar and, if not unacceptable, certainly seen as 'odd'. The implications of these varying perceptions would reach forward into the children's later school experience and influence their progress in learning. Those children whose home experiences of literacy most paralleled the school view were, perhaps unsurprisingly, most successful in school. Others, whose experience of literacy differed from what the school saw as valid, gradually ground to a standstill in learning, baffled by an unfamiliar set of practices which did not fit with home experience. It was not that the children from the two communities whose children began to struggle in school were 'less able' nor that their homes were lacking in reading material; the fact was that there was a serious mismatch between teachers' perceptions and children's real experience – and this made for failure in children who might otherwise have progressed perfectly adequately. In Shirley Brice Heath's view, school should be:

> a place which allowed these children to capitalise on the skills, values and knowledge they brought there, and to add on the conceptual structures imparted by the school.
>
> (Brice Heath 1983: 13)

And this has important implications for teachers; it is all too easy to assume that differences in literacy practices necessarily mean 'deficiencies'. Shirley Brice Heath's studies were carried out in America, but nearer to home, in an East Anglian industrial town, Sally Wilkinson looked in detail at the classroom and home literacy of three of her Key Stage 1 learners:

> Whereas much of Darryl's and Sarah's writing drew on themes and characters from books and the media, most of Rashida's writing was based on reality. Her stories would draw almost exclusively on remembered experiences, for example, a piece about someone in hospital reflected her knowledge of injections gained when the family took Mamun (her brother) for his regular check-ups. I found (like Shirley Brice Heath's observations of Roadville children) that Rashida had the greatest difficulty in creating imaginative stories. Her parents told me that there was not a tradition of oral storytelling in the family and that when Rashida wrote at home it was mostly letters to the neighbour's daughter, her siblings or her mother. This reflected what Rashida liked to do at school. When she was in the writing corner she would write letter after letter and post them in the class post-box. She wrote to confirm friendships and also to anyone whom she felt was sad or hadn't had a letter lately – in order to cheer them up. When I visited Rashida's home, Lyla (her sister) had showed me a loose-leaf file from Rashida's drawer in the chest. She had repeatedly written her own and her siblings' names and also played with words in both English and Bengali on the same page, experimenting with the patterns involved in the characters of each.
>
> (Wilkinson 1994: 35)

Rashida, obviously a capably literate child, was having lessons in writing in Bengali at the mosque and Sally Wilkinson came to understand that in the classroom she was 'showing expectations of her which are different from those of her family or the community teacher at the mosque' (p. 36). She goes on to explain how she used this knowledge to 'provide methods of writing at school which would have some resemblance to those she was encountering outside it'. The importance of such information is not only relevant for those children whose home culture is identifiably different, in terms of bilingualism for example. Sally Wilkinson also found that Sarah – from a local family of some long-standing – 'made a clear distinction between home and school books' preferring to read those from home which she was familiar with. At home, Sally Wilkinson discovered, Sarah liked telling stories and found reading aloud in school rather threatening:

> My task when Sarah was reading aloud with me on a one-to-one basis was one which required a delicate balance. I wanted to prevent her

becoming anxious over any stumbles in her decoding of the text and I also wanted to encourage her to interrogate the text more. I talked with her mother about this so that we were both operating in the same way. By the end of term, through both of us having in-depth knowledge of exactly the point that Sarah was at in her developing confidence and fluency, we were able to see the beginning of a change in her attitude to less familiar or unknown text as she focused on it, believing that she could get meaning from it.

(p. 30)

Sally Wilkinson learned a lot about literacy and ability by not making assumptions, but connections. Much of the everyday business of the classroom is conducted through print. This is an accepted part of the educational process and, of course, one of the central aims of schooling is to help children move towards confident and critical literacy. Where the centrality of literacy becomes more problematic, however, is when assumptions are made about a necessary relationship between accuracy in the technical conventions of writing, for example, or fluent and 'correct' reading aloud, and a child's general ability to grasp and internalise concepts. In other words, if reading and writing are taken as the main evidence of 'ability' then there are likely to be some errors of judgement. These will become even more entrenched if assessments in any area of the curriculum are based on unsupported reading and writing. (As in certain elements of the SATs at the end of key stages.) And, as another twist of the screw, if assessments are one-shot tests, then the aspects of literacy which are likely to be tested are those which are most readily assessed as 'correct' or 'incorrect' – largely the surface technicalities which do not give a full or reliable picture of any individual's literacy.

The important connections between language, literacy and learning are commonly acknowledged. Language is not only the vehicle for introducing and expressing new experience, facts or concepts, it is also the means by which knowledge and experience are forged and realised. It is at one and the same time the carrier and constructor of learning. Any block on the satisfying exercise and use of language and literacy will necessarily restrict progress in learning. Writing has certainly been seen traditionally as the prime means of assessing learning, but often the writing required for this purpose has been the kind of end-product, one-shot writing which is done to satisfy the requirement for a teacher to have some evidence that ground has been covered rather than as an integral part of the individual's strategies for getting to grips with learning. Where writing is seen as part of the whole process of making meaning – putting ideas down on paper, clarifying thought and shaping learning – it is a powerful tool for cognitive development. Rather than being seen as a means of judging success or failure after a learning activity, writing can be used as a way of contributing to the continuing process of learning. Planning strategies and frameworks, methods for reorganising early drafts or for categorising information all add to children's knowledge of how language can be shaped to fulfil their own intentions, to make their own meanings clear. Similarly, when writing is seen as a process which will develop best in a planned environment which supports experimentation, and allowed to emerge as children grapple with the communications they want to make, then there is likely to be more investment in wanting to 'get it right'. Further, investigations have shown that when writing is seen by teacher and pupils as a means of learning as well as an end in itself, it becomes easier to identify areas where extra help is needed or where significant progress has been made. (See, for example, the work of the National Writing Project 1988–91.) The teacher has a key role in introducing and demonstrating writing techniques for organising learning and in offering clear explanations of how these techniques can be used to help shape learning. On the other hand, teaching methods and classroom arrangements which depress the fluent acquisition of literacy may spring from the best intentions in the world to provide tasks which 'match ability' but their effects can be long-lasting and seriously damaging.

To make the picture even more complicated, it is becoming increasingly clear that the kinds of texts which are included in any definition of literacy are becoming more varied and diverse, so that it may be necessary to consider a range of *literacies* rather than just 'literacy' alone. Children have access to a wide range of texts besides printed books, many of them part of the new technologies of the microchip revolution. Although they may be ahead of adults in their familiarity with some of these literacies, teachers need to get to grips with them if they are to help children 'read' these with a critical eye; they need to find ways of helping children describe and frame what they already know if they are to harness new literacies for progress in learning while also using them with discrimination. In their chapter. 'Visual literacy: access for all', Katy Pearson and Gavin Thompson review the kinds of shifts that have been made recently to acknowledge and use pictorial and media texts in education and the children's diverse experiences of such texts. To be literate in a society that will soon reach the twenty-first century does not only mean being proficient in reading and writing, but also implies the need to be familiar with a growing number of 'new' literacies. In this chapter, the writers give examples from Key Stages 1 and 2 which support their contention that picture books and video texts are not just for the pre-literate or those who might be having difficulties with the written word. While acknowledging that pictorial text can 'take the heat off' reading for some children, or provide a way in to more traditional forms of literacy, they stress the value of pictorial and media narratives as challenging texts for the full range of readers.

This theme, and the importance of a developmental view of writing, are taken up by Noelle Hunt in her chapter, 'Cushioned by confidence'. She wanted to see how younger readers might be able to focus critically on the genre of picture books. Noelle is a language support teacher working with bilingual children in mainstream classrooms so she is very aware that inexperience with reading and writing in English can be a constraint for young children who are already fluent and/or literate in another language and who are capable and eager learners. With the ready co-operation of the class teacher, Noelle embarked on a project designed to use picture books as texts which would 'challenge readers at all levels'. She planned a differentiated project, starting from the aim of enabling all the children to gain access to a range of activities designed to promote critical awareness of genre. The results were a generally raised standard of achievement for all the children. This enactment of a commitment to equal access reflects research done by Coombs in America (Coombs 1994) into 'high-track' and 'low-track' groupings for learning – a type of streaming by ability compared with a control group which has a mix of abilities. As might be expected, 'high-track' learners did well in this system (for a range of reasons). However, it was also discovered that classes that were not ability grouped were much more like 'high-track' classes and that 'low-track' suffered impoverished learning experiences and diminished achievements. Whatever the reasons for this, it is clear that offering learning opportunities which can stretch all children is most likely to raise general standards of achievement. By careful planning, teacher and pupil collaboration and a project which took the heat off literacy initially, Noelle Hunt's 7 year olds were able to rise to the challenge of developing critical awareness of texts.

In the third chapter of this section, 'You think I'm thick, don't you?' Avril Dawson, a support teacher in a middle school (Years 5–8), describes work with some 'failed readers'. As she points out 'these are children of normal intelligence and articulacy, well co-ordinated and, like most of us, with excellent memories in certain areas', but they were having great difficulties in coping with the learning demands across the curriculum at Key Stage 2 and just beyond. She wanted to probe just why they had come to see themselves as 'struggling readers, well aware of the gap between themselves and their peers'. In discussions with individuals and with whole class groups she began to uncover the children's reading histories in an attempt to identify factors which might have led to failure. While there were no clearly identifiable causes for the pupils' difficulties, she discovered a great deal about their perceptions of literacy by talking with parents. Like Sally Wilkinson, she learned about what the children could do in terms of reading as well

as what might help them make more progress. It is salutary to speculate how different the school careers of Avril Dawson's 'failed' readers
might have been had their early years teachers been able to recognise
and build on the varied experiences of literacy which they brought from
home and to offer a greater range in school approaches to the introduction of formal literacy.

Avril Dawson's investigations raised issues about the relationship
between reading for learning from fiction and non-fiction texts; of the
importance of individual involvement not just in the learning itself, but
in the public recognition and display of that learning; the feelings of
frustration and helplessness experienced by children who have their
'failure' consolidated by particular approaches to learning; the effects of
the kinds of 'improper literacy' described earlier which are often invoked
as equalling 'ability'. Arguing for a wider definition of literacy which
will answer to the diverse experiences of all pupils, she concludes, most
emphatically, that 'we do our pupils a grave disservice if we give our
authority to the notion of functional literacy.'

Avril Dawson quotes Peter Traves who refers to 'the complex web of
experiences' that feed into literacy (Traves 1992). Frances Lockwood's
chapter, 'Hearing impaired children in the mainsteam classroom',
emphasises the complexity of links between literacy and oracy from the
personal standpoint of a teacher (and a learner) whose hearing has been
impaired from an early age. This presents a different facet of the inter-
woven issues of literacy, learning and progress. She is not dealing here
with severe hearing loss, but with the 'invisible disability' of hearing
impairment, which is much more widespread in classrooms than we
might suppose and can have far-reaching effects. As defined in the
National Curriculum, literacy includes the Attainment Target of
Speaking and Listening. Since literacy dominates life, and proficiency in
literacy is a central aim, then the official description of literacy, which
necessarily includes a high proportion of oracy, becomes even more
problematic for pupils whose hearing is impaired. This is not an argument for getting rid of some of the recent hard-won recognition of the
importance of talk for learning; rather, Frances Lockwood argues, it is
an important area for thoughtful planning for diverse experiences in
learning and careful monitoring of the learning environment 'As
teachers, we must not allow the "deficit model" of the hearing impaired
child to creep into our assessment of the hearing impaired child's *situation*.' She questions the easy assumption that talk is a means of equal
access to the curriculum for all learners, pointing to her own grateful
experience of reading and writing for reflective expression of developing
ideas. In this she prefigures a debate which will also be aired in Part III
– that talk is as important in learning as reading and writing, but needs
to be managed if it is genuinely to serve the learning process. What is

essential, she argues, is a balance in the *contexts* for learning – the approaches and classroom arrangements – allied to greater teacher knowledge, which will support all learners, not just the hearing impaired. These she sees as factors which will make learning accessible for all children.

Part II, then, looks at inclusive and exclusive approaches to learning through literacy. While it is important not to see literacy as the sole or even primary measure of 'ability' or potential for learning, it is equally critical to make strenuous attempts to increase access to literacy for all children. The varied perspectives offered here give strong evidence that moving away from a fixed view of literacy towards a wider acknowledgement of diverse literacies, and taking a critical view of just what we mean by ability (in literacy or in learning generally), will feed a more effective means of offering access to the full curriculum.

REFERENCES

Brice Heath, S.(1983) *Ways With Words*, Cambridge, Cambridge University Press

Cook Gumpertz, J. (1986) *The Social Construction of Literacy*, Cambridge, Cambridge University Press

Coombs J.R. (1994) 'Equal Access to Education', *Journal of Curriculum Studies* 26 (3), (May/June)

O'Neil, W. (1977) 'Properly literate', in Hoyles, M. (ed.) *The Politics of Literacy*, London, Writers and Readers

National Writing Project (1989) *Writing and Learning, Audiences for Writing, Becoming a Writer*, (and other titles) Walton-on-Thames, Nelson/NWP

Smith, F. (1984) *Joining the Literacy Club*, London, Heinemann

Traves, P. (1992) 'Reading, the entitlement to be properly literate', in Kimberley, K., Meek, M. and Miller, J. (eds) *New Readings: contributions to an understanding of literacy*, London, A & C Black

Wilkinson, S. (1994) 'What did you do at home today? A case study of the links between three children's homes, and school literacies', unpublished Advanced Diploma thesis, Cambridge, Homerton College

Chapter 3

Visual literacy
Access for all

Katy Pearson and Gavin Thompson

At one time, learning to read was considered to be a 'confirmed set of traditional exercises' (Meek 1992: 226) administered by teachers in the classroom with the aid of 'good' books. Reading was thought to be something that could be taught in stages by the use of teaching methods like mathematical formulae, which could then be applied to a corresponding reading situation. However, Frank Smith's revelation that children learn to read by constant exposure to and practice in reading which matters to them (Smith 1985) released teachers from an approach involving arduous 'drills and skills', and allowed attention to be turned towards the type of things readers learn without ever being taught (Meek 1988). Research in this era brought the beginnings of literacy development out of the classroom and into the pre-school environment of the home and its associated culture. Here it was discovered that the many forms and contexts of print such as the posters, advertisements, food labels and signs that surround us in our daily lives, give pre-school children a vast and varied knowledge of print before they have had experience of books. As a result, conscientious educationists have had to take account of the role that less 'traditional' forms of print play in the learning of children of all ages. This is a welcome change in attitudes towards what serves as valuable literacy for children. It is particularly important when considering how to provide a curriculum which will ensure access for all learners and build on the diversity of children's experience. Differentiation means meeting the learning needs of every child so that all can share in the same curriculum; too restrictive a view of literacy can operate against that educational goal.

'In our contemporary environment pictures are special' (Meek 1992: 232). We fill our walls with them, flick through them in magazines, watch them in moving series on television, see them advertising products on bill boards and appreciate their beauty and impact in galleries. In fact the use of images to represent meaning and communicate messages predates that of lettering. Yet mainstream education, particularly under the stress of the National Curriculum, not only fails to use the pictorial and visual world which surrounds children, it acts in deliberate opposition to it, fearing that emphasis on visual literacy might, in some way, threaten the supremacy of the written word (Hodge and Tripp, 1986). Such an attitude gives a definition of literacy which is shallow, limited and incomplete. It sees literacy purely in terms of reading and writing, the only valid text being written language. It now seems important to give literacy a much wider definition and to look critically at the assumption that the first resource for learning should come from printed books. 'Being able to read' now includes not only all types of print in the public domain, but also all visual texts like comics, magazines, picture books, computer VDUs, CD-ROM and television screens. The 'reading' of images can be just as beneficial and significant to children's learning as any written text, and in many cases, easier for the teacher to direct because of the child's experience, skill and obvious enjoyment in this area. It seems that the term literacy should be extended to that of 'literacies', in order to acknowledge and give credit to all other valuable texts. Further, it is worth questioning the assumption that the printed word is the best resource from which to get information. In querying the written word as presented on worksheets as the necessary first resource in the classroom, Penelope Weston asks:

> What other possibilities are there – for oral enquiry and reporting ... use of databases, photographs, modelling? Are there alternative methods which some pupils will find more effective and challenging?
>
> (Weston 1992: 7)

The time has come, it seems, for a re-evaluation of visual literacy and what it might offer for the development of learning for all children. In considering the contribution that visual texts make to the learning of children, we look first, briefly, at the new insights which a study of picture books can offer for finding more challenging ways in to learning. One of the most obvious ways in which picture books contribute to children's literacy and learning is through narrative; focusing on the specific media of television, including video, allows an examination of the role of narrative in children's educational development. Most importantly, we want to suggest that it is through seeing visual and verbal literacies as complementary, rather than in opposition, that we can best cater for – and draw upon – the diversity of children's experience of new and not-so-new literacies. This means challenging those who might already be seen as confidently literate as well as those who are not, it is our view that visual approaches can extend the range of *all* learners.

PICTURE BOOKS

A 'golden age' of picture books is currently being celebrated. Never before have art movements, printing techniques, gifted illustrators and writer/artists come together to produce such an abundance of richness and variety in the world of picture books. No longer are pictures simply illustrations of the written text. There still exists the belief among some parents and teachers that picture books are for the infant school child, who should be weaned from them before the pictures start to interfere with the beginner reader's ability to concentrate on the printed word. David Lewis claims that most analysis and description of picture books takes the view that the pictures are purely in the service of the words. This 'tends to generate a privileging of the printed word and a gravitating of attention away from the pictorial aspect of the form' (Lewis 1990).

Apart from consigning pictures to the inferior position of 'prop for beginner reader' (Lewis 1990) this view assumes that it is the words alone that generate the meaning. However, the work of writer/artists like Anthony Browne, Pat Hutchins and Ruth Brown, prove that this is simply not the case. Let us take for example Ruth Brown's *Our Cat Flossie*. While the words give us a story of an extraordinarily helpful, sensible and intriguing family cat – 'her hobbies include bird-watching and fishing ... she always insists on helping with the knitting and making the beds' – the pictures confirm to the reader that Flossie is, in fact, just like any other mischievous cat who catches birds and fishes, tangles up wool and messes up beds. The pictures give a totally different message from the words. Rather than supporting them, they contradict them. From the message conveyed by the gap between words and pictures, the reader learns how the written text is to be read – that the words are not to be taken simply at face value, but read with humour, with 'tongue in cheek'. Many children's picture books adopt this multi-layered approach. They play on words, juxtapose different messages through the words and pictures and show that instead of simply complementing the written language, the pictures are capable of contradiction, deviation, extension and elaboration, depending on the relationship the writer/artist has chosen for the text.

Children are reading pictures before they are one year old, without any direct instruction, and as with any skill, the more it is put into practice, the more it is improved and refined. By the time children come to pick up a book, they are already experts at grasping meaning and decoding messages from pictures. Yet instead of this skill being nurtured and developed by teachers in junior school years, the tendency is to press children to pure written text as soon as reading competency is reached. Picture books are considered of little value and banished.

In fact, suitable picture books are designed for all reading competencies, containing very subtle word play and humour which children have to tease out of the texts. In a variety of ways picture books can provide challenges for developing readers and young readers themselves can come to recognise the importance of pictorial texts. Spencer, a 10 year-old reader puts it like this:

> I have not always liked reading I do not like reading books without pictures and books that are sometimes easy. I like to read books that are challenging.
>
> (Bearne 1994: 31)

Here is a reader who is clear about the potential challenge of pictorial texts! Barbara Jordan argues that picture books 'offer as great a challenge to the reader as any sustained narrative text without pictures,' and that they are 'good for any age', quoting a list of picture book makers whose work has 'demonstrated without doubt that their books are anything but simple stories, simply told' (Jordan 1992: 115).

For the fluent, experienced reader there are a range of picture books which can be used with different teaching objectives. Pictures may be used to enhance the child's understanding of literary conventions, particularly structure, to appreciate the use of various genres, and to ease the reader into an acquaintance with classical authors. In literary conventions pictures serve to reinforce the structure of the theme. Their clarity of message allows for greater variation from the main story-line without the fear of the child becoming lost in complexity – something which is always likely within pure written text. The use of specific genres as being appropriate to particular themes and to build the right atmosphere and background, is a difficult concept for children to grasp. Illustrations help the child to identify the relationship between the style of text and the theme and atmosphere which is being covered. As Judith Graham states, 'It is my conviction that picture books have an underestimated power to communicate ... and that readers, young and old are recruited by picture books to engage with the emotional and intellectual meanings that characterise all good reading experiences' (Graham 1990: 117). Such a form of visual literacy, which clearly has enjoyable learning experiences to offer, as well as expanding one of a child's greatest natural skills, should be embraced with enthusiasm rather than devalued and set aside.

It is clear that the more experienced reader can learn a great deal from pictorial text. Picture books are not just for the beginner reader, nor do pictures simply 'tell the story' and help the reader understand a difficult piece of writing. They can, furthermore, help children – even the confidently literate – gain new knowledge and understanding in all areas of the curriculum. Barbara Quail wanted to inspire all the children in her Year 4 class to new enjoyment of reading and chose to do this by gathering a collection of richly photographed books covering a wide variety of subjects – the countryside and coastline of the British Isles, Dublin, Russia, abstract art, decorative knitting, Australia and aboriginal life, portraits of famous people by Lord Snowdon, one book with Italian text about the Dolomites and another in German featuring Hessen. She was gratified, but quite surprised about the success of this project: she commented on the reader-satisfaction gained from a reading experience where you could just browse, or look at one picture then put the book away, as well as the pleasures of revisiting the known and familiar. Many of the books had printed text as well as pictorial text and so stimulated children to read beyond their previously perceived 'ability'. At the same time 'looking at picture books means that children are not threatened by the risk of failure to identify words' and they can learn about the world outside their own experience (Quail 1994: 5). In conclusion, Barbara Quail comments (pp. 7–8):

> This reading focus has made me acknowledge the reading capacity of my children freed from the tethers of formal literacy. The picture books gave the children plenty of choice and at the same time raised their motivation. If you just gazed at one picture for a few moments you were left with an individual image to reflect on. The image is worthy in its own right, unlike that half page of unfinished text!

This echoes one of Margaret Meek's observations about the relationship between home and school literacies:

> Evidence from research emphasises the importance of images. It's schooling, and the teaching of reading as a concern with the words alone, that puts into our heads the notion that books with pictures are a preliterate form of storytelling, while all the time the very force of television shows us this is not the case.
>
> (Meek 1988: 15)

READING TELEVISION

Reading television is another very underestimated literacy activity. Children spend, on average, up to 20 per cent of their waking hours watching TV, a pastime which they obviously value and enjoy. Television forms an important part of a child's subculture. It brings to life their comic world heroes; it sets off widely followed trends and crazes such as the *Teenage Mutant Hero Turtles*, or *Gladiators*, and it can break across all cultural barriers, giving children shared interests with their peers. Cary Bazalgette reminds us:

Five-year-olds may not have done much reading – they may not even have been read to – but they have almost certainly watched a good deal of television. They have watched films, probably on video, but possibly at the cinema as well ... They have developed a limited competence in making sense of media products which schools rarely use: indeed, it is usually dismissed as being not worthwhile 'school knowledge'.

(Bazalgette 1988)

Yet, significantly, 'television is the modern children's encyclopaedia' (Meek 1992: 229), which provides them with direct information, stimulates their curiosity and engages their attention in matters which might otherwise be ignored. Children learn an immense amount from it, not least a wealth of information about their culture and about morality. It is a very powerful tool and, after all, it would appear that children spend as much time in front of the TV screen as they do at school. Surely we should be teaching children to *read* television and films and not just to watch them? However, some teachers and parents regard television in a very different and negative light.

There are two main fears: one is that watching television is a passive, low-level activity which is likely to stultify the developing intellects of young learners. It is seen as potentially the enemy of reading and thought, based on the unfounded assumption that the child who watches television today would, sixty years ago, have been reading books, despite the fact that more books are bought and read today. The other principal fear is that the television may be imposing violent, sexual or otherwise undesirable influences on the young. Statistics suggest that certain kinds of child crimes are on the increase and, of course, it is easy to cast blame upon television. Media reportage tells us that standards of literacy achievement have rapidly declined in recent years and again the influence of the television is muttered disapprovingly. These unquestioned, 'common-sense' assertions deserve challenge. Children are not necessarily helpless under the influences transmitted to them, rather, they can take what they wish from the screen, interpret messages in their own way, and reconstruct these meanings in their own lives, for their own purposes. Cathy Pompe provides a reminder that:

Children are natural critics; they mimic and make fun of everything around, mercilessly: adults, each other and themselves. Children's parody reflects the need both to get the measure of something, and to distance themselves from it. Children resist that which has power over them: adults, institutions, and even TV programmes.

(Pompe 1992: 57)

Helen Bromley (1994) provides a detailed observation of children's power to subvert and mimic what they have seen on screen and make it their own:

> My daughter arrived home from school one evening full of antici-
> pation for the next day. It transpired that this was not because of some
> inspirational delivery of the curriculum at Key Stage 2 but was due to
> the fact that 'We're playing this really good game in the playground.'
> The game was entitled 'The Land before Time' and was based on the
> video of the same name. The promotional material describes this as 'a
> tale of hope, survival and love' which will teach 'unforgettable lessons
> about life and sticking together'. Discussing this game with Rebecca
> showed that lessons had been learned, perhaps even more valuable
> than those suggested by its makers. Importantly, it was necessary
> to have seen the film before you could take part in the game. . . . The
> children had created an imaginary world in the playground, using
> places from the film. They were not, however, re-enacting the film
> but re-writing it with many original ideas. A great deal of planning
> was required to prepare for the next day's play and it was apparent
> that they found it very easy to slip in and out of the game.

Helen asked her daughter if she felt there was any way in which playing the game could help her with her work in class. Rebecca's reply was, 'I think it helps you with the past, the present and the future of thought.' Helen points out that:

> Playing the video inspired game was helping her to reflect on prior
> knowledge, speculate on possible outcomes and use both of these
> actions to support the task in hand. This serves as a powerful
> reminder of the importance of narrative.
>
> (Bromley 1994: 22–23)

THE IMPORTANCE OF NARRATIVE

Narrative is everywhere. It is impossible for children to escape from it. Every day a child will witness many and varied types of narrative from listening to retelling of events at home, warnings, anecdotes and expla-nations by the teacher, news narratives, television narratives, jokes and gossip amongst friends and hopefully a bedtime story. It is hard to imagine a child's life without it, so it is very easy to take it for granted and not fully realise its potential to educate children about themselves, about stories, about other people, and about imaginative possibilities. A great deal of the information that a child accumulates over the years is likely to have been acquired through stories rather than through factual statements.

Stories are a way of allowing children to see things through others' eyes. A story will always have been written from another point of view which a child will have to adapt to, thus broadening perceptions on the world. Because stories deal with events beyond the here and now they encourage inventive thinking, which in turn helps children deal with new and previously unencountered situations. Throughout a story the reader is building up sets of impressions of what has gone before and predicting a series of ways in which events may proceed. These anticipations are continually being revised in the light of the unfolding story. Experience of narrative can also assist in the development of the use of language in several ways. Children, and indeed adults, extend their vocabulary through exposure to new words in stories, in books or on the screen. It only takes the emergence of a cult TV series to remind us of that. The language of books and the quality that makes them literary and special can really be obtained only from books and is very distinct from spoken language. Here is one example where written narrative is separate from the visual and highlights the point that neither one can replace the other, but that they offer vast potential in combination.

This distinction between the language in stories and everyday language is a very important one with far reaching implications. Instead of referring to objects and experiences within direct experience, stories involve reference to things outside the immediate experience of their reader. In doing so they form a bridge between the concreteness of the here-and-now and the abstraction of the fiction world. This link is obviously a crucial one that children need to be able to make, as without it much of their future education will have little meaning and relevance. A child needs to be able to deal with abstract ideas.

Beyond literacy, too, narrative also has its uses; experience of narrative can help an individual's cognitive development, it can help a child cope with emotions and it can give a great insight into culture and history. Narrative can illuminate other curriculum areas as well, both in triggering off discussion or project work or in anecdotal form to explain a tricky concept. But above all else, narrative is fun. Stories in a book or on the screen provide endless pleasure for children and surely that alone offers good motivation in developing literacy. There is of course, the very large area of children creating their own narratives, whether writing their own stories, oral narratives in class, or just telling jokes or gossiping to their friends. It is all narrative, and it is all helping to develop children's literacy both as a vehicle for helping to make sense of experience for the child, and as a mechanism for conveying that experience to others.

But what of film, television and video narrative? Research suggests that over the last ten years cinema going has doubled and home video viewing has rocketed. At the same time an increasing number of families have access to satellite television (BFI 1989).

Linguists and media analysts have shown that the whole universe of signs is organised into systems of codes and conventions that we have learned, just as we learned verbal language. In other words, it makes sense to say that we 'read' a photograph or a TV programme in a way analogous to that in which we read a written text. Just as literature is not the same 'thing' as drama (and so you cannot use the same language to 'read' a Shakespeare play as you would to read a nineteenth-century novel), so television and film as a medium differs from both. We should be teaching children this language of how to read visual images so that they are able to interact with visual narrative and become active readers rather than just passive consumers. As teachers we spend a great deal of time in the area of literacy trying to teach children to read between the lines, so it is equally important that children are able to read between the images in visual literacy. Moreover, 'Reading television is an important aspect of general cognitive and social development' according to Hodge and Tripp (1986: 3) If we want children to be more discriminating about what they watch on television and at the cinema then we have to teach them the language and give them the power. If as teachers we could empower children and unlock the true potential of films and literacy, film would become applicable to all but one of the roles of narrative in literacy listed above (i.e. the exception is the learning of 'book' language) and would open up many more.

Importantly, however, there is one area where film narrative is unique. Film opens up to the child a whole new world of adult narrative and literature. Whereas there are many probable reasons why, for example, a Year 6 child cannot pick up an adult text and gain a lot of pleasure from it (perhaps style, complexity, vocabulary, concepts) there are far fewer reasons why the same child cannot gain a lot from watching film narratives designed for adults. Gunter and McAleer (1990) have published extensive evidence in support of this claim showing for example that by the age of ten, 80 to 90 per cent of the central plot of an hour long action adventure programme for adults is remembered and understood. They go on to say that in tests, most children aged 10 and over were able to make a fairly complicated inference about a scene in a drama programme. Film narrative empowers children, giving them earlier access to far more complex stories and scenarios than they would probably be granted through books at that age.

This could have important implications for children's cognitive development as a whole. In Vygotsky's words, children's thinking can be enhanced if attention is paid to the zone of proximal development

> the distance between the actual developmental level as determined by independent problem solving and the level of potential develop-

ment as determined through problem solving under adult guidance
or in collaboration with more capable peers.

(Vygotsky 1978: 86)

Teachers have often observed groups of children discussing quite
complex issues from adult-orientated film narratives with a noticeable
energy and enthusiasm. This peer collaboration, possibly with shared
expert knowledge of a particular subject or opinion, combined with the
adult film narrative (or even the characters in the narrative) actually
taking on a role as an intangible or surrogate adult, could in certain
circumstances lead to children 'knocking on the door' of the zone; set
within a planned learning context, the adult film narrative acts as a
vehicle that can help focus the child's cognitive reasoning on language
and culture, thus promoting the intellectual growth that is required
to enter the zone. Vygotsky says that 'the only "good learning" is that
which is in advance of development' (1978: 89). An adult film narrative can allow the child to access ideas of language and culture that are
ahead of natural development, thus achieving 'good learning' and better
understanding.

Since literacy is a cultural phenomenon and narrative is an essential
way of making sense of the world which is also cultural, we need to
look at contemporary cultural forms of narrative and utilise their power
to feed into literacy. Film and video narrative have as yet unrecognised
potential as learning tools that can help develop literacy, and educate
and please children whilst they are doing it. However, for the children
to extract the best out of the narratives, they need to be taught the
language of film and television so they can more easily understand the
codes, conventions and categories, thus putting them in a more powerful
position to make critical comparisons and evaluations.

This provides further, powerful reasons why the notion of literacy
should be extended to include a more deliberate inclusion of visual texts.
Because children have the capacity to be powerful decoders of TV, video
and film, the task is not seen as arduous, they do it as a matter of course.
Nevertheless they are still 'reading', they are still grasping information
by the same intellectual processes, but are instead using the media of
moving pictures and sound. 'Looking feels like learning . . . the viewer
watches, the voice-over guides the watching' (Meek 1992: 229).

However, if the information is not welcomed in the classroom by
teachers and not given any credit, it is not being used to its full potential. The meanings children gain from television can be adjusted,
expounded, directed and renegotiated in the classroom. By discussing
what they have seen, children learn how their knowledge can be most
suitably put to use, to which situations it can be applied, and how to
go about understanding, improving and adding to it. Teachers have the

capacity to use this learning to empower children and unlock their potential.

LINKS BETWEEN WRITTEN AND 'FILM' NARRATIVES

One powerful way of unlocking the potential of all learners is to exploit the links between visual and print texts. Margaret Meek refers to long-term research establishing that when children really wanted information, and responded to what they had read, they first watched the television (Meek 1992) and then perhaps turned to books to find out more. It could be argued then, that television and film creates readers because it 'opens up subject matter, while text books close it down' (Meek 1992: 229). Many children prefer to read books that they have first seen on tele-vision or film and are driven to read complicated written texts because of the first introduction to the narrative through film. Carol Kirwan found that her Year 5 children were keen to read the original text of *A Christmas Carol* after seeing the old George C. Scott film version:

> They became very involved in the language of the story and loved to get hold of rolling descriptive phrases. These soon emerged in their written work and led to enthusiasm for using dictionaries to look up unfamiliar words and phrases. They began to quote from the story and their careful viewing of the video led to them analysing the char-acters as depicted in the book and the film. Independently of this work, one of her young readers wrote in his reading journal: 'I enjoy reading *Jurassic Park* because I've seen it at the cinema.'
>
> (Kirwan in Bearne 1994: 28)

Some suggest that teachers fear television because they believe the child will know more than they, and this is indeed very possible. While it is natural that teachers could feel vulnerable under these circumstances, if they could 'withhold value judgements and tolerate the position of learning alongside their pupils' (Pompe 1992: 57) then they would see how valid and significant the learning from television literacy can be. The school and its curriculum are an ideal setting for incorporating tele-vision literacy and appreciation, which should be woven into all existing curriculum areas. As Avril Harpley points out:

> Media education helps children to discriminate, to become more crit-ical, better equipped to make informed judgements and able to communicate in a variety of ways with a range of audiences. They will be able to choose.
>
> (Harpley 1994: 104)

The media of picture books, magazines, comics, computers and tele-vision are not going to disappear. They are here to stay and in our world of rapidly changing technology, techniques and visual effects are improving all the time. Children are surrounded by these visual literacies and will continue to read them, enjoy them and learn from them with or without the approval of educationalists. It makes good sense for all those involved in education to accept this inescapable fact and work with it to increase the teaching options, harness children's visual experience and capacity to discuss complex narratives with confidence and, incidentally, to enjoy the learning that visual literacy offers. It is also important to avoid the situation where the classroom stands alone in its avoidance of these techniques which are commonly adopted in other fields of learning.

REFERENCES

Bazalgette, C. (1988) 'They changed the picture in the middle of the fight – new kinds of literacy', in Meek, M., and Mills, C.(eds) *Language and Literacy in the Primary School*, Lewes, Falmer

Bearne, E. (1994) *Raising Reading Standards Course Evaluation*, Centre for Language in Primary Education, London Borough of Southwark.

BFI Education (1989) *Primary Media Education – a curriculum statement*, London, British Film Institute

Bromley, H. (1994) 'A New Way of Seeing: what can young children learn from watching videos?', unpublished Advanced Diploma thesis, Cambridge, Homerton College

Graham, J. (1990) *Pictures on the Page*, Sheffield, National Association for the Teaching of English

Gunter, B. and McAleer, J. (1990) *Children and Television*, London, Routledge

Harpley, A. (1994) 'Unpackaged text', in Bearne, E., Styles, M., and Watson, V. (eds) *The Prose and the Passion: children and their reading*, London, Cassell

Hodge, R. and Tripp, D. (1986) *Children and Television: A Semiotic Approach*, Cambridge, Polity

Jordan, B. (1992) 'Good for any age', in Styles, M., Bearne, E., and Watson, V. (eds) *After Alice – Exploring Children's Literature*, London, Cassell

Lewis, D. (1990) *The Constructedness of Texts: Picture Books and the Metafictive*, in *Signal*, 62: 131–146

Meek, M. (1988) *How Texts Teach What Readers Learn*, Stroud, Glos., Thimble Press

Meek, M. (1992) 'Literacy: redescribing reading', in, Kimberley, K., Meek, M., and Miller, J. (eds) *New Readings*, London, A & C Black

Pompe, C. (1992) 'When the aliens wanted water; media education – children's critical frontiers', in Styles, M., Bearne, E., and Watson, V. (eds) *After Alice – Exploring Children's Literature*, London, Cassell

Quail, B. (1994) 'How pictures can inspire children to want to read', unpublished Advanced Diploma thesis, Cambridge, Homerton College

Smith, F. (1985) *Reading*, Cambridge, Cambridge University Press

Vygotsky, L. (1978) *Mind in Society*, Harvard, Harvard University Press

Weston, P. (1992) 'A Decade for Differentiation', *The British Journal of Special Education*, 19 (1)

Chapter 4

'Cushioned by confidence'
Using picture books as a resource for differentiated learning

Noelle Hunt

Picture books can cross the boundary between the verbal and the non-verbal worlds; they can be allies of the child reader

(Hunt 1991: 176)

They can also be allies of the teacher concerned to offer a differentiated approach when planning a book study project. Picture books offer a wealth of interest to readers at all levels because the visual and verbal elements work separately and in partnership to express a variety of meanings and, often, more than one story-line. A struggling reader and one who is more fluent may approach the same book and derive enjoyment from it in different ways. Simplicity of language can offer easy access to the one while visual features and their interplay with the text ensure the more confident pupil also finds choosing picture books a rewarding experience.

Words can add to, contradict, expand, echo or interpret the pictures – and vice versa.

(Hunt 1991: 176)

As a focus for finding out if picture books can interest and challenge older pupils, I decided to research the responses of a Year 4 class to the *Meg and Mog* series of books by Helen Nicoll and Jan Pienkowski (Heinemann). In collaboration with the class teacher, I planned a scheme of work around this one genre of children's literature. I hoped to discover whether the class as a whole would find renewed interest in books that most of them had not chosen to read since infant school. I wanted also to see whether such a study would promote progress and achievement in individual pupils who, between them, represented a wide range of reading experience. For example, I wondered about the response of the girl who confidently devours whole series of Enid Blyton books to the exclusion of all else. I was equally curious to know the reaction of a bilingual pupil with learning difficulties who has only recently begun to build confidence with simple and familiar texts.

As a peripatetic language support teacher for the past seven years, I have been mainly involved in teaching developing bilingual children. Since it has been recognised that the learning of bilingual pupils is best promoted within the mainstream classroom, I have benefited enormously from collaborating and planning with class teachers from across the primary age range. During this same period I have been bringing up young children at home and supporting their own early reading experiences. As my awareness of reading resources grew, I began to question barriers I had raised for myself when categorising children's books, for example that picture books were suitable for young children and older children 'moved on' to longer texts and fewer illustrations. Progressing fluently towards ever-longer and more dense texts is certainly one important measure of achievement in reading but, along the way, there is much to be gained by revisiting earlier favourites and by sampling a range of genres. After all, as adults we may pick up a lengthy classic, a predictable romance or a book of old photographs, all according to mood.

I had always recognised that picture books, with all their variety and ingenuity, were a valuable addition to bookshelves everywhere, but I had never appreciated their full potential for readers ranging from inexperienced to fluent. I considered they made a valuable contribution to early reading experience but a restricted one. Of course, I was focusing mainly on the verbal elements and paying little heed to all the visual messages. I had a hazy notion of how attractive these books are to children and I had certainly enjoyed a few chuckles when reading and re-reading favourites to my own children; I deduced from this that there was something in them for adult readers too. Since embarking on this work, I have come to appreciate just how sophisticated and complex is this genre of children's literature and to consider the broader opportunities for learning which picture books can offer. In the *Meg and Mog* project, I tried to disentangle the layers of meaning intrinsic within them and to assess children's responses to them.

I am currently based in three primary schools and when the opportunity arose to follow an extended investigation, I planned it for a class whose teacher is a former colleague, Caroline Luck, from the language and curriculum support service. We have worked together for some time and since successful collaboration depends upon shared aims and good communication, we were certainly off to a good start. The school is a primary school where I have worked almost continuously for five years. I know the staff and pupils well, am familiar with its ethos and feel as much supported there as supportive. All these factors are conducive to confident planning and successful implementation. In addition, I have followed the present Year 4 through from Reception and know them as individuals and as a class group. This pre-knowledge was particularly helpful when I was considering how to pitch the work and how to ensure differentiation of tasks within each module. Caroline's contribution, as class teacher, was invaluable. Although new to the class that term, she had insights about it from another vantage point. For my part, I had only ever worked with these pupils in a support role, and then I was focusing mainly on the bilingual pupils.

PLANNING AND PREPARATION

I planned my investigation around the *Meg and Mog* series of picture books because I considered them exciting examples of the genre. They were readily available in school (I needed at least 8 copies) and they are almost universally popular among young children. I was certain that all the Year 4 pupils had encountered them at some time or other but, equally, it was unlikely that they had re-read them very recently. Further, when I studied the series closely myself, I thought I could isolate certain elements – both visual and verbal – and develop activities around them for the class. We could consider how the text and pictures are part of an integrated whole but can also tell separate stories and, in terms of colour and design, we could examine the bold style in which the authors create characters and settings. Focusing on verbal elements we could look at the use of sound effects and rhyming words, of layout, print type and story sequence, and the appropriacy of language use to readership. I decided that all tasks would generate writing and drawing of some kind but initially as draft quality rather than 'best' or final copy. It would be kept in pupil folders to be used as reference by the children when devising books in the same genre. With an end goal clearly explained, I hoped pupils would view all work produced as purposeful. While exploring ideas in draft form, I did not want them to become too bogged down in the technical aspects of writing. I intended a more thorough approach towards spelling, grammar, punctuation and handwriting when pupils were at the final stages of producing their books. For the purpose of my project, I considered too rigorous an approach early on would be demotivating, most particularly for those pupils still struggling with independent writing. My primary aims were to expand children's thinking and to promote talk, the success of which depended on the children feeling supported and secure. Initial enthusiasm for a new project can be fragile and is only maintained if reinforced by successive achievements, recognised and valued by those we work with. Cushioned by confidence we can accept constructive criticism if its purpose is apparent.

As well as understanding purpose when writing, pupils had to consider the audience for their work. As they would be in pairs, the first audience would be themselves, a partner, Caroline and me. It was discussed that, for the finished books, a potential readership would be younger pupils in school and opportunities would be found for sharing books during the following term.

Timetabling was an important issue. Caroline and I discussed using one hour a week from the limited time I could allocate the class. It was also decided that the project should extend across half a term. I soon realised we were going to run short of time, especially as my work began to collide head-on with Christmas! In the event, Caroline generously freed more sessions in the last couple of weeks which enabled most children to finish.

There were several other factors to consider. These included the identified class topics for the term, my own language support objectives for the bilingual pupils and the timetabling and activities of other teacher/welfare support allocated to the class. There is also a wide range of ability among the pupils of whom six are bilingual. One girl who speaks Urdu as her first language has been identified as having learning difficulties and is going through the statementing process.

I was now at a stage to prepare worksheets, templates and folders. We had arranged to divide the class between us. I worked with my group every Friday and Caroline found another session in the week to work with hers. After school and at other times, we made opportunities to review progress. In writing about the project I have attempted to analyse and discuss only the work I did with my group but I have included some of Caroline's comments too.

ORGANISING ACTIVITIES

After agreeing on the timescale and framework for the work, I devised a programme of activities which asked pupils to respond to some features of the *Meg and Mog* picture books; the representation of sound/sound effects, the contribution of rhyming words, use of colour, of illustrative techniques and the content and layout of the text. The tasks are described below:

Session 1

I wanted the children to explore the use of sound effects in *Meg and Mog* and to experiment with ideas of their own. Two worksheets were given; the first offering varied bubble shapes as starting points and the second, more open-ended, allowing pupils a free rein to devise their own. I asked all pupils to consider reasons for choices made when representing sounds with visual images. I expected this session to be a noisy one.

Session 2

Still on the theme of sound, I asked pupils to look at the authors' use of rhyming words. Together, we found rhymes in *Meg and Mog* written texts and, to follow on, I asked pairs to look for rhyming words in the pictures. Pupils would then be focusing on auditory rather than visual skills in discriminating rhymes. Individuals within pairs were next asked to make up simple and original character names and to compile a list of words to rhyme with each.

Session 3

Pupils were each asked to design, draw and colour an original character and to place it in a setting decided through discussion with partners. They were reminded that the character would need to be reproduced more than once and to bear in mind the young audience for their stories. Most important, pupils were instructed to retain responsibility for drawing their characters throughout the development of the story.

Session 4

Pupils were given examples of text for which the wording prompted a more creative layout. They were asked to include their own character names and to rewrite the text in a way that would reinforce the content of each sentence.

Session 5

From this session onwards pupils began working on original stories, to a greater or lesser extent making use of the material produced so far. They drafted text and illustrations and wrote their final versions in origami books which could be opened out and photocopied for the published version. This was then coloured in and given a title page before being presented as part of a collection in a book box.

CHOOSING PARTNERS

With the activities prepared, Caroline and I met again to discuss putting the children in pairs. Sometimes they can be left to choose by themselves but, for this work, I wanted to ensure optimum working partnerships. We were concerned that each pair should be mutually supportive while still allowing individual assertiveness. It was a balancing act. This seems a good point to give brief introductions to the children on whom I have focused particularly in this chapter.

Sunita and **Shasta** share the same first language. Shasta is a steady worker with moderately fluent English literacy skills. In this project she provided encouragement and support to Sunita who is fluent in spoken English but has some learning difficulties. Both girls enjoy attending a lunch-time Urdu club which is run by another member of the language and curriculum support service. We discovered that **Nagina** and **Sally** complemented each other well despite not choosing to work together before. Both hard-working and amiable, they brought diverse and shared literacy experiences to enrich their partnership.

Robert, a thoughtful boy and something of a perfectionist, was teamed with **Nadim** whose spoken English is fluent and expressive. Nadim often has good ideas but finds it difficult to focus these ideas on the tasks given. This also proved a mutually supportive partnership and, when Nadim went on holiday to Pakistan, Robert completed the book by himself. The success of this collaboration was proven by the contributions of both boys being evident in the final story.

Asrat worked with **Shelley**, the latter a quiet girl who is less confident than her partner. Asrat is friendly, fluently bilingual and has developed a confident writing style which influences both the content of her stories and her distinctive handwriting.

Stephen and **Ruth** once collaborated well on a project when in Year 3. Remembering this, I suggested we give them another opportunity to work together. Stephen is imaginative but tends to be slap-dash in his approach to written tasks while Ruth is assertive enough to contribute ideas of her own and develop them more thoroughly.

Cameron and **John** were less successful working together and demonstrate one important reason why children need opportunities to work in varied groups, developing skills of collaboration as they move on to new projects. Cameron is easily distracted from tasks and finds it difficult to conform within the class. He has, when motivated, shown himself capable of more than he usually gives. John, on the other hand, is tolerant and works imaginatively and persistently to complete tasks. At first, Cameron seemed to have little to offer his long-suffering partner but, when the task given was to devise and draw an original character, he produced quite a good version of Frankenstein and, for a while, the collaboration went swimmingly. However, pupils, as instructed, retained responsibility for the development of their own characters and Cameron unfortunately, did not sustain his interest. Faced with such inconsistent participation from his partner, John went his own way, quietly inspired and, because of his solo status, using the ingenious device in his fairground story of drawing only distant matchstick pictures of the two characters (and one back-view at a rifle range!).

Most collaborations were more successful, some yielding surprises; children unexpectedly assertive or vice versa. Only one pupil, initially consigned to a threesome because of odd numbers, opted to work alone. A very confident girl, she has already developed her own distinctive writing style. I suspect she was reluctant to compromise this by writing in partnership.

TEACHER INPUT

Pairs decided, and worksheets prepared, it was now necessary to consider the format of each session. By the time you get started, an hour disappears in no time at all but I wanted to differentiate in terms of the level and type of teacher interventions for the given tasks. I planned each session to start with a whole group discussion but with pupils sitting with partners. This then gave an opportunity to follow whole group talk with paired discussions without the class moving away from the carpet.

I first introduced our focus for the session and, with *Meg and Mog* books spread round the group, we found and discussed examples. Each pair then returned to tables to complete the task given. This gave me a chance to go round and talk to pupils while work was in progress. I was thereby offering opportunities for talk on several bases – individual with the teacher, as part of a small group and as a large group. The pupils were thus enabled to share ideas in a situation where they felt comfortable and this tiered discussion process meant that they had the opportunity to consolidate new knowledge gained from each focus. In practice, I found the class responses best in small group discussion and the balance shifted during the course of the term.

Each task was designed to have simple and explicit instructions but to be sufficiently open-ended to allow individual interpretation and a variety of acceptable responses. At all times, for inspiration and to provide a model, pupils could refer to a *Meg and Mog* book. Provided the instructions were understood, no one should have faced a total block over what to do. With the books at hand, the least confident child (or least inspired) may nearly reproduce something from the model offered but more imaginative pupils could be expected to treat the model as a jumping off point for ideas of their own.

Children were aware from the outset that each piece of work they did could contribute towards the stories they would eventually write themselves. Indeed, they were actively encouraged to refer back to earlier work as they developed their own characters, illustrations and story-line. Since each pair used their own ideas/output for reference, the development of tasks remained open-ended and differentiated. In drafting their own stories, children could look for inspiration to the *Meg and Mog* books and to their own experimentations with sound, colour, characterisation and text which originated from the activities of the first four sessions. Pupils amassed a portfolio of work which was valued the more as its relevance became increasingly obvious. Nothing was graded or marked as such; I either responded verbally while an activity was in process or pencilled in constructive comments and questions which were returned in their folders for the following week. Several children were enthusiastic about this kind of response. Some wrote replies underneath my comments. One came and thanked me personally and wanted to discuss further something I had suggested to her.

Successful collaboration with Caroline, combined with her whole-hearted support and shared aims, allowed pupils to reflect on and explore ideas assimilated from *Meg and Mog* while working in other areas of the curriculum. For example, Caroline sometimes arranges books thematically for shared reading sessions. During the term she regularly set out a table of *Meg and Mog* books which proved very popular. She also explained our objectives to interested parents and noted comments made by children, often in passing, when reading other books. Sunita, the bilingual pupil with learning difficulties, pointed out a sound effect bubble from her current reading book. She tried making the sound. Another bilingual girl, Shasta, became interested in the notion of 'series' of books. She had been reading one of the Banana book stories and deter-mined to look for another in the same series. Yet another pupil paused when reading aloud and returned to the rhyming word she had noticed in the previous paragraph. There were several examples of this height-ened awareness of visual and verbal features from all kinds of texts.

STARTING WITH A BANG!

Most people who work with or have young children of their own are familiar with the *Meg and Mog* series of books. Meg is the witch with a penchant for getting her spells in a muddle, usually with drastic results for Mog the cat, Owl and herself. These are vibrant colourful books where sounds variously hiss, fizzle and explode from the page. Children love them and laugh at all the misadventures.

For our first session, we considered the sound effects. We looked through the books together and found some wonderful examples. This was one of our noisier discussions as children experimented with making the sounds aloud. We considered whether particular examples might be loud or soft, or perhaps growing louder or softer and whether they were high or low. We discussed the importance of visual features in conveying this information, that is the shape and positioning of the sound bubble, the use of colour and the size and type of print. Accompanying illus-trations seemed important too. How do the characters react to the sound? Do we find this out from the text and the picture or perhaps from one rather than the other? Each pair then went off with two sheets to work on. On the first a variety of bubbles were drawn and these instructions given:

'Think of sound words to fit these bubbles. Use colours if you like but have a reason for your choice of colour.'

On the second sheet they were asked to make some more bubbles and sound words of their own. Responses were generally enthusiastic, bold and colourful, although it was interesting to note that visual features to express the sound were used with varying degrees of appropriacy. Here are examples, including some from the second sheet which progressing from the first, asked for wholly original ideas.

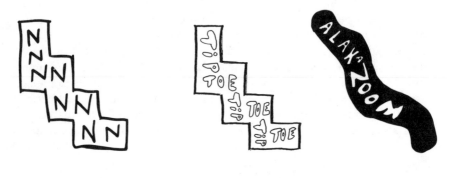

Example A   Example B

   Example A is rather obscure and suggests its author has looked at the caption in a purely visual way and decided to block in all available space with the symbol 'N'. Although I listened to several children try making their sounds, I regret not finding an opportunity to hear how this one was supposed to be made. By contrast, Robert and Nadim produced ALAKAZOOM (example B), a marvellous amalgam of more than one word which is perhaps inspired by one of Meg's magic spells. It is written boldly and colourfully in a bubble which suggest some long incantation! while their 'tiptoe' stair is a lovely example of sound, vision and experience combined.
   The following examples, C, D and E show how the children were able to represent ideas of their own, using graphic cues as well as onomatopoeia to create sound impressions in response to the prompt: 'Make some more bubbles and words of your own.'

Example C   *Example D*   *Example E*

The second session was based around rhyming words. Here are the instructions I gave on the work sheets:

'Look at the pictures in your book. Can you make any more rhyming words?'

'Make up two simple names for characters of your own. Make a list of words to rhyme with each character.'

I used the word 'simple' rather than monosyllabic but explained what I meant by it.

When planning this work, I made certain assumptions about the class and the stage pupils would have reached in their understanding of rhyme. Session two demonstrated (not for the first time in my career) that it is never wise to make assumptions! I expected only that they should recognise and list rhymes from simple monosyllabic words but I left open the possibility for more sophisticated attempts. Most children needed more individual support than I anticipated. However, we found many examples in the *Meg and Mog* books and, during our discussion, one pupil suggested that listening for rhyming sounds would be helpful for beginner readers.

I had hoped the children would refer back to the rhymes they had thought of when writing their stories. Only one pair actually included any rhymes in their text. On reflection, I realise I was expecting too much of them. Already restricted by having to write a sequential story in only five pages of simple text, it was perhaps a tall order to ask pupils to make parts of it rhyme. Economical use of words was challenge enough! I was encouraged by some of the responses to the first work-sheet which asked pupils to look for rhymes in the pictures rather than the text. They had then to use auditory discrimination alone. Shelley and Asrat found 'seeds/weeds', 'leg/Meg' and 'sat/Pat' in this way. Sunita, whose partner had been called away to read, was proud to produce six words to rhyme with 'Spot' and five to rhyme with 'Pat'. Taking into account her learning difficulties, this was quite an achievement. Another pupil made up several words to rhyme with a character called 'Humpy' who sadly had his name changed before he reached the final story. Many pupils went on to use their character names in the stories they wrote.

Planning for the third session and onwards owes much to a Book Arts Conference I attended at which Paul Johnson was a speaker (Wheathampstead, October 1994). His enthusiasm for book-making with children inspired me and I looked for opportunities to try out some of his ideas. The *Meg and Mog* work gave me an ideal opportunity to experiment. At the Conference, I learned how to fold A3 paper into origami books, the beauty of it being they could be opened out and photocopied. By making these books with the children I would be introducing them to the world of publishing. All that would be needed was the use of a school photocopier!

In the third session I asked children to draw pictures of the characters they had previously given names to. We looked again at *Meg and Mog* and most particularly at the pictures. We noted how blocks of colour spread across the whole page so that they are integrated with the text. We discussed whether the pictures alone could tell the story or, even more interesting, whether they told a different story to the text. We looked at the amount and type of detail and decided that the effect was uncluttered. Of the details included, most were essential to express feelings, sounds or actions. Sometimes there were 'extras' which were useful for counting skills or just for talking about. Of course we could not be sure of the authors' intentions but it was a valuable learning experience to discuss our own interpretations of the books.

There was no worksheet for the activity which followed this discussion. Each individual within the pair was given a sheet of A4 paper. Using a template in the centre of the sheet, they drew round it to create the correct page size in draft form. The drawing had then to be contained within the frame. For pupils with poor spatial awareness it was helpful to have practice at relating the size and positioning of the character to the frame. From another standpoint, more artistic pupils, given the same boundaries, had an opportunity to experiment with layout and know that it had only to be reproduced exactly to fit the final copy. It was also a useful device for me as I could arrow in pencilled comments from around the edge.

I emphasised that drawings of characters should be kept simple as they would feature several times in the final copy. Most important, responsibility for drawing a character remained with its originator. I was concerned that those children who may have little input to the text, should feel a real sense of ownership for the story through being creator and illustrator of one of its two main characters. In itself the task did not offer many opportunities for talk but I suggested that each pair, while working, should discuss the context in which their characters would meet. It would obviously be necessary for them both to appear in the same story.

Sometimes incongruities provoked change. Cameron's cave-dwelling Frankenstein prompted John to create a skull-headed figure in a grave-yard. With only five pages of story possible, it seemed unlikely they could transport Frankenstein and his grim companion to the fairground John was determined to include. In the event, as described earlier, Cameron lost interest and John could go his own way. In almost every other case, characters retained most detail through the drafting stage and on to best copy. A few evolved in terms of colour. With the advan-tage of hindsight I realise that the final sessions involved too much drafting, particularly of illustrations. I was fortunate the children stayed mainly enthusiastic but I would plan differently another time.

In the fourth session we moved on to work on the text. We consid-ered positioning and layout, size and type of print and the use of bubble-writing. Not least, we talked about the content and language use which led our discussion on to readership. I then gave each pair two worksheets with sentences set out in a normal (some might say boring) way. The content of each gave it the potential for a more interesting layout. Pupils were asked to do the following:

'Re-write these sentences adding the names of your characters. Otherwise, use the same words but make them look more interesting. Have reasons for what you do.'

By this stage of the project, most children needed little further encour-agement to do exciting things with sentences like

'. . . ran down the stairs and fell with a plonk at the bottom.'

'. . . jumped up and down all over the place.'

'"Ssssh!" said . . . who was feeling very shaky.'

After completing these sheets, I thought some pairs might lift these examples of text directly into their own stories. Not one of them did. Indeed their stories were all original and made a most varied collection for our book box.

Awareness of audience prompted many pupils to take care when print-ing their writing and tell their stories simply. As the last draft would be photocopied to produce a fair copy, pupils could work with soft pencils and rub out and correct mistakes as they went along.

OUTCOMES

By the end of term, nearly every pair had produced a book ready to publish and most had been photocopied, refolded and given the finishing touches of title page and card covers. I made a box into which the books would snugly fit and each pair of authors took great pride in

Example F

Example G

putting their books inside. All were accorded equal status by being part of a collection. Just as Shasta had been eager to find others in the Banana book series, so these authors were interested to read each other's work.

One of the many aspects of this project which I found fascinating was that some pairs seemed to latch on to one feature over all others. Robert and Nadim constructed their story around sound effects. Their characters are original and imaginative but the story line has perhaps been

Example H

influenced by reading *Meg and Mog*. There is a nasty explosion which spells disaster for the cat. Although we never learn the fate of this unfortunate animal, all is happily resolved for the two main characters with a final 'ALAKAZOOM'! The authors, when devising their story, made particular reference to ideas from the first session.

By contrast, Asrat and Shelley were very influenced by the work on illustrations. They devised characters who were simple but distinctive and who had expressive features (see Example G). Each page, above the line of text, is totally covered with vivid blocks of colour, each one contrasting with the next. Their characters show movement and they include some incidental details but not so much as to clutter the page. The accompanying text suggests they have a young audience very much in mind.

While many pupils remained conventional in positioning the text, one pair combined illustration and text so thoroughly that it reads like a series of pictograms and my eyes dance all over the page attempting to follow the sequence of words. It is so rewarding to see the effect of combined imaginations taking flight! Stephen and Ruth called their book 'The Fancy Dress Party' and the theme gives ample scope to their ideas (see Example H).

As a whole, Caroline and I were pleased with the outcomes of this project. We considered various criteria for success. Important among them was our observation of pupils busily participating in the various activities. We also noted the ripple effect of new experiences informing learning in other areas of the curriculum. For solid evidence we had folders containing an accumulation of draft material and a book box, much valued by the group, in which were presented a varied collection of original stories.

Individual pupils were justly proud of their achievements. Sunita, supported by Shasta, relied less on teacher intervention and gained confidence in working independently. She contributed at every stage and, when Shasta was absent for the rhyming activity, she showed she was competent to follow instructions and to complete the task by herself. Robert and Nadim spent much time in discussion and the resulting story is full of humour and wonderful sound effects, certainly more imaginative than Robert would normally produce on his own. Stephen took a great interest in the whole project and brought one of his own *Meg and Mog* books to add to the class display. With Ruth, he worked enthusiastically to complete their story and, if the title page was a little rushed, the contents certainly convey the confidence with which this pair experimented on their text. Asrat and Shelley assimilated many features from the *Meg and Mog* books. This is evident from reading the story about Pink and Park. In the past, Asrat has often needed teacher support to help her get started and to decide what to do next. In this work she showed a mature understanding of the needs of a young audience and proved to herself and to us that she can work independently with confidence. She particularly enjoyed a later opportunity to share the books with the Reception class.

For me, the project has been a beginning and I shall look for other ways to develop children's critical awareness of texts. As teachers, we rightly devote much time and energy to developing children's individual reading skills but it is also important, and never too early, to provide opportunities for children to reflect on and gain an appreciation of the visual texts they read. They can challenge readers at all levels and certainly provide a resource for demonstrating a range of unexpected capabilities. The confidence of working with familiar and well-loved texts allowed all our new authors to go beyond what any of us imagined possible.

ACKNOWLEDGEMENTS

Caroline Luck for her support and inspiration. Staff and children at The Reddings Primary School for their co-operation and encouragement.

REFERENCES

Hunt, P. (1991) *Criticism, Theory and Children's Literature*, London, Blackwell
Johnson, P. (1990) *A Book of One's Own*, London, Hodder & Stoughton
Johnson, P. (1994) Book Arts Conference, Wheathampstead Education Centre, October
Nicoll, H. and Pienkowski, J. *Meg and Mog* (Series) London, Heinemann

Chapter 5

'You think I'm thick, don't you?'
Children's reading histories

Avril Dawson

> Every reader has a history of experience as a reader. Part of the process of literacy is an awareness of that history. Students should see that history valued by being made explicit in talk and writing. A reader's history is not simply a record of what they read and when, it is the complex web of experiences that constitute our memory of reading. It includes where they read, under what conditions, with whom, how they responded, and so on.
>
> (Traves 1992: 84)

THE READERS

Sean[1] comes into the room silently and settles into a chair – mine, significantly the more comfortable one, if he gets there first. He gives no clues that he intends to work: writing equipment is hidden away in his trouser pocket until required, homework concealed there too (if by some miracle he's done it *and* remembered it). If he's quick and doesn't like the look of what I've put ready on the table, he'll slide it out of sight and feign amazed ignorance when I ask what's happened to the book or activity I left there. Reading is a matter of obstinate bargaining:

'No, I'm not reading that. I've read two pages. It's your turn, Miss.'
'I'll read that page if you read that one.'

He starts the first few words with apparent confidence, but very soon comes to a word he doesn't know and thereafter his reading is punctuated with:

'What's that?'
'Eh?'
'Oh, I'm not doing this,'
'That's enough, let's do something else.'

Another lesson. I collect Peter and Michael *en route*: Peter punctual, carrying everything he needs for this lesson and the following one;

Michael casual, taking his time, finding things to look at or talk about on the way, to delay the start of the lesson as long as possible. The session together is an odd mixture of relaxed informality, with lots of chat, and intense pressure: the focus on the two boys, no class to hide among. Reading collaboratively is reasonably successful: the one who is not reading aloud helps out the one who is struggling. They make a good team, though they find it hard to sit still and follow someone else reading. Individually, they are very different readers. Michael is more fluent and tackles more sophisticated texts, expecting them to make sense, sometimes substituting contextually correct words, looking ahead and listening to himself. Peter has much more of a struggle, reading the words as a series of signs to be decoded one by one, with no apparent thread of continuity, little sense of the whole and therefore little awareness that what he is saying aloud does not always make sense. Difficult words are attacked phonically: this sometimes helps with the first syllable, but he has problems working out all the components and running them together in the right order.

Three Year 8 pupils in a mainstream middle school of four hundred-plus children, drawing from a catchment covering private and council estates in the small town and surrounding villages. Sean and Peter have been statemented since Year 7; Michael benefits from Peter's statemented time, as Peter is more relaxed when the spotlight isn't totally on him. Michael's spelling is very weak, often indecipherable to himself as well as others, and his reading is less successful than we all – he included – feel it could be. Peter and Sean are certainly struggling readers. Failing readers. Children who are struggling with almost everything they do in school every day, because they do not have the literacy skills they need. They have failed in the school system.

> Each one, at different times but in the very same words said: 'You think I'm thick, don't you?' They had every right to ask, for that was the implicit message that came with every school lesson where reading was involved.
>
> (Meek 1992: 225)

THE TEACHING

Yet these are in truth children of normal intelligence and articulacy, well co-ordinated and, like most of us, with excellent memories in certain areas. I found it tempting to collude with the deficit model of reading difficulties, to look for a missing link, which, once found and replaced, will produce a successful reader. Administer a dose of this and the problem will be solved. Take reading apart, treat each 'sub-skill' with a course of instruction and, hey presto, we'll have a reader.

Looking for the magic solution, the remedy, is like expecting the doctor to administer the perfect medicine for the perfect, instant cure. (And isn't that what we *do* want from a doctor?) But it seems to me to be a dangerous analogy, a fundamental misunderstanding of the nature of literacy, which leads to unrealistic expectations on the part of the child, the teacher and the parents. Literacy is holistic – and there the medical analogy should end.

Teaching children who have been identified as having special educational needs, particularly one-to-one with statemented children in withdrawal sessions, is a peculiarly intense activity. Both sides – pupil and teacher – see each other in a different way, and probably behave differently to the way they behave in a class situation. There is no relief for any individual, since in any forty-five minute session they will be asked to perform. The teacher has to focus on one pupil – no others to stimulate discussion or understanding.

There are obvious advantages for the teacher, of course: behaviour management problems, for example, are certainly different, though not necessarily non-existent. I know my pupils well. It is important for me to have a good relationship with them and I see it as a necessary and valuable part of our time together that we should be able to relax, joke, gossip occasionally – not only for light relief, but for closer understanding and trust. Children often reveal anxieties in one-to-one or small group sessions which would not otherwise be apparent – may even be disguised by an air of confidence, aggression, lack of interest, or humour.

The readers were more or less resigned to their lack of progress. I was frustrated by it. I felt that I needed a deeper understanding of the 'reading history' of these children, of how they see the literacy environment both in and out of school, of what their perceptions of literacy are – and to see it from their point of view, rather than comparing it, inevitably unfavourably, with my own. Shirley Brice Heath's seminal ethnographic study, *Ways With Words* (Brice Heath 1983) shows with great clarity how teachers are able to make positive changes in their goals, their language, the building of school experiences on home ones and their definitions of relevance, when they recognise the rich variety of expectations and language environments which are a part of the cultures of their pupils. It is worth observing, for example, as Margaret Meek has done, that 'some of the things mediated to us by print come to our pupils just as meaningfully in other ways – visual, oral, social.' (Meek 1992: 50)

THE READING ENVIRONMENT

The first step towards this deeper understanding was to look critically at the shared environment of the school. This proved to be a cathartic experience. This is not a criticism of my colleagues; as a school, we take pleasure in displaying and valuing children's work, whether literary, practical or artistic. My view of our environment was almost wholly within those terms. What I had not really questioned were the covert messages of the environment the children are taught in when they are withdrawn from classes.

Room 16 was converted from the computer room; it has no natural light, but a carpet, several tables and chairs, a whiteboard, and some posters of paintings around the walls. The interview room, also carpeted, has a desk, a computer, a stoical cactus in a pot and a small sink. The posters on the walls were of theatrical productions and the children often took advantage of the words on them when playing 'Hangman', etc. The main SEN room, which we now call Room 3 in an attempt to rid it of stigma, is a small classroom, uncarpeted, with three computers, and shelves, trolleys and cupboards full of books and other resources. There is a sense of temporariness about all the rooms, in that they are used by a 'floating population'.

The reading in-service course I was doing at the time required me to keep a journal throughout the two years.[2] This provided an invaluable space for reflecting on the question which had been put to me: 'Well, what messages are given by you and your classrooms?' And the answer was. . . . Reading is only reading if it's books. Reading is phonics. Reading is all to do with what goes on in here and nothing to do with what goes on out there. Reading is all about failure. Reading is all to do with graciously trying to induct you poor souls into my world. Reading is tests and grades. Reading is all about what you don't know, not what you do know. . . . Maybe that's too hard on myself, but then I'm not talking about well-meaning intentions, only perceived messages. So the teaching areas should be filled with the things kids do know – adverts, road signs, record charts, tape covers, food labels . . .

I shared my disquiet with the boys[3] and they confirmed what I had finally seen – that the walls (apart from a map, a few pictures and poems) were filled with information primarily for the teachers' use. It was ours, not theirs.

The contrast between my passionately held beliefs about reading and the messages I was giving could hardly have been greater. Somehow, I had thought my feelings were transparent, yet the children's only first-hand experience of me as a reader was in reading to or with them, from limited texts, and of me reading purely functionally.

That was the first lesson I learned. The children talked about what they would like to see in 'their' rooms; the walls are now covered with their stories and poems, which they have word-processed and illustrated attractively. Photographs of signs and notices around the school and their villages and estates act like a magnet and provide a variety of ready-made games. Active, can't-sit-still pupils love rushing round the room to be the first to spot the photograph of 'Danger' or 'Turn Left'. The backs of cereal packets give a selection of 'Where's Wally?' puzzles, with plenty of motivation for reading practice built-in; instructions, background information, lists of 'Things to Find' and so on. Two Year 6 children were surprised by their ability to read an article about 'Power Rangers' from the *Guardian*. Children's achievements in and out of school are celebrated with photocopies of certificates and local newspaper articles about football, judo, dancing successes, and they find it fun to highlight their own and their friends' names. Interactive displays invite them to connect jokes with punchlines (physically, with threads), to fill in pre-cut speech bubbles and pin them up on a street scene, fill in their birthdays on a beautiful Dorling Kindersley calendar, write a resolution on a pre-cut leaf and add it to the large tree, or celebrate a success by writing it on a pre-cut butterfly and putting it on the wall. The interactive nature of some of the displays is important; the photographs and news articles are relevant to their own lives, as are posters of ships or football stars the children bring in, and the fact that they help to put the work up themselves, discussing what should go where, what needs changing, what they could do next. The rooms are slowly becoming theirs, not just ours.

READING HISTORIES

The next step was to look into the children's 'reading histories'. Each child is unique in his background, feelings of self-esteem, the 'story in his head' – the way he explains to himself his experiences of literacy. Writing my own history – another requirement of the reading course – proved very rewarding and I became fascinated with other people's stories, both children's and adults'. I asked some of my family and friends; the adults generally remembered little about 'learning to read'. Their memories were warm ones, about favourite books, the pleasure of solitary reading, the delight in being read to as a small child. Some had outstandingly bad memories, for example, the adult whose only book as a child, a Bible, had had all the pages torn out by a particularly unpleasant relative for use as toilet paper. This memory was sharp after nearly seventy years. One remembered his teacher

> pointing with a long thin cane to cards around the wall, high up, with a picture on each alphabet letter. We would all say 'Aaa . . .' and then 'Burr' and 'Curr', etc. It seemed like an exercise that had its own point and little to do with learning to read because I could quickly read and understand whole words, the ones below the letters, and yet we all had to keep repeating the letters every day.'[4]

I discussed memories of reading with a mixed ability Year 7 class. These too concerned bedtime rituals, favourite stories (which they could still recount in detail), colourful illustrations, pop-up books and story tapes, recognising the sweet shop sign. Dean remembers *Dean's Bedtime Story Book*, his favourite because he thought it was just for him. Others had enjoyed the books which are printed with the child's name as the central character, and featuring their friends, families and pets – books that they could relate to, find themselves in. 'My favourite book that I could read was *Topsy and Tim Go to the Seaside*. I liked it because I used to like fishing and Topsy and Tim went fishing and caught two fish for their dinner.'

Whatever the merits or otherwise of *Topsy and Tim*, there is a telling contrast between the involvement felt in those comments and the following experiences:

'We used to read in groups, a page each. I did not like that because I stutter and it's embarrassing.'

'I have a big memory from when I was about six. I had cards at school which had words to learn from, which were words like "have", "and", "which", "where" and things like that. I did not like to read a lot.'

'. . . when I was in Class Two and I always used to hold a book up and make up the story as I went along and I got told off for not reading the right words.'

In our withdrawal sessions Peter and Michael talked at some length, on tape, about their reading experiences, stimulating each other into early memories of school, and comparing their taste in reading. Peter's favourite book had been *The Owl Who Was Afraid of the Dark*, which he talked about with a fondness which made me realise that we could have re-read this together profitably, without any embarrassment on Peter's part. He is a great Enid Blyton fan – our most successful reading sessions had been using *The Famous Five Adventure Games*. (It would be too long a diversion to consider the valid objections to such texts; it is sufficient for me that Peter enjoyed them.) He likes re-reading old favourites, which he knows off by heart, 'but my mum gets harder ones for me from the library'. Michael talked with pleasure about his boxed set of *Winnie-the-Pooh*; he is ambitious in his reading, sometimes reading his dad's books, and with every intention of reading *Lord of the Rings*.

They talked about the colour-coded reading schemes which they had had to work through systematically. 'Were there any that you enjoyed?' 'No!' Peter launched spontaneously into a scathing take-off in a halting monotone:

'The – cat – went – to – town. Over the page. The – cat – came – home. Over the page. The – cat – went – back – out. Over the page. The – dog – come [*sic*] – up. Over the page And – licked – the – cat. Over the page. They – both – went – back – and – had – dinner. Four words – ten words on a page! And they're about that big! That big! And every level you got they got about a centimetre smaller!'

Both said they enjoy reading but felt frustrated when they were not given enough time to read a text at school – this was a frequent problem. Peter reflected on the difference between reading in his head, which he feels he does reasonably accurately, and reading aloud, when he has the added strain of someone listening for his mistakes. They remembered the characters in TV reading programmes, imitating phrases with perfect intonation.

These programmes are part of a shared culture; the Year 7 and other Year 8 pupils I talked to had the same memories, whichever school they'd been in, even in different parts of the country. Peter looked back to a golden age, when he felt he could read as well as anyone else, and pinpointed two particular conflicts at school as the starting points in his reading problems – I will return to those later. We had the opportunity to look at their strengths as readers, and at their less successful strategies – a genuine discussion, I felt, when I was able to offer my opinion and experience but give at least equal time to theirs. Peter ended with a thoughtful appraisal of the reading he finds easiest – reading texts that he has written himself, when he knows what to expect and remembers what he meant even if he has spelled words incorrectly.

This has had a considerable effect on the reading work I do with children. Jason, for example, a Year 5 statemented child, with a reading age of 6–7, has been struggling to find any books he is capable of reading but which interest him. He enjoys looking at illustrated reference books – motorbikes, planes, dinosaurs and so on – in which he can 'read' the pictures very ably, though very little of the print. But it will not be too long before he loses the motivation – and who can blame him? His mind is constantly in search of new information, which his reading ability will not satisfy quickly enough. He is politely bored with most texts, bored sometimes to the point of disruption with trying to learn phonically regular words or frequently occurring words. At present, he is getting to grips with reading of his own choice, reading words like 'accessorized', 'hovercraft' and 'sidecar' – and doing so very successfully.

Probing into Sean's reading history was much harder. It is important for him to work one-to-one because he is so sensitive about his reading ability. We have an easy relationship, full of mock insults which disguise a genuine fondness, but Sean tenses immediately if anyone else comes into the room during one of our sessions. This meant that our tape sounded far more like an interview than a discussion, with Sean's characteristic one-line answers: 'Nope', 'Dunno'. Sean does not like reading at all now, but he remembered the enjoyment of being read to, pop-up books and nursery rhymes at home, and apparently had neutral feelings about starting to read at school, neither positive nor negative.

This felt like skimming the surface. I had learned little about their reading that was new – we had talked about some of these things before, although without going so far back. I felt I knew them all a little better and that my genuine interest in what they had to say could only be an advantage, but that there was more. Perhaps, despite myself, I was looking, like Peter, for the single factor that stopped their early positive experiences of reading leading on to natural fluency. Or, despite my sense of the uniqueness of each pupil, I was looking for a pattern. I was very grateful that the parents had all agreed, so welcomingly, to an interview.

HOME INTERVIEWS

The interviews took place over the last couple of weeks of the summer term – five in all, as I also talked with the mothers of two other statemented pupils, David (Year 5) and Tony (Year 6). It happened that, for convenience, all the discussions took place in the family homes. I could not have predicted beforehand how influential this factor would be. They were wonderful experiences, which left me buzzing with excitement.

> '. . . when I left, I felt as though Peter had become 3-dimensional for me, and that the difference was not so much in the information I was given as in the fact that I· had been given it as a guest invited into their home, not when I had invited them into my work territory, or when Peter had given me insights into him but in a situation (school) where I had power and authority over him.'[5]

This factor of my being a guest was crucial. In some ways, as in the interviews with the children, I did not learn many new facts about them – though I did learn, for example, that Sean had been born seven weeks prematurely and had been given the last rites when his kidney collapsed shortly after birth; that he had had hearing problems until he was seven, when his mother was told that he would need to learn the alphabet again as he had never heard it properly; that Peter had almost had a nervous breakdown at primary school; that his older brother had experienced reading difficulties when he was younger and that his father finds it difficult to read aloud, though not to himself. There was no pattern. There was nothing outstanding about which to say – this is the key, this is why they are not succeeding. But there were certainly subtle shifts in perception. The background to their history and environment of literacy was no longer the pale reflection I was unable to match with my own, but a form with positive shape and colour.

Peter

The interview with Peter's parents was the first with parents of the Year 8 pupils. An hour and a half one evening, talking to Peter and his mum, sitting relaxed on the floor, stroking the family dog, Peter's dad arriving later to join in the conversation while busying himself with some paper-work. A conversation between other family members in an adjoining room, disruptions as people came and went, the phone rang, Peter showed off his new birthday trainers. Laughter, gossip and discussions about the lovely carvings – souvenirs from a family holiday visiting relatives in South Africa. This led to Peter recounting a legend about one of the places they had been to

> 'simply but with understanding of detail and concepts. This child whose dominant characteristics for me are often his stubborn refusal to accept responsibility for learning, his appalling spelling and his poor reading skills. To see him so animated, able to tell a story with such sensitivity, at ease in his own surroundings, was to see more of the whole, and a salutary reminder to me . . .'[6]

Michael

Michael and his mother welcomed me with customary charm, Michael playing the perfect host, serving me with coffee and making sure I was comfortable. His sister stayed for a while, and his father arrived home from work and joined in the discussion. We discovered that they had bought their house from some old friends of mine, which gave an imme-diate point of relaxed contact at the beginning of a conversation which was to last two hours. Michael showed me the wall plaque he had mentioned with the 'family rules' and brought me the village newsletter, in which he had a poem printed.

Sean

Sean's family had been neighbours of mine until recently; his younger sister and my younger daughter had been friends, so we also had a good basis of contact, although we did not know each other well. Sean quickly made himself scarce (as did his father, when he arrived home from work); his younger brother and both sisters stayed for a while as I talked with his mother. We stroked the dog and ended up, after two hours, looking through the wedding album, giggling over out-dated fashions.

David and Tony

The interviews with David's and Tony's mothers took place during school lunch hours, so the children were not present and there was less flexibility regarding time. Again, though, I was made very welcome and the ease of the conversations is highlighted on the tapes by laughter, casual interruptions by other family members, pets, and digressions from the main topic of conversation. Tony's mother and I found ourselves comparing the merits of various snack crackers when the tape ran out and it was time for me to return to school.

These descriptions are anecdotal and may seem very trivial, but it is precisely in this that I feel the strength of the experience lies. These were not formal interviews, but loosely structured chats in an atmosphere of friendly, co-operative trust. I was not just the teacher, but also a parent, a mother, a shopper, another member of the same community. There was time to find out details – such as Sean's previous reliance on lip reading – to discover what was important on both 'sides', to listen to the parent as the expert, the one who knows their child best, on their territory. The environment was such that I could say a lot of the things I believe and understand about reading in a genuinely sharing, non-threatening way. I could share my own experiences, be honest about my feelings of failure and short-comings as a teacher, which were accepted with trust. (As far as I can judge!) Sean's mother, for example, introduced the subject of dyslexia, about which she clearly felt she had strong grievances against her previous education authority. This had the potential for being a difficult subject, but, in such a non-confrontational situation, we agreed with good humour.

I had the opportunity to say how my understanding of, and admiration for, Sean's tenacious determination had grown since I had transcribed and analysed a tape of him reading – his offhand manner is very much part of him, but also conceals the enormous amount of work he has to do for something which is so easy for most of us that we do not even recognise this quality in him. I felt very positive about what I see as progress: that Sean would now idly pick books off the racks and try reading them; that I had tried out some inspection copies of books on him, which he then pestered me to order – that his nagging was real progress – and the glorious day when, at Sean's instigation, we read together for a solid forty-five minutes.

Michael had the opportunity to offer his own opinions about his difficulties and see them taken seriously. Prediction usually serves him well in narrative texts – substituting 'afraid' for 'frightened' makes little difference – but, as he pointed out, this is not so easy when you are reading non-fiction, like science, with concepts which are unfamiliar. Reading 'practical' instead of 'physical' can set off a whole chain of confusion. This is something of which I was well aware in Sean's case, as he much prefers non-fiction, but the reading I have done with Michael has almost all been of a narrative nature. It is interesting to note that Michael apparently copes reasonably well in science lessons, in that he is able to take part orally and practically, rarely asking for help with the writing or reading requirements, but perhaps under-achieving. There must be a lot of children experiencing similar, relatively low-level, confusions, unable to ask for clarification because they are not aware that they are confused, or embarrassed that they have not understood, or aware that it would not be possible to clarify every detail.

We compared, at length, Michael's utilitarian view of education with the view his parents and I share, of education being, at its best, an opening up, a way of enabling you to make your experience of life more interesting and exciting. Most pupils I have talked to see education solely in terms of getter a better job in the future, and therefore see little relevance in learning anything which is not directly related to the person they expect or hope to be, rather than the person they are now. Often, in any case, the least motivated pupils are those who see little relationship between the person they are now and what they are offered by school. This is an inevitable consequence of the political and social climate. Michael also highlighted the public nature of reading in school, particularly in the early years, with his description of the experience of being called to the front of the class to read to the teacher at her desk. Contrast this with the warm memories of reading alone, or the security of the bedtime ritual.

I was interested in 'the story in Peter's head'; his tenacious belief that something had gone wrong at a particular moment. One incident he referred to as the 'da game'. His first-school teacher had suggested that he should say 'da' when he could not read a word and go straight on to the next one (sometimes several in a row). He'd told me that this had caused outrage at home – his parents had forbidden him to do it, a fact which they spontaneously confirmed. The incident had taken on something of mythical proportions over the years, and was associated with Peter having to squeeze his teacher's elbow when he could not manage a word. We discussed paired reading, and the usefulness of reading to the end of a sentence, then going back to the unknown words, a discussion during which the polarity of 'them' (school) and 'us' (home) seemed to disappear.

The other incident which loomed large was 'the case of the missing blue folder'. In calling it that I do not intend any trivialisation. Peter had obviously been taught by 'Breakthrough to Literacy' at the beginning of his school career, and he had talked with a continuing, angry disappointment about the supply (?) teacher who had given everyone in the class – except him – a blue folder, because she said he wasn't good enough for one. His mother explained that Peter could read cards with his own words on – 'tractor', 'farm', etc. – reflecting his current interests, but that he could not read the scheme's pre-printed words so was not allowed the blue folder to keep them in. Peter was adamant that he could not be bothered with reading after that. I wondered about what the teacher's explanation might be if it were possible to ask; how close the two viewpoints would have been – and how often *my* aims or reasons have not been understood, and held against me by child or parents. And, of course, vice versa.

There were some apparent discrepancies in all the interviews; most notable were the discrepancies between claims that parents had been led to believe that nothing was wrong, and the claims that, at the same time, the child was being given extra help in reading, or even that private tuition was being paid for. In one case, the memories were in stark opposition to the recorded facts. It is difficult to explain such conflicts; it may be simply to do with ordering events/feelings chronologically in one's memory, or to do with finding a scapegoat. In a way, the discrepancy itself is unimportant. It is, after all, possible to hold conflicting views at the same time, to 'be in two minds'. What is essential is to acknowledge the feelings of frustration and helplessness regarding the problems the child is facing now and has faced in the past.

MOVING ON

'The interviews made me feel that what is lacking in the medical analogies about reading is an understanding of everyone as individuals – we are ignoring the warning that a prescribed medicine should never be given to anyone else, even if they have the same symptoms. Successful reading is not a matter of adding one sub-skill to another, it is the "orchestration" of "a complex web", a harmony, a rendering of the "tune on the page".'

(Barrs 1992)[7]

That is not to say that there is no point in drawing attention to patterns in words – we learn to 'read' our environment by drawing parallels and comparisons, and by noticing differences. But we are doing pupils a grave disservice if we give our authority to the notion of functional literacy. So much of the way we teach – despite ourselves – must give this impression and unconsciously works against us. How often do we discuss texts with struggling readers? How much do we concentrate on decoding words? Despite their desire to 'join the literacy club' (Smith 1984) because of the clearly perceived benefits – maybe the cost of joining is too high. To have to plough through more and more of what doesn't interest them: if you learn *this* spelling pattern, great, we'll do another one; when you manage to read *this* book, you'll get a longer, harder one. For some, the challenge and sense of achievement may well be enough. Isolated words in word tins produce some successful readers. Some learn despite the word tins. Others just like collecting. One Year 7 reader told me how much he enjoyed working through a reading scheme. But maybe there are too many disadvantages. Maybe if they learn to read, they'll have demands made on them that they don't want to face. Struggling readers are well aware of the gap between themselves and their peers.

Generalisations are not enough: 'children can't read because they have no experience of books at home'; 'children can't read because they haven't learned blends'; 'children can't read because. . . '. Of course these are important factors for consideration but there may be many more – the boy who unconsciously emulates the father he does not see reading, rather than the women he does see, for example (Dombey 1994). We may not even be able to say: this child cannot read because of a), b), c). Perhaps the best we can hope for is to say: these are some of the factors working against this child – a, b, c – and these are some of the factors working for her or him – x, y, z – and to communicate the enthusiasm for reading. Be clear about the messages we give. Do children understand that we feel reading will be an empowering, exciting experience for them too, or is the message we give that it's a series of hurdles to be climbed, the more hurdles for the ones who find it hardest and least satisfying?

Sean, Peter and Michael have moved on to upper school, and *I* have learned a lot from *them*. My two Year 6 readers made up their own script for a spoof news programme which was then videoed; the changing scripts and captioned photographs of the work in process give the opportunity for reading at a level which would normally be 'above' those pupils, were it not their own work. I read *On the Way Home* to children in various year groups; the repetitive format made it easy for them to produce their own imaginative extracts, which also required careful attention to print formats and punctuation. Tony, now in Year 7, who is still unable to score on any reading test, (nor is there any point in subjecting him to one) is able to read back not only his own extract, but make a good attempt at others; something he did spontaneously one day for the benefit of another child.

Perhaps, after all, these are not children 'who have failed in the school system' as I deliberately described them at the start of this chapter, but

Chapter 6

Hearing impaired children in the mainstream classroom
The effects on literacy and learning

Frances Lockwood

LITERACY AND ORACY

> No one is untouched by the consequences of literacy.
>
> (Meek 1991: 2)

We all belong to a society that is literate. Language is all around; we can read it, hear it, speak it, write it. This is what it is to be literate – to participate in language and to use it, engage with it. Literacy allows us to ignore what we do not need to read, hear, say, write; our 'literate-ness' moderates these decisions. In dividing the National Curriculum for English into three Attainment Targets: – Speaking and Listening, Reading, and Writing – the implication is that proficiency in all these elements makes a child 'literate'.

Reading, writing, speaking and listening must all develop as children develop for them to acquire literacy. The ability to talk may develop before the ability to write, but they are equally essential to literacy. Indeed, normally hearing 4-year-old children may be seen to hold an extensive and rapidly growing fund of vocabulary. They often have a sophisticated grasp of the basic patterns of syntax and the ability to generate long and complex sentences. Spoken interaction with adult carers is of prime importance in the provision of a meaningful context for social exchange:

> Talking and listening are so ordinary that we scarcely notice that they are ways of using language in order to learn how the world works and how to accumulate shared understanding about it.
>
> (Meek 1991: 18)

If it is well accepted that children use their experiences of learning, speaking and listening in order to make sense of reading (and reading has to be learned for them to be deemed 'officially literate'), it is important to discover the consequences, if any, of interruption to these processes. Learning difficulties may take a variety of guises arising from a variety of causes. The particular focus of this chapter, hearing impairment, is a factor that may be clearly linked to low achievement in speaking and listening and slow growth in language development generally.

Before asking what it is a hearing impaired child cannot do, it is important to outline what it is we expect a normally hearing speaker/listener to be able to do. The opening statement of the 'General Requirements for English' in the National Curriculum for English may be of use here:

> English should develop pupils' abilities to communicate effectively in speech and writing and to listen with understanding.
>
> (DFE 1995: 2)

'Communication' implies conversation. A child at Key Stage 2 may be expected to have a good knowledge of the conventions of conversation either with a peer or with an adult. This may include an understanding of the importance of context, shared experience being relevant to each participant; a notion of turn-taking; accompanying body and facial gestures; making pertinent contributions in context in the light of previous remarks; the ability to express verbally ideas as they occur; to accept and use colloquialism, dialects, or slang; and not be afraid to ask for repetition/clarification of a point to enable informed reply. 'Speaking' is a method by which one is able to convey ideas and beliefs in the simplest and most effective way. This may include paraphrasing and/or summarising contributions along with the explicit intention of aiming one's own speech at the level of capability presented in the audience. Speech should provoke a response, either positive or questioning. Children will become aware that people speak for different purposes besides communication: to impart fact, fiction, information, instruction, poetry, drama, for negotiation and so on. 'Listening' requires concentration. The listener too must acquire skills – to paraphrase the ideas presented for ease of understanding and storage: to make what is heard relevant to one's own experience and to allow learning to take place in the light of the meeting of old and new experiences. Questions must often be asked, for clarification, to express understanding and move on, or to disagree. The quality and diversity of our encounters with language may vary – hence the differences in the levels of confidence with literacy attained by different people. Learning to read and write (the accepted prerequisites for being literate) may be dependent to some degree on the quality and variety of language for communication experienced by the child. Primarily these effects will be significant in the early years of language development and on arrival at school.

All children need access to spoken language before they can effectively become literate in the ways of print. Oracy continues throughout education to contribute to the development of children's reading and written abilities. Language (spoken or printed code) is made explicit to the child as a tool for manipulation in the fulfilment of needs and desires. Also, as Webster points out: 'Since this is so, then provision for children who have some difficulties with hearing becomes an important aspect of differentiating for diverse learners' (Webster 1986: 150).

HEARING IMPAIRMENT – A DEFINITION

'Hearing impairment' is an invisible disability. The term itself almost disguises the reality of the meaning. It is simply and importantly this: a hearing impaired child cannot hear as well as her/his normally hearing peers. However slight the consequences of this may be perceived to be, the fact remains that she/he cannot hear very well and this is bound to have an effect on learning.

There are two kinds of hearing impairment, one much more common in the population than the other, being especially prevalent in infancy up to 8 years. Conductive deafness, or otitis media is by far the most common cause of hearing impairment in children. Its basic action is the presence of fluid in the middle ear which prevents the ear drum and ossicles from vibrating in response to sound waves. Otitis media is a temporary condition which fluctuates in its presence and severity; 'glue ear' is the common name for a more severe presentation of this problem. Sensori-neural hearing loss is of a more serious nature as its effects cannot be treated, only compensated for by the use of hearing aids. This hearing loss is permanent and usually more severe in its presence. Sensori-neural deafness is of the inner ear. In some circumstances it is possible to experience both kinds of hearing impairments; there is no guarantee that a sensori-neural hearing impaired child will not suffer further loss through infection.

Hearing loss in primary aged children may be detected in a variety of ways. Andrews and Roberts (1994) estimate that 20 per cet of primary aged children may at some time suffer from middle ear trouble; of course, this may or may not include deafness specifically, but it does imply some degree of hearing loss. Initial concern about a child's ability to hear may come from the family, nursery, school, or health care team. Many authorities offer sweep testing at 5 years by a school nurse or medical officer; results may be followed up by audiologists. There is a critical factor in this method of detection – not only may children be missed out when testing takes place (owing to absence from school or movement between authorities) but the very fluctuating nature of conductive deafness means that a child may be able to hear within perfectly normal limits on one day, and on the next have a significant hearing loss induced by conductive impairment.

Evidence for hearing impairment in school children is sometimes complicated by other learning and behavioural factors which teachers may be more used to discovering and dealing with. A child suffering from a conductive loss may display any of the following tendencies:

- Hearing may get noticeably worse during and after a cold.
- Tiring easily.
- Not being able to follow simple requests in school.
- Asking for much more individual help than usual.
- Appearing not to be concentrating during listening times.
- Not responding when called from behind.
- Displaying atypical aggression or irritability.
- The child may speak more softly her/himself often with a nasal sound.

Many of these features apply to the situation of sensori-neural deaf children, but they have the 'advantage' of having a constant level of hearing which allows for one approach in compensation. Children said to have learning difficulties, including dyslexia, have often been found to have experienced middle ear problems which undoubtedly have contributed to their slow academic development. The episodic nature of conductive hearing loss is a critical factor for many more children, especially in the early years of schooling, than might be imagined. For this reason it is worth considering the implications for hearing impaired children of the role of oracy in promoting literacy. In identifying some critical factors in classroom approaches affecting hearing impaired children, however, I want to argue that any conclusions about how best to cater for their learning needs will also help create effective learning environments for all children, hearing impaired or not.

IMPLICATIONS FOR LITERACY AND LEARNING

It is not the intention here to examine how children learn to use language. It is important, however, to remember that children do not acquire language at the same rate, nor do they necessarily attain the same degree of skill in manipulating language. Hearing impairment obviously will affect a child's efforts to acquire and manipulate language 'normally'. As such, their potential for acquiring literacy may be affected:

> Even very mild hearing losses are known to affect the child's early development of language because any restrictions on the child's ability to listen and hear therefore limit her/his exposure to normal speech patterns.

> (Webster and Ellwood 1985: 82)

I do not accept that the child is a passive 'recipient' of language – unquestioningly absorbing the rules, vocabulary, and structure of literate language uses to the degree of perfect imitation. Nor do I believe that a mild/moderate degree of hearing loss will inevitably interrupt (perhaps permanently) the child's language development in the primary school towards the goal of literacy. This is not to say that a mild/moderate hearing loss is not significant. Of course it is highly significant if one simply cannot hear all that is going on. The point, however, is that Speaking and Listening (National Curriculum English AT 1) and being able to hear normally are not the same issue. *Hearing* does not inevitably affect one's ability to *listen*.

As someone with a moderate hearing loss of a sensori-nature, with direct personal experience, it is hard to know how to approach such an issue as the consequences of the newly elevated status of oracy in the classroom for the hearing impaired child.[1] As a teacher I agree with Lynas (1986: 87) in her observation: 'In Britain, ordinary class teachers vary considerably in their style of teaching, but they generally work on the assumption that their pupils have normal hearing'. And the National Oracy Project's publication *Teaching, Talking and Learning at Key Stage 2* emphasises what children's talk does *for the teacher*: 'Talk is the form of communication that gives me a way into pupils' ideas, feelings, hopes, and emotions' (NOP 1991: 7).

There is no room for doubt that talk is not only a tool for children to make sense of their own learning, it is an important element of the whole process of learning – including giving the teacher valuable information about the progress of that learning. At the same time, the needs of children are made explicit: they need contexts which encourage talk; the confidence which comes from regular speaking and listening; and the time, space and the resources to share. Talk helps children: by enabling self-criticism; by allowing the teacher to stand back and listen; it provides a great sense of achievement and responsibility; it raises the status of children as participants in learning; fosters an atmosphere of positive criticism by harnessing the power of peer-pressure; and past experiences are made relevant to current thinking.

SOME RESERVATIONS

Despite these important insights, however, I cannot agree with the idea that it is possible to provide equal access to the curriculum for all via talk. Talk is the counterpart to listening. They are inseparable. Many publications about oracy are concerned with mainstream education and therefore 'talk' cannot be construed to mean signing or any other form of symbolic communication accessible to the deaf. For my own part, the traditional primary education I received was not characterised by talk; therein, I expect, lay my salvation. My vivid memories are of dark classrooms, or those with the light in my eyes, only realising the purpose of what I had just done long after it was done. Reading became a solid, reliable and even enjoyable activity. As Webster says:

> There is a certain appeal in the visual stability and permanence of written language for deaf children. After all, the child's biological capacity for learning a symbolic language is not affected by deafness.
>
> (Webster 1986: 208)

Certainly I have found this to be my experience. This statement obviously refers to such 'symbolic languages' as signing, but I feel, as 'only' a moderately hearing impaired literate person, that it is relevant to consider the permanence of print as a reliable source and operator of literacy. By this, I mean that of all the modes of literacy, as evidenced by the Attainment Targets in the English National Curriculum, print is the one that does not rely on the participant being able to hear normally. This has been of critical importance in my own educational experience. However, using and learning through the printed word demands full literacy including developed achievement in what the National Curriculum labels Speaking and Listening.

Achievement in the components of literacy allows membership of a literacy culture for which school prepares the child. The literacy culture is that which formal schooling can introduce to the child, it is distinct from the language experiences in the home. Necessarily, every child brings different home language and literacy experiences to the learning environment of the school. Since school learning depends crucially on literacy, an important question is 'what is it that the child already has which will help her/him acquire literacy?'. Given that the moderately hearing impaired child will have participated to some degree in the early development of language, hearing impairment will not inevitably disrupt the context in which language growth takes place, and so impede the child's efforts in learning to read. What moderately hearing impaired children bring to the learning environment, as well as their early experience of language, is a special need that accompanies their degree of language confidence and competence. The Warnock Report acknowledges this:

> The purpose of education for all children is the same; the goals are the same. But the help that individual children need in progressing towards them will be different.
>
> (Warnock 1978: 4 para. 1.4)

Ultimately, 'Education is a good and a specifically human good, to which all human beings are entitled' (Warnock: para. 1.7).

No teacher would deny this. Yet these statements are somewhat hollow-sounding when one considers the moderately hearing impaired child in the ordinary classroom. Deafness is invisible and as such is easy to ignore. Lynas in her somewhat crudely entitled *Integrating the Handicapped into Ordinary Schools* uses Wolfsenberger's principle of normalisation:

> the utilisation of means which are as culturally normative as possible to establish and/or maintain personal behaviours which are as culturally normative as possible.

(quoted in Barton 1988: 28)

as part of an argument that the best way to 'normalise' is to educate the presumably 'abnormal' person in a 'normal' setting. Warnock (1978) had already diluted this view with the belief (rightly) that a disability is a handicap only in certain circumstances. The hearing impaired child desperately wants to feel 'normal'. This offers a paradox, however, since no two definitions of normal are the same, even in the same context. Every person is different in some way from the norm and they may believe and wish that if this difference could be 'normalised' then many other aspects of life would be made more bearable. In this way, hearing impaired children have more to gain and more to lose in their quest for literacy. They have to enter the literacy culture, not only to be empowered but to feel normal. More is at stake.

The disappointing fact about many of the new offerings from educational initiatives about talk in the classroom is that they fail to acknowledge the impact that hearing loss has on the ability to speak and listen to the same degree of expertise, all other factors remaining equal, as normally hearing peers.[2] The raised status of talk in the classroom is positive – of course we should listen to children more than we do. Yet it is important to provide the environment for speaking and listening which will allow *all* pupils to participate fully. Teachers and normally hearing pupils have much to consider in the face of hearing impaired classmates. As teachers, we must not allow the 'deficit model' of the hearing impaired child to creep into our assessment of the hearing impaired child's *situation*. It is the learning environment and our place within this that must enable children in their endeavours to acquire literacy.

DEVELOPING A CONTEXT FOR LEARNING

Teaching strategies could be more accurately termed 'enabling strategies'. Teachers enable pupils to make sense of their surroundings and of the world by showing them the skills that being human demand. Communication is one of those important human skills and one which, as has been discussed, is a critical matter for hearing impaired people. At a basic level, one could say that providing a child with a hearing aid will enable her/him to 'hear'. This is not good enough. The teacher must still be sure to stand no more than two metres away from the wearer as hearing aids do not distinguish between sounds nor do they decide which would be the most useful to amplify. In terms of classroom organisation, the teacher must consider whether group arrangement of children and tables is the fairest system given that a child may need to see whoever is speaking all the time in order to concentrate on the thread of meaning. This is no less true in secondary and higher education! Isolation in a learning environment is the quickest way to demotivate a child, giving opportunity for a valid excuse to find distraction.

The classroom is only one area of the school in which the child is expected to learn. The library (how difficult to understand whispered instructions on how to find the coveted book; how distressing to whisper back without hearing the sound of one's own voice!), playing field (the wind and a hearing aid are sworn enemies with painful effects!), and hall (I don't think I have ever understood what assemblies are for!) are all taxing on the hearing impaired child's listening skills. Classroom noises may seem innocent enough, but placing a tape recorder by a hearing aid wearer will demonstrate on playback just what is being amplified.

The question of lip-reading is mentioned only in passing by such experts as Webster and Ellwood (1985) who expect that additional cues on lips may support communication.[3] Obviously, teachers should endeavour to keep their faces as visible as possible during speech. Nothing should obscure the mouth; the teacher should not stand in front of a window or light source; speak and write on a board at the same time (I wonder if I would be able to understand long division had it not been so studiously explained to a piece of chalk); pace about whilst talking; or 'mouth' words. It seems a shame for teachers to have to be advised how best to address their pupils, but as always, the best treatment of the hearing impaired child is that which benefits all children: look directly at the audience; the audience should all be facing the speaker; use a natural rhythm of speech with natural patterns of lip shapes.

There are some strategies which teachers can use to aid the hearing impaired child in particular, for example, managing and checking hearing aids regularly. In the main, however, such strategies focus on organisational aspects of the school day. So called 'peer-adoption' nominates a normally hearing child to the task of ensuring that the hearing impaired child has heard/understood the range of messages, announcements and changes of context which occur in the school day. Children tend to do this without thinking or having to be asked and hearing impaired children become experts at nagging the child next door for a repetition of what has been missed! During group discussions, the teacher must make sure that the speaker is always identified, and that they intervene in cases of difficulty to paraphrase or illustrate content further. Smaller groups may be considered until the confidence of all the children at speaking is ascertained. As always, teachers should strive to provide real life experience as a stimulus for spontaneous language.

Webster and Ellwood believe that:

> The teacher should have sufficient information to organise the classroom experience effectively to include the hearing impaired child, but not at the expense of the majority.
>
> (Webster and Ellwood 1985: 81)

Inclusive education can cut both ways.

CONCLUSION

What has been described here demonstrates that what is good practice for the hearing impaired child in the classroom also benefits all children engaged in spoken interaction with the teacher and with each other. The acquisition of literacy is a different process for each child. Teachers acknowledge this to be the case and moderate their teaching. Hearing impairment is one of many 'special needs' and in seeking to offer a curriculum for a range of learners, teachers may need to look beyond the particular 'need' and to consider their whole approach to teaching and learning. The University of Birmingham School of Education (1991) in its course for teachers of hearing impaired children outlines those factors which should facilitate learning:

- The child should be seen at all times as an active participant in learning.
- Teaching styles adopted should promote rather than repress pupil involvement.
- Direct experience is crucial, but the power of language cannot be underestimated; and time is needed to talk things out.

This document stresses that access to the curriculum, which after all is supposed to enable the acquisition of literacy amongst other things, does not just mean children being in the same room as their teachers, but requires their active participation in learning. Again comes the message that teachers, when forced to reflect on their organisation of the curriculum in the light of a hearing impaired child being present, inevitably improve the efficacy of their teaching for all the children.

Speaking and listening hold the key into the world of language – language for communication, for social exchange, for presenting one's ideas and beliefs. Speech is context-bound, not requiring the degree of reflective and disembedded thinking that print at times demands. It is oracy that gives children their first linguistic insights, thereby enabling achievement in learning to read. The auditory environment (Webster 1986) is what teachers need to consider for all children when they attempt to enable children in their quest for literacy. The quality of any child's experiences with oracy will, I believe, go a long way in facilitating the acquisition of literacy. This has not been my experience, but it is one that I want to provide for my pupils, remembering that for me, as for all others, hearing or hearing impaired, literacy is the key to future learning, escape and delight.

NOTES

1. The hearing impairment or deafness described in this chapter is of a mild/moderate nature. That is a loss of up to 70 decibels across the frequency range in the good ear.
2. This is, unfortunately, true of *Teaching Talking and Learning at KS2* (National Oracy Project) although the Project has published some material from teachers working with deaf and hearing impaired children.
3. I am aware that there is a complex and important debate within the deaf and partially hearing community about the relative merits and demerits, as well as the principles, of lip-reading and signing, but I do not think this affects the point I am making here.

REFERENCES

Andrews, E. and Roberts, N. (1994) *Helping the Hearing Impaired Child in Your Class*, Oxford, Oxford Brookes University Press

Barton, L. (1988) *The Politics of Special Educational Needs*, Chapter 5: 'Challenging Conceptions of Integration', London, Falmer

Department for Education (1995) *English in the National Curriculum*, London, HMSO

Lynas, W. (1986) *Integrating the Handicapped into Ordinary Schools: A Study of Hearing Impaired Pupils*, London, Croom Helm

Meek, M. (1991) *On Being Literate*, London, Bodley Head

National Oracy Project (1991) *Teaching Talking and Learning at KS2*, York, NCC

University of Birmingham School of Education (1991) *Distance Learning Course for Teachers of Hearing Impaired Children*, Birmingham University

Warnock, M. (1978) *Special Educational Needs*, London, HMSO

Webster, A. (1986) *Deafness, Development and Literacy*, London, Methuen

Webster, A and Ellwood, D. (1985) *The Hearing Impaired Child in the Ordinary Classroom*, London, Croom Helm

Part III

Mixed ability: the range of learners

Introduction to Part III

> Within any group of pupils there will be a wide range of ability and experience. This calls for a flexible approach allowing for differentiation to provide success and challenges for them all.
>
> (NCC 1989)

Just what is the 'range of ability and experience' which teachers have to take into account when providing for differentiated ways of tackling the learning demands of the primary curriculum? Part II opened up the debate about 'ability' by emphasising that this need not always be equated with fluent or technically accurate literacy. Part III takes the arguments and issues further, outlining the breadth and variation in the range of learners whose curriculum (and other) needs have to be met in the classroom. Much of the existing work on differentiation comes from the area of Special Educational Needs (e.g. Ainscow and Muncey 1989; Booth *et al.* 1992; NASEN publications), and has often been associated with initiatives to ensure access for children whose educational chances are delayed or hindered by the difficulties they may have to face. Quite rightly, principles of inclusion and entitlement are hard fought-for in the area of special education. However, there is also a tendency to see children who are defined as having special educational needs as necessarily under-achieving. This, linked with other assumptions about differentiated provision for learning, has tended to shift attention towards those children who find the intellectual demands of the classroom a struggle. Penelope Weston, reporting on one local authority's work on differentiation, points to the frequent connection made between issues of differentiation and low achievement; she quotes some staff as dismissing the initiative as 'just another remedial project' (Weston 1992: 7). Much of the burden of hammering out the theoretical, as well as the practical, issues about diversity has been carried by those who work in special education. It is time that the balance was shifted a little more towards a view which acknowledges differentiation as relevant for *all* learners.

One topical issue about provision for the full range of learners is how to cater for those children who are very able in some – or all – curriculum areas. The discussion in Part I about balancing the needs of the individual with communal learning aims and practices is relevant here. For children who show particularly developed aptitudes in learning, the educational commitment to individual entitlement can sometimes fall down. Partly this is because of the emotional, political and philo-sophical debate surrounding high achievement. Educationalists are careful about the terminology they use. The term 'gifted', for example, is capable of misconception and loaded with emotive and political over-tones. This may be because it puts most of the emphasis on the individual rather than the individual's accomplishments; it is important to keep a clear view of the relationship between an individual's *capabilities* and her or his *value as a human being*. Nevertheless, children who display exceptional aptitudes have their own special needs and must be consid-ered and catered for. This can be tricky, of course; not just because of the unease we might feel about apparently according privilege to the already privileged, but because the qualities which are perceived as exceptional are not absolute for all kinds of societies and cultures. In a non-industrial society, for example, the 'very able' might be those who are keen-sighted or exceptionally patient and enduring; in a high-tech culture, social aptitudes may count for less than technical expertise. The unstable nature of the category 'very able' can sometimes obstruct balanced educational debate about how to provide for children who show particular aptitudes to an exceptional degree.

One difficulty for teachers, before tackling the issue of provision, might be how to identify children who might have exceptional ability or poten-tial. There is not just one manifestation of high ability, but several, some of which are:

- **High achieving all-rounders who seem to excel at anything they undertake**. These children make their abilities manifest pretty quickly so may need no further identification.
- **High achievers in all aspects of one particular area of the curriculum** – e.g. physical education. It may be relatively easy to spot unusually good early performers in sport, but it is not always clear whether this might represent exceptional talent or just a temp-orary highlighting of ability due to opportunity, coaching or early physical maturity.
- **The 'covertly able'**. It cannot be taken for granted that high levels of ability will be immediately obvious. Some children might well have exceptional potential but be under-achieving for a range of reasons; one of these might be family or peer pressure either to reveal themselves as exceptional as an honour to the family or to hide

abilities because of not wanting to be seen as 'different'. Another might be related to boredom or lack of motivation because the learning presented lacks challenge, or a matter of culture or gender which prevents easy identification of exceptional ability.

- **Very able children with communication difficulties or physical handicap.** An absence of full language competence does not mean an absence of intelligence and cases of autistic children, for example, who display remarkable abilities in a particular area have been highlighted recently. Equally, concerns about children with perceptual difficulties which get in the way of the technical aspects of literacy and numeracy, and so hinder progress, are also familiar.

Of course this is not a definitive list, nor does simply describing some categories help teachers decide how best to identify and cater for children with high ability. What about high achievers in music or art – is their ability also likely to be described as spurts of technical prowess which will slow down? If not, what can be done to provide support? Their needs may be a little different from other high achievers and be affected by the material resources available to the school. Sometimes teachers see high achievers' own verbal or logical versatility as a threat, or become irritated by parents' concerns about a stimulating enough environment and curriculum for their exceptionally able children. Very able children may well find the social demands of schooling more of a struggle than others. Joan Freeman gives an example of a child who said 'When I get to school, I've learned to isolate myself mentally from anything that might hurt me; I just sort of close the door' (Freeman 1991 quoted in Goodhew 1994). Another recognised way of coping with exceptional ability may be unsocial behaviour. Then there are the children whose exceptional ability may be more technical or spatial. In identifying children's capabilities, teachers need to observe learners carefully and find ways of assessing ability which can cover the full range of learning opportunities – not just those based on literacy or numeracy. Many of the traditional forms of testing arrangements do not give children who are mechanically inventive and conceptualise things in three dimensions, or divergent thinkers, opportunities to display these abilities.

This is a strong argument not only for a range of forms of observation and assessment, but for the provision of a varied and diverse range of opportunities for learning. It also means offering challenges which might involve the teacher, too, in taking some risks and opening the classroom door a little wider. Part of a fuller and more stimulating range of learning opportunities might be the chance for children to talk with adults, since conversation with a more experienced person can extend ideas. Classroom assistants and other non-teaching staff are invaluable here, but it's worth investigating how other adults might be invited to become involved in the classroom – not just for the benefit of the very able learner, but for all the children. The adults need not themselves be experts in any particular area (although in some cases this might be just the kind of stimulus a young engineer, musician or dancer might need) but ready to offer a different point of view and to share ideas that simply come with experience that the highly able child's peers cannot possibly have. Most of the effective ways of providing for very able children will be those which can involve all the pupils in activities which they can take on according to their own choices and preferences. Although special resources might be necessary for some extension activities, providing separate work can put an unwelcome or unhelpful spotlight on an able child. Work which can be taken as far as the individual can possibly push it, supported by reference material and human resources to stimulate the highly able learner may well be the most supportive way of extending those who are already very advanced. Older children can equally be a stimulating resource for younger, very able children. Whilst it is important to take account of individual needs it is equally vital not to make any child feel isolated. The social arrangements of the classroom may need to be reviewed so that children are encouraged to respect and praise each other's achievements of all kinds, not just the academic, and give value to a wide range of qualities. Teacher example and modelling can be vital in helping children to learn how to do this genuinely.

Giving value to diversity is essential for the 'entitlement to becoming physically educated' and being able to take on further challenges. In Patricia Maude's chapter, 'Differentiation in physical education', she stresses that:

> Children need to feel confident and valued as movers, to maintain a strong self-image and self-esteem in movement, to face change and development with anticipation rather than with dread.

The history of physical education has been one often more related to skill-building than to development of diverse individual capabilities. Patricia Maude emphasises the process of children's individual physical development rather than seeing physical education as a set of targets to be reached. She gives an overview of some of the physiological aspects of development and outlines an approach where differentiation in physical education is offered through provision, participation and outcome. She explains that 'movement learning is differentiated from the outset' since 'each child brings to the learning a unique blend of individual body characteristics ... add to these experience, opportunity for practice and feedback' and each child, no matter how physically able, will learn a 'movement vocabulary' which will enable them to challenge themselves further. Her comments here are apposite to a general view of ability and how best to identify and promote different abilities in different areas of the curriculum. Children who exhibit physical differences are encouraged to join in activities at a level which will stretch them; they are not excluded because of any variation in body shape or flexibility. How different from some practices of classroom learning where those who do not fit with a predetermined 'norm' are often given less challenge, rather than helped to take on activities which will help them get better at whatever is on offer.

Indeed, providing opportunities for children to experiment and go beyond what they can do now, is critical in managing learning. This is certainly what Alison Wood argues in her chapter 'Differentiation in primary mathematics'. She emphasises the need for a style and approach to mathematics teaching which will genuinely invite children to take risks and learn through tough engagement with what they want to learn. In looking at very able young mathematicians, Alison Wood suggests that it may well be that attention to their needs will help create more productive learning opportunities for all. She points out that efforts to provide differentiated tasks can hold back the development of all children's mathematical ability – perhaps most acutely the development of very able young mathematicians. Her chapter offers not only a sturdy critique of mathematics schemes and other attempts to offer a differentiated mathematics curriculum, but some practical suggestions for alternative approaches.

The work done by Ros Smith and Isobel Urquhart on 'Science and special educational needs' ties together some of the threads already unpicked in Part II as well as in other chapters in this section. They begin by giving clear evidence that literacy should not be seen as a determiner of a child's capacity to tackle scientific concepts. Traditional forms of grouping based on literacy ability can impede children's scientific learning. Although they argue for collaborative approaches they warn that an unreflective approach to the tasks which are used for collaboration can result in double disadvantage. Firstly, it can mean that children whose literacy competence does not match their scientific understanding are given less challenging scientific material and put in groups which may not stimulate their thinking; then, because of the frequent requirement for individual recording of results, their learning may be hampered a second time by the technical problems they might have in writing or reading. Classroom organisation comes in for scrutiny as Ros Smith and Isobel Urquhart make a distinction between children working *in* groups and working *as* groups. However, this is not an argument against collaboration but a re-appraisal of the opportunities on offer for collaborative learning through talk. Nevertheless, they warn that opportunities for talking and learning in science may not themselves be unproblematic. Cultural factors may intervene.

Certainly, classroom activities need to be properly differentiated to provide for children who have different styles in oracy, whether these styles are culturally developed or a matter of personality. For example, those who are more reserved and reflective; those who are up-front and voluble; those who are speaking their home languages or dialect or those who are operating in an unfamiliar speech form. This does not imply that only certain children should be asked to take part in certain talk activities; gradually all pupils will have the chance to experience a range of ways of using talk for learning, in a variety of groupings and settings. Ros Smith and Isobel Urquhart urge that in using talk to support scientific learning 'differentiation should enhance children's strengths rather than confirm their weaknesses'.

It is recognised, however, that one of the greatest strengths that children can bring to classrooms – their ability to speak their own and other languages – still offers some problems for teachers. How can children's oracy be developed and how can talk be used for learning in the curriculum? Jennifer Reynolds describes a series of classroom activities based on talk in a variety of contexts. These emerged as a result of continuing evaluation of classroom work allowing her to assess individual knowledge and skills. To exemplify the potential of talk for learning, she describes the progress of four children whose abilities spanned the whole spectrum of her Year 5/6 class. 'An ear to the ground' offers a detailed analysis of how classroom management, varied group organisation and continued careful planning for talk, can take account of many of the reservations and concerns expressed earlier about both the potentially restrictive as well as the liberating aspects of talk for learning.

Children's intellectual, social and emotional development, their self-esteem, self-confidence and cultural and linguistic identity, are inextricably bound up with elements in their language repertoire, and their community and home languages merit support and development in their own right. Even those who are apparently monolingual and share Standard English as a common language, vary their language according to the audience, purpose and context of communication. Some people may include elements of dialect usage in everyday language with friends or at home but move towards more standard forms when at work or outside the immediate community. Some, including children, have the ability to use distinctly different dialects and/or languages and so have an even wider range of choices about the most effective kind of language to use in a particular setting, varying forms and registers to suit their communicative intentions. Conscious attention to the varieties of language which children bring to the classroom is important in promoting knowledge about language. This emphasis on linguistic diversity and its impact on classroom learning leads to the final chapter of the section, Ian Eyres' account of working in a mainstream class with three Bosnian girls. In this account, not only did the bilingual learners get to grips with some important knowledge about how Bosnian and English can interact, but through their story writing the rest of the class gained a great deal of knowledge about the structures of language. This chapter demonstrates the importance of classrooms being hospitable to diversity.

Part of this hospitality depends on teachers recognising and valuing children's own language and knowledge. Ian Eyres was a little baffled about how best to support three pupils whose language he had no access to, but found that by drawing on his own experience with developing monolingual writers and building on the girls' own knowledge, in this case, specifically of *Snjezana i Sedam Patuljaka* (Snow White and the Seven Dwarfs) they made fast and impressive development through writing bilingual texts. Ian Eyres' chapter identifies provision for differentiation by choice, support and outcome while also offering a useful description of ways to develop children's writing – whether the writers are bilingual or otherwise. He adds weight to the urging given in earlier chapters in this Part to offer children challenges; by pushing them, with courtesy and care, to the leading edge of their competence, he found that these learners were able to demonstrate much more complex language ability than would have been possible through reductive formal exercises. Not only this, but the whole class benefited from the close attention being paid to a new language in the classroom. By taking risks himself, by acknowledging the children's home language and literacy experience, by careful grouping and awareness that he was dealing with conceptually able learners, and by a recognition that too simplistic a view of differentiation can be exclusive, Ian Eyres brings together many of the issues raised about how best to cater for the full range of learners.

REFERENCES

Ainscow, M., and Muncey, J. (1989) *Meeting Individual Needs*, London, Fulton

Booth, T., Swann, W., Masterton, M. and Potts, P. (1992) *Curricula for Diversity in Education* and *Policies for Diversity in Education*, London, Routledge

Goodhew, G. (1994) 'Opening the door to able children', *Special Children*, 78, October

National Association for Special Educational Needs publications

National Curriculum Council (1989) *A Curriculum for All*, York, NCC

Weston, P. (1992) 'A Decade for Differentiation', *The British Journal of Special Education*, 19 (1)

Chapter 7

Differentiation in physical education

Patricia Maude

A person is not a thing, but a process ... a form of motion ... not a noun but a verb.

(Kelly 1984: 83)

In this chapter I intend to build from Kelly's quotation by exploring the nature of 'process', examining the importance of the person as a form of motion, a 'verb'. I want to establish what it is to become physically educated within the context of becoming an educated and fulfilled person. In so doing, I shall examine the crucial issue of differentiation, as it pervades and underpins every aspect of child development and physical education. The chapter, therefore, is structured into two inter-related parts, firstly, the diverse features of the child seen as process and verb and, secondly, the contribution of a differentiated programme of physical education in providing for the education of the whole child.

PROCESS AND VERB

Children are at the centre of the learning process and bring to that learning, from their earliest years, a unique blend of physical features, abilities and aptitudes and a range of previous experience. Much of that experience is gained whilst maturing; the sequence and order of this may be predetermined, but the pace is unique to each individual. Movement learning is differentiated from the outset. If you watch any new-born child learning through movement, you will observe apparently random activity, uncontrolled and flailing limbs and the reflex actions that are evident at birth. Some of these might give the impression that the infant is a mini-adult, pre-programmed and ready to go! Some of the reflexes persist in their crucial role in the maintenance of essential life functions, such as sucking and swallowing. Others, however, disappear only to return as learned movements, months or years later. The stepping reflex is one which might give the impression that a new-born child knows how to walk at birth. If you hold a normal new-born infant with the feet touching a flat surface, you can observe the lifting and placing of one foot in front of the other alternately as in walking. Try this activity a few weeks later and the response is no longer present. Learning to walk is complex and dependent on a range of inter-related developments and achievements. No one stage of achievement or development can happen without certain preceding elements being sufficiently mature and in place. Even then, no two infants acquire exactly the same movement pattern, nor at the same pace.

Gallahue (1982) has plotted the route to the acquisition of basic movement skills and has named the various stages. The emergent movement pattern or early experimentation, he names the *initial stage*, followed by the *elementary stage* in which co-ordination is improving, but the movement is incorrectly performed and incomplete. Finally the child achieves the *mature stage* in which all the essential elements of the movement pattern are integrated and in which the movement includes the *preparation*, followed by the *action* and ending with the *follow through*.

There is, however, little strict conformity along the way, since each child brings to the learning a unique blend of individual body characteristics, including shape and size, length of body levers, strength, mobility or suppleness and speed. Add to these the child's experience, opportunity for practice and feedback, the suitability of the learning environment, motivation and stimulation, intellectual ability and tenacity, and it is not surprising that outcomes differ in both skill level achieved and the pace at which the mature ability is attained. To deny the child even one element of progression is to undermine the potential for success. Deprivation of nutrition, sleep or exercise can stunt growth, leading to a potential inhibition in movement development. Lack of a safe movement environment can also deny children the opportunity of sufficient experience towards achieving full potential in movement.

The role of the teacher in promoting this achievement is of paramount importance, for not only does the teacher need to know the process of the sequence of growth and development but also the progression in motor skill acquisition in order to provide children with appropriate, challenging, physically active and attainable tasks. If a child experiences difficulty in performing a skill at one stage, this will inevitably lead to inability to progress to subsequent stages. If a teacher does not know how to provide the building blocks to success, this can frustrate the child. Frustration can be a contributory factor in loss of motivation and poor body image and self concept.

Gallahue's movement theory can help teachers to recognise the performance stage of each child, the critical moment of readiness to tackle the next stage and then to understand how to set appropriate tasks to facilitate the next stages of progression. In dealing with a class of children, all at different stages, it can be very comforting to know that the sequence of skill acquisition is the same for every child even though the pace of development varies from child to child.

This sameness in sequence, but diversity in pace can be seen in one of the early acquired skills – learning to walk and run. In examining these more closely it is easy to see that the child as process relies on the importance of the relationship between growth, maturation, development and learning. Since each of these factors progresses at rates which vary from individual to individual, it is clear that differences between individuals often vary dramatically. The process of learning to run comprises a series of progressions. All normal infants both display the walking reflex and lose that reflex in the first few weeks of life. They then take about a year to develop sufficient movement knowledge, co-ordination, balance, strength and experience to learn to walk. They also need time and practice to go through a range of related movement activities which are the progressions towards walking.

The sequence of learning and the series of progressions that precede walking include rolling over, holding the head up unsupported, pushing up on the hands and arms to raise the head from front lying, sitting supported, then unsupported, standing supported and unsupported, stepping supported and finally taking the first step alone. Running requires further experience in stepping, co-ordination, balance, speed, stamina and strength, firstly to travel more quickly and then to project the body through the air from one foot to the other. Every child normally goes through the same sequence of learning stages and in the same order, but each proceeds through these at a unique and individual rate. When considering the movement curriculum, it is this individual rate that demonstrates the need for awareness of differentiation.

This is just one example of the whole process of child development in relation to the acquisition of body management and skilful movement. The child as a process, growing and developing in movement acquisition, is also dependent on other sequences of body maturation in the early years. The body develops cephalo-caudally (head to tail) and proximo-distally (centre to extremity) and this influences the range and rate of acquisition of other movement abilities. The abilities of the new-born child are largely focused near the mid-line within the body, namely in relation to the heart, lungs, digestive and other centrally located organs responsible for basic survival. The peripheral parts of the body such as the hands and feet, gain their functional importance much later. The brain is active and functional from birth, whereas the usefulness of the legs and feet does not become fully evident until about a year later. The upper half of the body is quite active and knowledgeable in movement before the legs become actively involved in locomotion. Similarly, the shoulders, arms and both hands working together, as in grabbing a toy, are active well before the palmar hand grasp and later the pincer finger grip techniques are achieved. These early learning features may seem far removed from the daily work of the primary school teacher in physical education, but their influence is certainly not. It is especially relevant for children who seem clumsy, uncoordinated, with delayed movement development and who also seem to be at risk in the PE setting. For these children the importance of a carefully structured, individualised progressive and regularly taught programme of gross and fine motor skills cannot be over-stressed. Fine motor skill develops out of gross motor skill. Gross motor skills are broadly those which involve whole body movement, such as locomotion. Fine motor skills are those which involve smaller, manipulative skills such as gripping, catching and throwing. Co-ordination and control in gross and fine skills, achieved in physical education, will have immeasurable benefits for children in the classroom, helping them to achieve efficient manipulative techniques in activities such as writing, drawing, measuring, cutting and construction work.

The second feature of process as it affects developing movement acquisition is the child's constant exposure to change. To a greater and lesser extent, changes are brought about from within the child and from environmental factors. From within, growth leads to increase in height, lengthening of limbs and increase in weight. Body proportions change dramatically through childhood. For example, the head of a new-born child is relatively large in proportion to the rest of the body and by maturity it only doubles in length. Arms and legs are all about the same length at birth, but by maturity the legs have increased fivefold in length. Apparently overgrown hands and feet at the beginning of the adolescent growth spurt, contrast to the normal expectation of proximo-distal development in which the extremities grow before the related limb. This can sometimes make for awkwardness in movement when compared with the pre-growth spurt skill level. The child may need reassurance that this is only a temporary feature. Sensitive teaching can help children to accommodate these changes.

Each of these challenges in turn makes new demands in terms of achieving mature movement patterns, in retaining movement knowledge already acquired and in adapting to new developments which have come about as a result of the growth process. By contrast, as the child gains experience and skill, so the ability to adapt and incorporate these changes in body shape and size is enhanced, as is the ability to face, accept and accommodate new challenges from the environment. Environmental factors demand constant adaptation in movement responses. For daily living tasks to be achieved with ease and efficiency, gross and fine motor skills will be drawn on automatically, without special planning. Physical education challenges children to select appropriate skills in answering tasks, to repeat and refine those skills and to increase the range and complexity of their movement vocabulary.

Sometimes the fearlessness and apparent lack of caution shown by some children can be daunting for the teacher, but few children actually go beyond their own safety limits. Teaching children how to learn in changing circumstances opens the door to self-determination. However, the absence of sufficient constant factors can be problematic for some children, for example a child who has not learned to select equipment appropriate for the task or a child whose growth spurt has temporarily sapped energy. In providing suitably differentiated learning experiences, a teacher may need to draw on knowledge and understanding of child development, the processes of movement learning and of the progressions which constitute skill learning.

Gallahue (1982) categorises movement acquisition into four phases from birth to maturity. As discussed previously, the new-born experiences the *reflexive phase*. This is followed by the *rudimentary movement phase* of infancy, then the *fundamental movement phase* in childhood and finally the *sport-related phase* as maturity of movement skill is achieved. Primary school teachers are concerned with ensuring that children progress out of the rudimentary phase as soon as possible in Key Stage 1. They should then be guided through the fundamental movement phase and on into mature, skilled movement.

In Key Stages 1 and 2 children are exploring and experimenting with movement. They are gaining control in their movement and are becoming versatile and adaptable through improved speed, agility, balance, power and co-ordination. Some of the skills that Gallahue analyses and refers to as being refined in the fundamental movement phase, include running, jumping, climbing, throwing, catching, striking, rolling and balancing. These skills are developed both through the maturing of the body systems and through opportunities for practice and feedback. Teachers play an important role here, for skilled teaching ensures continuous progress and depends on teachers' knowledge of appropriate progressions for the learner. For example, when a child is learning to catch, rolling a ball along the ground slowly would precede bouncing the ball and later throwing the ball. You might use a Velcro sticky pad or even a beanbag or a balloon to help the child with receiving. Rather than work with a partner, you might encourage the child to work alone (to self-feed) by rolling the ball to a rebound surface and receiving it back into the hands. Self-feeding is another means of developing hand-eye co-ordination and helps too in the learning of pace and direction. It also facilitates the all-important skill of 'keeping the eye on the ball'. Working alone can help those children who find the judgement of pace of a ball fed by another person too challenging.

Similarly, in learning to swim in shallow water, there are a range of techniques and logical progressions available for the teacher and learner. For example, understanding the use of buoyancy aids, knowing how to stand up from front to back lying and how to achieve a floating position in order to learn how to propel, can give the all-important boost in confidence and achievement to the beginner.

Key Stage 2 has been described as the 'skill hungry years' in which children are keen to be competent movers and are also aspiring to the sport-related phase, by building a bank of movement vocabulary, rather like a set of tools that can be applied in a range of activities. To achieve this, maturation, experience and time are important contributors, but effective teaching is the vital factor in the degree to which the final phase can be accessed. The challenge for the teacher is to provide for the diverse range of movement behaviour of the learners as 'verbs' in the class, to provide sufficiently differentiated learning opportunities and to teach the children to manage their own learning within a broad curriculum framework.

The child as process and verb then, has an individual physical structure and a personalised aptitude for skill acquisition and for achieving potential. To maximise that potential in the Physical Education curriculum, entitlement will be ensured by teachers who are knowledgeable in the differentiated developmental process through which children pass, in the same sequence, but at different rates. Equally important is the teacher's role in guiding children to understand that each child's individual physical structure, personalised aptitude for skill acquisition and unique potential for achievement are not inhibiting factors in becoming physically educated. Rather they are empowering factors in becoming skilful movers and independent learners.

DEVELOPING A DIFFERENTIATED PHYSICAL EDUCATION PROGRAMME

The uniqueness of Physical Education as a learning medium is twofold. Firstly, it provides for the cognitive, social and emotional development of the child as well as for the physical. Secondly, Physical Education can underpin all other aspects of the curriculum where the ability of the child to participate fully within the classroom environment and in the general life of the school calls for articulate movement control and range of movement ability. A child with fully developed gross and fine motor skills, and an 'eye' and 'feel' for movement efficiency often has confidence in tackling the full range of movement-related activities in school, whether in writing-related activity or in other 'hands-on' tasks. Many of the 'hands-on', problem-solving activities across the curriculum are dependent on the learner's motor skill ability, confidence, achievement and success in movement. For children whose movement development has been delayed or who have impaired motor skill ability for some reason, it is all the more important for the teacher to maximise the child's available mobility and versatility in movement and to devise a Physical Education programme that enhances these.

For Physical Education to be effective in fulfilling its educative role, we need to ask 'What is it to be physically educated?' Physical Education for children from pre-school age and throughout primary school should provide for enhancement of physical and motor development, co-ordination, extension of movement vocabulary and skill. The curriculum should challenge the emerging physical, intellectual, aesthetic and emotional abilities of the child. It should also initiate children into some of those activities that constitute the foundations for the socially recog-nised sports and recreation of our culture. The Physical Education programme must contribute to children's knowledge and understanding of the requirement to take personal responsibility for developing and maintaining a healthy, active and safe lifestyle.

The quality of Physical Education in Britain today is a product of the movement learning experiences of our predecessors. In 700 BC, gymnas-tics and athletics were the skills that enabled the physically educated to participate in the Olympic Games, whereas education in the Minoan period in Crete required the learner to be articulate in acrobatics! There were two components to becoming an educated person amongst the early Greeks, namely music and bodily exercise. More recently we adopted into this country the system of Swedish Gymnastics which led to the daily drill exercises experienced in British primary schools in the 1940s and 1950s – did these underpin the present aerobics era? My own drill experience was of physical training that seemed to deny the exist-ence of the intellect.

Laban devised a creative approach to movement education which informed the Dance and Gymnastics curriculum, mainly for girls in the 1970s, along with dance drawn from the folk and country traditions from Britain and abroad. The playing fields of Eton traditionally provided a diet of invasion games such as rugby, football, and hockey – a curriculum which has sometimes been seen as appropriate to the late 1990s. In fact, the Physical Education curriculum for the last decade of the twentieth century, as evidenced in the National Curriculum Orders 1995, draws on a wealth of experience and cultural practices in schooling, sport and recreation in providing learning opportunities for children across a broad spectrum of areas of physical activity. Permeating each of these is the requirement that children should be physically active, should learn safe practice and should develop positive attitudes. The curriculum should embrace learning experiences in athletics, dance, games, gymnastics, outdoor education and swimming. Closer examination of both the content of each of these activities and the breadth of provision can confirm the potential benefit to be derived, provided that children can gain access to these activities according to their individual need and can gain worthwhile developmental movement experience.

Success in teaching Physical Education depends on three elements. Firstly the teacher needs knowledge of the curriculum content in dance, games and gymnastics in Key Stage 1 and Key Stage 2, along with athletics, outdoor education and swimming in Key Stage 2. Secondly, knowledge of growth and development and the sequence of skill acquisitions applicable in both key stages is essential. Thirdly, with understanding of these two elements in place, the teacher can differentiate to provide for the needs of every child, regardless of physical ability.

The six broad areas of activity now required in the National Curriculum provide for a broad balanced experience and for access to the full range of activity types, as an entitlement for every child. No more will children grow up on a diet of games only and within games, concentration on invasion games such football or hockey. The new games curriculum calls for a balance between the three games types of invasion, net/wall and strike/field. In all primary schools children will now learn the skills and small-sided games that lead into the adult versions of these three games types. Variety such as this caters well for the diversity of children's interests in games playing. This can be further achieved by developing a progressive curriculum, from single skill learning to complex and combined skills; working alone and with a partner before being required to co-operate and compete with and against large groups; working in mixed ability as well as in single ability groupings and progressing to games in larger groups, with increased game structure and rules where appropriate. Providing a range of equipment can offer opportunities for differentiation in the games curriculum.

From the early years children can learn to select suitably sized equipment to achieve a task. Teaching children to select according to need, to set themselves appropriately increasing challenges, to work hard and to value their achievements and those of others are some of the keys to success.

Similar quality of achievement should now be possible in gymnastics too, where the curriculum has a clear skill component and where technique is a valued element underpinning the range of movement vocabulary. Formerly, floorwork and use of apparatus were often considered to be two unrelated elements of gymnastics. It is now accepted that use of apparatus is an extension of the floorwork and that apparatus suiting the children and the task in hand is brought out by the children, for their use, as required. Children are now encouraged to transfer skills and sequences from floor to apparatus and back according to task or topic. They can also learn new skills using the apparatus to help, where this is easier than learning on the floor first. For example, it was a commonly held belief that the forward roll on the floor is the easiest roll to learn and it was therefore the first to be taught. However both the forward and backward rolls are more easily achieved when attempted down an incline, such as a foam ramp. Furthermore, there are many rolling activities available to the child who is not yet ready to learn the forward roll. There include 'log rolling' (from lying on the front via the side, back and side, to return to the front). Other rolls using this, the vertical axis, could start and/or finish on different parts of the body such as the knees, thereby increasing the movement vocabulary and the knowledge of the concept of rolling. Creating sequences of rolls, with linking movements between each, provides for increased understanding of the concept of rolling, builds complexity in movement knowledge and enables even those children who are unable to perform the relatively complex forward roll to participate from a wide range of movement vocabulary.

Differentiation by task and by outcome have long been accepted practices in Physical Education. The non-statutory guidance of the August 1991 National Curriculum reads:

> Different children will progress at different rates in relation to each of the four categories of physical development, the stage of cognitive, emotional and social development, the stage reached in learning practical skills, the level of skill necessary for the activity.
>
> (DES 1991: 42)

To enable children to achieve at their own level, the learning process may either be set at different levels of difficulty in relation to each task or as a common task allowing for differentiated outcomes from different children. Both methods have their place and are appropriate in different circumstances.

Planning for differentiation means that children can learn in an environment in which discrimination by gender (formally a serious problem in PE), discrimination by physical or intellectual ability, body size or shape, will not feature and in an environment in which the learner can take a measure of control for personal achievement. For me, insight into differentiation is ably expressed in lesson evaluations written by two student teachers after teaching a planned games session, each working with four children. The quality of their appreciation of the need to cater for individual pupils within the group is matched by the extent to which, even at an early stage in their course, they are aware of providing differentiated learning experiences. They also take care not to let such differentiation operate against maximum learning opportunity. One student also comments on the benefits to be gained by providing for peer feedback to enhance learning.

Evaluation of teaching by student teacher 1

'At all times I made an assertive effort to encourage the children experiencing difficulty. The girls found it more difficult to pick up the techniques with their feet, this perhaps reflected inexperience. I felt it was important to give them extra praise as they were more likely to become disheartened. The boys on the other hand found this technique very simple and for them, increasing the difficulty of the task was necessary in order to stretch them to their full potential.'

'The necessity for differentiation was evident though it must be approached with care so as not to disillusion the less able or go beyond the level of motor development the children have reached.'

'I was much aware of dividing my time equally and allowing children to overcome some of their difficulties by co-operation with one another. Learning from their peers is certainly a valuable resource in Physical Education.'

Evaluation of teaching by student teacher 2

'From the two sessions I have learned the importance of building on the past achievement of individual pupils; providing opportunities for children to experience success; using a variety of resources, e.g. different equipment for different levels of ability; also to prepare different group tasks with different pupil roles and responsibilities and variations in pace to meet the different levels of ability.'

These two student teachers also demonstrate sound awareness of the need for assessment within their teaching. The importance of assessment in evaluating children's achievements and progress, in pin-pointing areas for development and in guiding future planning, cannot be overlooked. Observation and recording of achievement will largely be undertaken by the teacher, but learners, too, are often competent assessors of their own and others' achievements and areas for development. Many learners are skilled observers and well able to provide valuable feedback on others' work.

By taking into account the stage of physical development and fitness of the child as well as the level of physical skill already mastered, areas for assessment can include both functional and aesthetic aspects of achievement. Functional assessment could include level of skill achieved, accuracy, technique, consistency and quality of performance, adaptability, movement memory, the ability to achieve successfully more than one thing at a time and the complexity of sequencing. Aesthetic criteria might include the effectiveness of expression, use of imagination, the body-line, co-ordination, control and fluency of movement. In terms of other aspects of learning, I would include the achievement of appropriate solutions to set or selected tasks, safe performance, clear actions with successful outcomes and the extent to which the child incorporates health-related fitness into their work, as further criteria for consideration in determining appropriate assessment strategies.

Children's diverse physical development means that their physical education will inevitably include differentiation in *provision*, in *participation* and in *outcome*. In *provision*, this can be seen through the variety of challenges set; in *participation*, through the range of individual differences in ability and participation of the children; and in *outcome* through the different levels of performance achieved. It is also likely that in primary school, children are on a fast track, steep learning curve in movement development, with all to gain and nothing to lose in skill acquisition and in movement performance. In the pre-pubertal stage, movement should be articulate, skilful, creative, providing great satisfaction and without prejudice in relation to ability level or the anatomy and physiology of the learner. Children need to feel confident and valued as movers, to maintain a strong self-image and self-esteem in movement and to face change and development with anticipation rather than with dread. We as teachers must not neglect to provide for this entitlement so that no child that we teach will leave the primary school unwilling to participate positively in physical education, sport and recreation in Key Stages 3 and 4 and no child will be unmotivated as a result of our teaching.

The primary school years should be formative and exciting. Within schooling, physical education can now be challenging and satisfying, ensuring for learners access to quality physical activity. Within physical education, the concept of differentiation and progression can now become the accepted way of thinking, learning and teaching. Within differentiation, the child, who is both 'process' and 'verb' and central to the learning experience, should expect to study and acquire a movement vocabulary which is articulate and skilful, to achieve quality performance and to participate actively and safely. Additionally, the teacher's aim for each child should be to produce learners who seek to become physically educated, to maintain a positive self-image in physical education and who develop an enduring commitment to continued participation in physical education after they leave the primary school.

REFERENCES

DES (1991) *Physical Education for ages 5–16*, London, HMSO
DFE (1995) *Physical Education in the National Curriculum*, London, HMSO
Gallahue, D.L., (1982) *Understanding Motor Development in Children*, London, John Wiley & Sons
Kelly, G. (1984) *A Theory of Personality*, New York, Norton

Chapter 8

Differentiation in primary mathematics
Some dilemmas

Alison Wood

It is obvious to anyone who has tried to teach a mixed ability class that the problems of providing suitable activities for a wide range of pupil abilities is one of the most difficult tasks a teacher has to solve. In no subject are the effects of inappropriate tasks, or tasks incorrectly matched to the ability and stage of development of the pupils, more crucial than in mathematics. Teachers are often made aware of the need for differentiated activities in mathematics by the reactions of those children who are unable to cope with the work that the majority of the class can tackle with some degree of success. These mathematically low attainers often do not appear to understand what is required, their ability to read in order to extract information may be poor so they are unable to act on written instructions and, even if they know what is being asked of them, their mathematical understanding is often inadequate to perform the task. The difficulty this poses for the teacher is not unique to mathematics but the total blankness which children can display towards a mathematical question is somehow more complete than in other areas of the curriculum where they can make some attempt to perform the task even if the resulting work is of a low standard. This makes mathematics a subject in which every teacher is aware of the need for differentiation.

DIFFERENTIATION IN MATHEMATICS: A 'SPECIAL CASE'?

There are several reasons for mathematics being a special case which become more evident when considering the problems faced by teachers with mixed ability classes:

1. The, now well-known, 'seven year gap', in pupils' mathematical ability at age 11, referred to in the Cockcroft Report *Mathematics Counts* (1982: para. 342). Some 7-year-old children are able to understand concepts that others still have not grasped by the age of 14

The standard example illustrating this is the question: What number is one more than 6799?

2. The difficulty of finding tasks in mathematics which can be differentiated by outcome.

3. 'Aha' ability (Gardner 1978). Intrinsic pleasure in mathematics often comes from the moment of clarity when a sudden insight jump enables a child to understand a concept or solve a problem. This feeling comes from inside the child and any member of a class is likely to experience it (if at all) at a different moment. This clearly makes for difficulties when trying to teach mathematics to thirty children! If a teacher or another pupil 'gives the game away' the opportunity to gain this sort of pleasure is lost. The 'Aha' feeling is an important factor in motivating people to continue to persist in mathematics in order to experience the feeling again and, for this reason if for no other, teachers should exploit the educational advantages this emotion can encourage.[1]

4. The child who is an able mathematician needs to experience the effects of being 'stuck' in mathematics at primary school. It is by being stuck that we learn to try different strategies and increase our range of possible tactics for problem solving. Without such experiences, the danger is that the learner may become lazy or complacent and cease to develop powers of reasoning. Some years ago the Open University produced a bookmark bearing the message 'STUCK? Good – now you can learn something'. Perhaps we should all put a copy of this in our classrooms. I have seen too many children with the potential to become good mathematicians who have successfully worked through a maths scheme in primary schools without ever being seriously challenged mathematically. The challenge for them has become winning the race to get through the book.

THE ABLE MATHEMATICIAN IN A MIXED ABILITY PRIMARY CLASSROOM

I shall consider point 4 of the list above in some detail because I believe that it is crucially important that primary teachers improve their range of strategies for teaching the most able pupils in mathematics. Although I had a vague unease about the way we taught these children for many years, there were four particular events which brought the problem home to me.

The first occurred in 1982 when my elder daughter was 7 years old. We had some inspection copies of a new secondary school mathematics scheme which consisted of small booklets on different topics which pupils were expected to work through 'at their own pace'. To determine whether or not it was necessary for an individual child to study the whole of a particular booklet, a short diagnostic test was included. The result of this test was intended to direct the child to an appropriate page to start working. My daughter, certainly a good mathematician but not outstanding, was able to complete all of the diagnostic tests she tried at the age of 7. At that stage she found them challenging; they were suitably geared to her understanding and she was well motivated to work through them. The local secondary school used this scheme exclusively for their mixed ability classes of children in Years 7 and 8. I wondered how this approach to teaching mathematics would maintain and stimulate my daughter's interest in the subject in four years' time and encourage her to experiment and persist. The level of expectation of intelligent and effective 11-year-old mathematicians at this school seemed to me to be dismally low.

The second experience which disturbed me concerned a group of fourteen Year 6 children. These children had been selected by their teacher as being in need of extra stretching in mathematics, in particular in solving problems which were not straightforward. I was asked to teach them and did so on a weekly basis for two terms. It became apparent within the first half hour that, not only did they expect to be able to solve any problem within seconds or, at the most, minutes of it being posed but they also resented being asked a question which they could not immediately answer. They were not used to being wrong or stuck; they had not had the chance to develop persistence in solving mathematical problems since they had been able to cope with everything in the scheme textbooks with no difficulty; the boys became uncooperative and the girls began to cry! (I apologise for this apparent stereotyping, but I merely report what actually happened.) It took a mixture of tact, cajoling, flattery and a carefully worded explanation of the nature of 'doing real mathematics' to persuade them to try again when their first hunch turned out to be wrong or to lead them along an unhelpful path. Having established a good working relationship with these children, the twenty hours I spent with them gave me some of the most rewarding experiences of my teaching career. The work they tackled, the discussions we engaged in and the imaginative and original proofs which they produced gave us all great satisfaction and my own teaching skills were undoubtedly improved through interaction with this group of children.

The third example concerns two able mathematicians in Year 4. The class was being taught by an outstandingly good, resourceful and conscientious student teacher. I knew the children well, having visited the class frequently during the year and having taught them myself on several occasions. The student had prepared special problem work cards to use in odd moments. These were carefully graded to pose suitable challenges for children with varying mathematical ability. Susan and Harry were sitting next to one another but not officially working together. The student gave Susan a card:

Place one of the numbers 1, 2, 3, 4, 5, 6, 7, 8 in each of the squares in the diagram. Every number must be used once. No number is to be put so that it is above, below or beside a consecutive counting number (e.g. 5 cannot be above, below or beside 4 or 6.). Consecutive numbers may be placed diagonally next to each other.

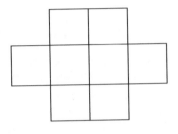

I watched and listened to what happened. Harry said 'You'll not be able to do that one; I tried yesterday. It's hard.' Susan said nothing, took no notice of him and began to try the problem. It was clear that both children understood what they were being asked to do. Harry looked on closely 'That won't work,' he said. 'I tried that.' Each time Susan tried a new tactic he informed her that it would be unsuccessful. I persuaded him to let her try on her own for five minutes after which time I would return and discuss it with them. Somewhat unwillingly he agreed and continued with his own task. When the five minutes had elapsed I went back to the children. Susan had not managed to solve the problem so I read it carefully. Harry said 'Have you done this one before?' I admitted I had not. Predictably he said 'It's hard. I don't expect you'll be able to do it.' However, fortunately, I could see a possible method of approaching the problem having done others similar to it. I asked them if they could see two numbers in the set which were 'different' as far as this sum was concerned. Immediately Harry said 'Yes, and they have to go in those two squares (pointing) – now I can do it.' Both he and Susan completed the problem satisfactorily. I asked them if they could see any other solutions and we had an interesting discussion about the symmetry of the system.[2]

At the end of the session Harry came up to me and asked, 'How did you know to ask me that question about the two special numbers?' This child wants to know how to develop strategies for problem solving. He is an able mathematician and needs frequent stimulus to encourage his persistence and discussion with equally good mathematicians to enable him to articulate his ideas. How can a teacher provide for this need when s/he has thirty other children to cater for, most of whom would be unable to understand either the problem or the answer?

The last example concerns a postgraduate student with a first class degree in mathematics. Rarely do we recruit mathematics graduates to the PGCE primary course and those we do seldom have a first class degree. I was supervising the student on teaching practice. He was teaching a small group of Year 3 children. One of these children, George, although untidy and disorganised, had been identified by the student as being very able at mathematics. Because of George's poor performance in written work, the class teacher had not realised that he had an exceptionally good mathematical mind. Whilst teaching the group the student was frequently interjecting asides to George. It became obvious that he was teaching two maths lessons, one to George and a different one to the rest. The content of the discussion with George concerned number patterns involving remarkably complex algebraic ideas. It was an abstract mathematical discussion between mathematicians. I realised how rarely I saw teachers rise to the challenge of the able 7-year-old mathematician. It is understandable; there are few specialists in primary schools and it is not a subject in which non-specialists feel confident.

Before trying to suggest means for tackling the challenge of the able child in the classroom I should like to consider other relevant issues and research findings.

LOW ATTAINERS IN MATHEMATICS – THE TEACHER'S DILEMMA

The desire to provide the most able developing mathematicians with suitable mathematical activities is often overshadowed by the pressing need to cope with the demands of those who are mathematically least able. Those children who appear to be unable to tackle the simplest mathematical task, whose retention of facts seems poor and whose self-confidence in being able to achieve success in mathematics is minimal, need continual help, encouragement and short-term goals. Extensive studies have attempted to establish the factors which are associated with low attainment in mathematics (e.g. Denvir, Stolz and Brown 1982) and the lists produced are very wide-ranging. Children who 'fail' in mathematics do so for a variety of reasons: emotional, intellectual, environmental and physical, or a combination of these. There is no single way of dealing with the low attainer in a class. The teacher knows that, without adult support, these children are unlikely to have the motivation to apply themselves to any unfamiliar mathematical task. The only common factor as far as the teacher's strategies are concerned is that all the low attainers need disproportionate teacher time. One of the basic challenges of classroom management which needs to be addressed at all stages of planning is the matter of how to share time equitably.

The 'tyranny of the scheme' (Haylock 1991) referred to above in respect of very able young mathematicians, is possibly an even more crucial consideration with low attainers. One of the reasons which Haylock gives is a mismatch in many mathematics schemes between literacy and numeracy. He explains:

> This approach relies on the written word as the medium of instruction. For most low attainers the best way for them to come to understand many mathematical ideas and processes is for someone to explain these to them and the worst way is for them to have to rely on their poor reading skills.
>
> (Haylock 1991: 146)

Many teachers have other adults in the classroom; it is worth exploring ways of enabling these helpers to assist the teacher in giving explanations of mathematical ideas to the least successful mathematicians in the class. In addition, it is important to develop appropriate resources as well as using already existing resources, for example computers or cassette recorders, more imaginatively in order to provide the necessary teaching input for these children when no other adult is available.

ACQUIRING MATHEMATICAL SKILLS AND CONCEPTS

An assumption is made by many teachers and others (including, I suspect, Secretaries of State for Education) that mathematics is a linear subject in which every child, in order to understand a concept, must follow the same thinking path though at varying rates. This assumption underpins the structure of the Mathematics Orders of the National Curriculum which is based on supposedly increasing levels of achievement and it is accepted implicitly by those schools in which the majority of the mathematics sessions are spent with children working individually through commercially produced textbooks. There is both common-sense and some observational evidence to support this theory to a certain extent, particularly in that part of the curriculum concerned with the development of 'arithmetic' or number. The findings of Denvir and Brown (1986) established that it is possible to construct a hierarchical framework of interrelated skills, linked by one being a prerequisite of another, which 'can describe children's present knowledge and suggest which further skills they are most likely to acquire and thereby inform

the design of teaching activities' (Denvir and Brown 1986: 156). However, their research indicated that teachers cannot accurately predict
which skills an individual will actually acquire from an activity so
teaching should not be too prescriptive about what may be learned. In
the pilot study Denvir and Brown discovered that children did not necessarily learn the specific points the teacher had taught but sometimes
learnt other skills instead. The implication of this is of great importance
when considering how much of the responsibility for the teaching of
mathematics should be left to a textbook.

USING A 'MATHEMATICS SCHEME'

One of my earliest memories of working in a primary classroom is of a
child who came to me with his textbook and said 'I can't do this one.'
I asked him to read the question to me which he did, haltingly. I repeated
the words he had read. He thanked me, returned to his seat and satisfactorily completed the question. Since then I have noticed similar
behaviour on many occasions. It is more difficult to read and act on
instructions than simply to do what someone tells you.

It would be impractical, time wasting and, for most teachers, not very
successful, to suggest that published schemes should not be used in the
classroom and that teachers should rely on providing suitable material
for their pupils without the help of authors who, although they do not
know the children concerned, are usually qualified mathematicians and
are certainly experienced teachers. However, the still widespread practice of leaving the vitally important task of teaching mathematics to
young children to a book instead of the trained teacher seems to be at
the least short-sighted and possibly negligent. During the last few
years teachers have been bombarded with expectations for changing and
tightening up their practice. However, the demands of the National
Curriculum seem to follow to a great extent what was already being
done in primary classrooms in mathematics and the inevitable temptation has been for teachers to assume that their teaching methods and
the content of what they teach need not be a priority for immediate
change. Unfortunately the legacy of the fifteen years before the introduction of the National Curriculum has left a system in which, partly
in an attempt to provide material for individual children to progress
at different rates thus, hopefully, matching the task to their ability
(i.e. providing an answer to the problem of differentiating) and partly
to compensate for the inadequate numbers of mathematics specialists in
primary schools, the maths scheme reigns supreme. Careful scrutiny of
the teachers' manuals which accompany the schemes reveals frequent
warnings that schemes cannot replace teacher input and explanations,
that they should be used in conjunction with discussion and shared

activities, that it should not be assumed that every child should do every question and that the support materials which are provided in addition to the basic textbooks form an essential and integral part of the scheme. However, these warnings are often ignored, for a variety of good and not-so-good reasons.

Several negative effects arise from allowing the scheme to do the teaching, some of which I have already mentioned in this chapter:

1. Mathematics is a very difficult subject to learn from books, so the level of mathematical content has to be low and simple when children are to learn from the text alone. There are many advantages which come from discussion between a child and the teacher which cannot be replaced by a book. These include :

   - listening to the inflexions in a teacher's voice ;
   - adapting the pace of an explanation;
   - holding back one step in an example until the previous idea has been grasped;
   - reminding the child of previous contexts in which the same idea has been met;
   - providing suitable apparatus to support an explanation;
   - giving extra examples to illuminate a particularly difficult idea;
   - stressing which aspects are of the greatest importance;
   - asking questions to discover whether the child has grasped the idea;
   - encouraging the child to express an idea in her or his own words.

2. If children are all working on different problems or 'sums' the likelihood of discussion about mathematics is reduced. There is considerable evidence to show that children are more likely to understand a concept if they have to explain it to someone else and put the idea into their own words.

3. Much of the mathematics teaching a book can give is of the 'Here is how you do one like this' type. It is not possible to give out hints suitable for individual children, the value of which was made clear by the discussion with Susan and Harry.

4. All pages and examples in a book seem to a child to be equally important. The book cannot say in the same way that a teacher can say: 'Here is a really crucial idea – do not carry on until you are sure you understand it. If you do not follow the first explanation try this one, or this one. . . . Talk to your friends and your teacher about it. . . . Look back at the book you used last year and see if you can see a connection between this idea and the exercise on page 23. . . .'

5. Children assume that the methods used in the book and the layout of answers are the correct ones. They are not encouraged to invent

ways of writing down their own thoughts. The inevitable outcome is to learn the suggested algorithm to obtain a correct answer whether or not you understand why the algorithm works.

6. In a classroom in which every child is working on a different problem, and often on a different topic from others in the class, key explanations have to be given by the teacher many times more than if groups were being taught together.

7. Teachers tend to become scheme administrators rather than spending their time teaching.

8. Mathematics is not a suitable subject for children to teach themselves. Witness the immediate queuing or hands up of the majority of children who turn over a page and see an unfamiliar question even though they may well be able to tackle the question if they had enough confidence to try. Questions are frequently of the 'Is it an add, Miss?' type.

9. The expense of the basic scheme books is great and many schools cannot afford the supporting resources which are often those encouraging investigative methods, discussion activities and differentiated material.

10. The practice of allowing children to use answer books and correct their own work, although time saving and providing the means for instant feedback, leads children to assume there is only one answer or one way of expressing an idea.

11. Most primary school schemes assume that the same material is appropriate for teaching a concept regardless of the age of the child using the book. Observation and evidence contradicts this. A child of 7 who has been successful in mathematics will tackle a new idea on the confident assumption that s/he will understand the question and solve it satisfactorily whereas a child of 11 with a history of failing to achieve in mathematics facing the same problem will not expect to be correct in her or his answer.

Different approaches and contexts suitable for the age and experience of children of different ages are needed which the 'maths scheme' used in isolation cannot hope to supply. The attempt to provide for differentiation through a scheme, in fact, works against the development of challenge in mathematics.

DIFFERENTIATION BY OUTCOME

It has been seen that, in many cases, differentiation in mathematics has to be by task. This applies, in particular to the more obviously hierarchical areas of the subject like number, though, even here, it is possible to generate useful discussions and games which are suitable for a wide ability range. Some of the most successful primary school mathematics teaching I have seen has been organised so that the whole class works on the same broad numerical topic to facilitate discussion, but the content of the questions is adapted for differing stages in development. For example, if it was decided to work on multiplication some children might be doing repeated addition using multilink cubes. Some might be building up tables using 100 square patterns or calculators. Some could be playing a tables game. Some could be inventing a suitable method to calculate 23 multiplied by 7 and some could be tackling demanding problems or doing a factor investigation.

Several computer programs are ideal for whole class teaching because questions can be posed which are later answered by the computer itself. Notable examples of programs which are ideal for this treatment are *Counter* (an old but splendid program which incorporates sounds into place value concepts) and *Monty* (ATM 1985: 5–24 and 63–88). Class sharing of computer programs is most successful when the computer is linked to a large TV screen. This needs a single lead and is very easy to set up quickly.

Much work in shape and space and the more practical aspects of data handling lends itself to differentiation by outcome.

Inspiration for suitable material for discussion topics in mathematics can be collected from a variety of sources. Some of the most obvious stimuli for discussion are bar charts, number patterns, 100 squares, the National Lottery, football scores and estimating measurements. Other tactics like 'Guess today's numbers' are particularly successful. In this game the teacher has a rule for 'acceptable' numbers. Each day the rule changes. Children are invited to suggest possible numbers and the

YES	NO
17	23
317	2
57	34
	22
	160

Once most of the children have discovered the rule, questions can be asked:

'What is the next YES number after 57 if they were put in order?'
'How many YES numbers lie between 100 and 200?'
'Are there any YES numbers less than 0? Give an example.'
'What is the rule?'

teacher writes each suggested number on the board under one or other of two columns headed 'Yes' and 'No'. The aim is for children to guess the rule and then correctly sort numbers into the categories.[3]

A mathematics lesson which starts and ends with a whole class activity not only has the effect of helping to create a sharing atmosphere, it also provides the chance for children to benefit both from expressing their own ideas and listening to those of others. Particularly recommended as a source of many ideas is *Talking Points in Mathematics* (Straker, 1993) It is often possible for a child who has just gained a concept to give a clearer explanation to another child who is on the brink of the 'Aha' than the teacher, who long ago understood the idea.

WHERE DOES THIS LEAVE US?

Despite the difficulty in providing suitable materials for every mathematics session there are, nevertheless, some teachers who choose to do this and teach very effectively. I was surprised to receive a Christmas card from a newly qualified teacher whom I had taught the previous year in which she said, 'School is lovely; I am really happy there and I am lucky because we have NO MATHS SCHEME' (her capitals). Many teachers feel that they need the support material provided by books. However, if they use these resources they need also to accept the potential management problems and unsatisfactory teaching situation induced by allowing children to work 'at their own pace' through a scheme; they need to acknowledge that using a scheme without planning for a range of ways for mathematics to challenge children, is not a successful style of teaching. Different activities and types of problems need to be available for the varying abilities and interests of the children in any average primary school class whilst at the same time teacher input and group discussion are necessary and valuable. Replacing one scheme with another will not, in itself, address the dilemmas associated with providing for differentiation, even if it were a financially viable alternative. It is the *way* that available books and other resources are used that makes a difference to the learning of the children, not the scheme itself.

It is clear that, especially in mathematics, it is essential for teachers to find a successful method of differentiating tasks in order to provide suitable material for all members of the class especially the very able or the slow learners but there seems no easy way to achieve this. The following suggestions are made to enable a school staff to review their mathematics policy to take account of some of the points raised in this chapter. They are in no particular order, obviously cannot constitute an exhaustive list and clearly they do not all apply to every school; far from it since they have all been suggested as a result of successful use in schools.

Whole school issues

- Spend a staff development day working with learning support assistants in order to develop their questioning techniques and mathematical confidence.
- Create opportunities for the mathematics specialist in the school (or other available mathematicians – perhaps the local secondary school, or parents, could help here) to work with children who are achieving most highly in mathematics.
- Set up a maths club.

Resources

- Look through the available resources and identify some mathematical activities which lend themselves to differentiation by outcome rather than by task.
- Find out what facilities are available locally to provide support for primary schools in teaching mathematics to the most able – and use them.
- Create a bank of problems and investigations suitable for challenging the able young mathematician and others which are suitable for children who are achieving average or below average performance (see Haylock 1991 for a wealth of ideas).

Classroom practice

- Overhaul the way in which the available books are used. This may involve weaning the children (or teachers?) off the 'Go at your own pace using these books' system to working in well-matched groups. It may also involve distinguishing between which questions are suitable for every child, which should be tackled only by the most able and which questions are unnecessary for the most able.
- Provide opportunities for oral whole class activities.
- Encourage all children, especially perhaps the most able, to express their mathematical ideas clearly on paper so that someone else can understand how they thought the problem out.
- Explore the possibility of flexible arrangements of the classroom furniture which could then be adjusted to the nature of the mathematics session. This could either facilitate genuine group work or encourage individual thought.
- When preparing sessions try to imagine yourself in the position of the most able, an 'average' and the least able mathematician in your class and make sure that you will make it worthwhile for each child to become involved in the session. The most able mathematician in

your class may well be better at the subject than you are. Try working through a page of the work you are asking the children to do and see what you feel about it. This can be a depressing but revealing experience! Once a child can, for example, tell the time, there is no more point in that child working through pages of clock face pictures practising the skill than there would be for you, the teacher, to do it yourself.

NOTES

1. Many students learning to be primary school teachers report feeling this success for the first time when they are at college. They claim that at school there were always quicker pupils or impatient teachers who told them how to do the mathematics before allowing them the necessary time to think it out for themselves. In college sessions we spend time discussing how teachers can give hints and ask questions rather than tell children how to think. Perhaps this would be a fruitful focus for a staff development session in a primary school.
2. Harry and Susan's problem – There are many possible solutions. The easiest way to obtain one is to place the digits 1 and 8 in the two centre squares and this is the strategy which I encouraged the children to use, e.g.

		3	5	
7	1	8	2	
		4	6	

This solution is also valid for the more challenging question in which no two consecutive numbers are to be placed adjacent to one another either horizontally, vertically or diagonally.
3. Guess Today's Number – Again, there are several possible solutions. This is why the question has been included under 'Discussion Topics'. The simplest rule which satisfies the given list is, perhaps:

YES numbers have a 7 as the units digit; NO numbers do not.

In this case:

The next YES number after 57 is 67
There are 10 YES numbers between 100 and 200
Depending on your point of view, YES numbers less than 0 *either* do not exist, *or* end in a 7, e.g. –27, *or* end in a 3, e.g. –213

REFERENCES

Association of Teachers of Mathematics (1985) *Some More Lessons with a Microcomputer* (SLIMWAM 2), Derby, ATM

Brown, Margaret (1981) 'Is it an add Miss?', *Mathematics in School* 10 (1)

Cockroft, W. H. (1982) (Chair of Committee) *Mathematics Counts. Report of the Committee of Inquiry into the Teaching of Mathematics in School*, London, Her Majesty's Stationery Office

Denvir, B. and Brown, M. (1986) 'Understanding of Number Concepts in Low Attaining 7–9 Year Olds', *Educational Studies in Mathematics* (17) (1) and (2)

Denvir, B., Stolz, C. and Brown, M. (1982) *Low Attainers in Mathematics*, London, Paul Chapman

Gardner, Martin (1978) *Aha Insight*, New York, Freeman and Co

Haylock, D. (1991) *Teaching Mathematics to Low Attainers*, London, Paul Chapman

Mason, J. (ed.) (1988) *Project Mathematics Update*, Milton Keynes, Open University

Straker, A. (1993) *Talking Points in Mathematics*, Cambridge, Cambridge University Press

Chapter 9

Science and special educational needs

Ros Smith and Isobel Urquhart

A group of children were investigating magnetism. They had played with a variety of magnets, they had magnetised needles and made floating compasses and used these to find the bearings of features around the school. The children had not experienced this topic before, so the teacher thought it would be valuable to assess their understanding of the concept after they had completed the practical activities. She decided to use individual questionnaires in order to evaluate their learning. This proved to be a difficult task for Ben and James: the teacher was aware they enjoyed and participated fully in the practical science, but that they disliked and when possible, avoided reading and writing. It was explained that all the group should complete the questions on their own and afterwards she would talk to them about their answers.

The expectations of Ben and James' achievements proved to be correct, evidence of learning was negligible, they had misunderstood questions and left most of the task unfinished. When the boys were asked to plan and draw a route for others to follow, making use of LOGO procedure commands, a different picture emerged. The two boys worked together in a collaborative manner, used the magnets to check their plans and on listening to their discussion, it rapidly became evident that they had understood both the relevance and purpose of the activity. Two different forms of appraisal resulted in two very contrasting outcomes.

It is our contention that children with special educational needs should be provided with opportunities which go beyond teachers simply allowing for apparent deficits in children's capacity to learn. We argue that some children identified as having special educational needs, particularly those whose scientific understanding is often assessed through their difficulties with some of the skills associated with literacy and sometimes numeracy, can contribute to their own and others' scientific understanding through collaborative talk. In this context, science investigations can have a certain value for enabling such children to work collaboratively in a way that reflects their ability.

DIFFERENTIATION IN PRIMARY SCIENCE

The dictionary places 'differentiation' between 'differential' and 'difficult'. The former is defined as 'varying according to circumstance' and the latter as 'needing much labour or practice'. It could be argued that these two definitions have much in common with what is understood by practitioners as 'differentiation'. Another somewhat exasperated definition of the term was provided by an experienced teacher, when asked about his methodology for ensuring he planned for differentiation within the classroom: 'Differentiation, that's what we used to call mixed ability teaching, we've been doing it for years in primary schools.'

But have we? One factor often assumed to contribute to the success of the primary curriculum in motivating children has been the 'one teacher–one class' system. It is argued that this has ensured that individuals' needs were thoroughly known and effectively met. Further, the provision of detailed and extensive written records of children's progress since the introduction of the National Curriculum in 1989 would, it was hoped, result in the increasing differentiation of activities through careful classroom management. The Core and Foundation subjects now taught in primary schools would mean that individual strengths and weaknesses would be attended to by different methods of pedagogy and organisation.

The National Curriculum Council (1993), recommends how teachers might plan for differentiation in science activities. While advocating a pro-active approach to differentiation, the NCC reminds readers that teachers would also need to be conscious of cultural and social influences on children's interest in and understanding of scientific concepts, which are often closely associated with their language socialisation. Thus, teachers learn about children's understanding of scientific concepts by listening to the talk that goes on when groups of children work collaboratively.

Children's personal experiences, their consequent motivation and hence, some would assert, conceptual understanding and scientific skills are influenced by a range of factors (Tolmie and Howe 1992; Murphy, Scanlon, Hodgson and Whitelegg 1994). These findings have been largely ignored by a model of differentiation which advocates differentiation through a child's written recorded outcome within its respective group (Edwards, 1990). Despite the focus on a written outcome, the model disregards specific consideration of individuals' possible literacy difficulties within science. It also ignores the contribution to their own and others' learning that children's verbal communication skills could provide. Here is a dichotomy of pedagogies, for while it may be accepted that planning and the ensuing practical investigations will be of a collaborative nature, the recording and hence the assessment of the activity remains based on an individual's written effort. This confirms the contention that unless there is a joint external goal to be achieved by the group (teams/competition/display/problem solving) then it is expected that children will produce individual outcomes rather than consolidate their findings in a mutual achievement.

In addition, the obligation of schools to provide written summative evidence of a child's attainment in science can result in differentiated outcomes assessed in terms of literacy skills. These may then be interpreted as indicating the child's perceived ability in a particular scientific activity. Such evidence would not reflect the aims and values of mixed ability grouping. The Association for Science Education advises teachers that 'The goal of your teaching is in terms of learning objectives not product outcomes' (Association for Science Education 1994). In other words ASE advocates the differentiation of learning through the planning of tasks in accordance with the aims of the National Curriculum for Science (DES 1994) rather than by summative assessment techniques. This view has also been recognized by the National Curriculum Council (1993), which repeats the recommendation of planning procedures for differentiating science activities.

Differentiation has been taken in some subjects, albeit often in the larger primary schools, to mean that in junior classes some core subjects are taught by ability across the year group. Perhaps this has been most evident in mathematics and English but even where the size of a year group precludes separate classes, it is common for children to be seated in groups according to assessments of some of their linguistic or mathematical skills, regardless of their competence in other areas of the curriculum. The justification for such seating arrangements is that the children will work well together and advance their understanding at a steady pace, but is this really advantageous for developing their understanding and skills in other areas of the curriculum?

Grouping according to ability has obvious implications for children defined as having special educational needs.[1] The first principle which needs to be borne in mind when considering how to include children with special educational needs is the entitlement principle, which has been consistently mentioned in National Curriculum documents. While the trend has been to respond to that entitlement by placing some form of teaching support in the classroom to help children who have been identified as having special educational needs, Gipps et al. (1987) found that most primary teachers in their study preferred withdrawal of such children, typically for extra help with literacy difficulties. It may be that given the pressures that primary teachers are under, the attractions of withdrawal as a solution to the difficulties of classroom management and meeting the needs of thirty-plus children are very obvious. There are, however, well-rehearsed disadvantages to persistently withdrawing the same group of children, while the strategy cannot be proscribed entirely, if used intelligently (Gross 1993). Nevertheless, grouping children according to ability has long been known to be less effective than it is sometimes supposed. 'The assumption that pupils of like ability are more easily taught, or that pupils with special needs will have a detrimental effect upon group situations, is a false one' (Bennett, and Cass 1988, 1990; Johnson and Johnson 1985; Slavin 1990). Furthermore, it is of particular benefit to children with special educational needs *not* to be grouped together, while it has also been found that the understanding of children with more advanced scientific conceptualising also benefits from the need to communicate their understanding to less experienced learners. The importance of communication and collaborative learning is discussed in further detail later in this chapter.

IDENTIFICATION OF CHILDREN WITH SPECIAL EDUCATIONAL NEEDS

How teachers should group children with special educational needs raises a second and more fundamental consideration, which is of particular relevance to the findings of the two sample studies below. It is about how teachers identify special educational needs in the first place. Children are often first identified as having special educational needs as a result of their attainments in the technical skills associated with reading and writing, and sometimes, additionally, in mathematics. This reflects, at least partially, the importance attached, both in education and in society generally, to a high level of competence in some of those technical literacy skills. It may also reflect the relative ease with which some of these skills appear to be identifiable through testing procedures. Test results, however, can over-privilege certain features of literacy which are then interpreted as indicators of a child's deficiencies as a learner across the curriculum. Most teachers would agree that testable skills of literacy and numeracy are by no means the whole extent of literacy, nor yet of learning and understanding; neither is the medium of literacy the only means by which learning and understanding can be communicated. While it is certainly true that many children who appear to have difficulties in learning can also be presumed to find it difficult to learn to read and write, the prediction does not always work backwards: children who have difficulties with reading and writing are not always children who have difficulty in understanding new concepts or communicating their insights in other ways. It is important to remember that a significant number of those children are well within our understanding of normal, general *ability*, and that their difficulties are specific to the demands of literacy. Identifying all children experiencing difficulties in literacy as having similar educational needs in all circumstances can lead to teaching strategies and decisions about grouping which may not suit the abilities that children may be able to bring, for instance, to scientific investigations. To group children by literacy or numeracy achievement may obscure individuals' abilities to communicate their understanding to other children and teachers through talk.

This chapter, therefore, examines the development of learning in science in the light of such common assumptions and practices. The investigation was prompted by consistent observations made about the weakness of teachers' ability to use assessment processes effectively; that is, to plan appropriate work matched to individual and groups of children's ability (Black 1991).

The surveys

Two recent surveys carried out with primary teachers have highlighted some of these issues and confirm that teachers experience some in-security in making judgements about grouping children which are based on scientific criteria.[2] The first survey asked the teachers to identify the usual criteria they adopted for grouping their class for science activities. Twenty-two responses were given, as follows:

Survey one

Mathematical ability	9
Reading skills (Infants)	1
Friendship	6
Age (vertically grouped class)	1
Gender	1
Mixed ability	2
Other	2

None of the teachers considered it appropriate to use scientific skills or scientific understanding as criteria, arguing that these were, for the most part, difficult to identify; insufficient records of progression were available; and their own instinctive understanding of any individual's skills or understanding was not yet in place. In contrast, children's mathematical skills, where clear and definitive levels of progression were usually available, were perceived as far easier to identify. Despite teachers' unwillingness to group children according to specifically scientific criteria, the NCC suggested the use of scientific investigations to 'gauge the understanding of a child' (NCC 1992: 25). Evidence from research has suggested that task or context is highly significant in motivating and developing a child's conceptual understanding and skills in science (APU 1988; Maltz and Borker 1982; Thorne 1986; Reay 1991;

Tolmie and Howe 1992; Whitelegg, Murphy, Scanlon and Hodgson 1992). If teachers do not feel confident about describing progress in the development of scientific understanding, then it is to be presumed that they may feel equally unsure about how to create the contexts and tasks to promote such development. The net result of this lack of clarity must be an inability to identify just what will provide evidence of children's developing scientific understanding.

There is, none the less, one group of children whose individual educational needs *are*, theoretically, available for scrutiny and effective response: children who have been identified as having special educational needs. The question then arises, are the recommendations of the NCC (Teaching Science at Key Stages 1 and 2) being implemented for these children? This is a particularly sharp question given the general lack of clarity revealed in the two studies.

The NCC suggests that teachers ensure that, 'children's strengths are used to build their confidence and maintain motivation' (NCC 1993: 60) This may present difficulties in both the management and formative assessment of pupils deemed to have special educational needs in certain areas of the core curriculum. Could this lead to some pupils being doubly disadvantaged: first, by the grouping criteria used for science; and, second, by an assessment of scientific understanding through written evidence ?

A second follow-up survey asked a different sample of teachers to identify which of a list of methods of grouping they used specifically with children with special educational needs in science. The results are encouraging. Although a variety of criteria were identified, all fourteen teachers said pupils with special educational needs were placed in mixed ability groups, Literacy and numeracy skills did not appear to be a criterion for *grouping* children described as having special educational needs in this survey.

Survey two

SEN grouping	
Mixed ability	14
Collaborative pairs	12
One SEN child per group	9
Friendship	8
Grouped together with adult helper	7
By maths ability	1
By reading ability	1

Further, twelve teachers said they would also use collaborative pairs of children, one teacher, however, adding the rider that she would sometimes use a better *reader* with a less able reader in order to record results. In terms of the potential of collaborative work, this particular response confirms the powerful but limiting signficance of literacy as a criterion of achievement. Nine out of fourteen teachers also said they would organise their groups so that only one child defined as having special educational needs was in any group. Eight teachers said they used friendship groups, although that decision may obscure the possibility that children identified as having special educational needs might also be friends with one another.

Teachers were asked, in addition, whether they used any other rationales for grouping children with special educational needs. The six responses received covered almost the full continuum of response to children experiencing difficulties: from withdrawal of children for the preparation and follow-up of scientific work where they could work with an adult; through treating the children as similarly as possible whilst differentiating by outcome, and by level of support provided during the class lesson; to using children's thinking skills and ability to talk and discuss as criteria for identifying children with difficulties, and for grouping. Teachers who replied to this question seemed to pay particular attention to the personal, emotional and social needs of individual children as well as the child's learning needs, for example considering whether the child could work with a particular group, whether he or she would be able to contribute, and whether the reporting back stage would enable the child's contribution to be valued.

When teachers were asked to focus on the nature of the special educational needs of two specific children, the two main criteria used to *identify* the children's needs were literacy and/or mathematical difficulties (18), followed by general conceptual difficulties (7). It is notable by how much literacy and numeracy outweighed any other consideration in describing the learning difficulties of the selected children. Thus identification procedures based on literacy difficulties lead to grouping decisions which may be assuming, in *some* cases, cognitive difficulties; or which are necessary because of the high *literacy* requirements of the task as planned and its assessment.

Nature of special educational need	
Literacy/mathematical difficulties	18 (10 boys, 8 girls)
Conceptual difficulties	7 (4 boys, 3 girls)
Other (e.g. dyspraxic, microcephaly, social skills)	7 (5 boys, 2 girls)
Motivation/esteem	5 (2 boys, 3 girls)

Finally, teachers were asked if they would like to change the way children with special educational needs were grouped, if they had the opportunity. Five replies did not want to change anything, and four wanted more adult help because a 'well informed adult working with the children was the ideal', or to 'supervise.... ensure they are on task and don't come to a dead halt', or that more staff would enable the teaching staff to work with smaller groups. This raises the possibility that, for some teachers at least, there may be limited faith in the efficacy of peer learning and that organising children with special educational needs in this way may stem from lack of resources rather than from conviction. It may, however, also reflect findings from research: Rogoff distinguishes between exploratory activity, such as scientific investigations, where peer collaboration is especially valuable in making meanings from experience, and a skills-teaching requirement, where she found an adult helper was often more effective (Rogoff 1990).

Griffin (1990) warned that the National Curriculum of 1989 would need to be implemented with careful consideration to the needs of pupils with special educational needs. He interprets 'mixed ability' as children working together and reaching different standards of achievement within one group, but if this is to be successful, three criteria need to be implemented:

- The less able must be actively involved.
- Their work has to have equal status to that of other children.
- Their work must have a learning outcome.

Griffin's acceptance of differentiation by outcome within any group of children has been used by some to ignore a specific consideration of individuals' varying needs in the context of actual tasks and classrooms. The argument also assumes that the final outcome of a science activity is likely to include an element of individual recording. Although planning and investigating may well have been of a collaborative nature, the evaluation of the activity returns to being an individual project. That individualistic return reinforces Bennett's (1987) contention that unless there is an external goal to be achieved by the group (e.g. teams, competition, display, problem solving), then children will be inclined to work *in* groups but not *as* groups. Reference in the second survey to the need for a more able reader to work with a child with special educational needs 'in order to record results.' may indicate a similar concern that all participants are assessed on individual outcomes, such as making an individual record of their scientific investigation. On the other hand, it could equally have been a response to the literacy requirements of the task: enabling the child to read written instructions on a worksheet, for example.

Sutherland and Boyes (1993) examine how the criteria presented by the NCC's Guidance (1992: 10) for providing enriching experiences through science can be applied to all pupils. They demonstrate how an activity can be differentiated by careful planning to ensure that all pupils are motivated and fulfilled, either by differentiating the particular task in a specific group, or by assessing the individual's outcome and the attitude towards the task in hand. Implicit in this model is that differentiation of children's science investigation skills is an integral part of the proceedings. Differentiation, in this definition, is achieved by ensuring that progression is accomplished at an appropriate pace, and by encouraging group work, using a variety of activities to enable all participants to demonstrate their strengths. The appreciation of a child's past experience and achievement are seen as the points in the formative assessment allowing the teacher to 'ascertain what is expected of the child in terms of concepts' (Sutherland and Boyes 1993: 71). The augmentation of a child's science investigation skills has always been recognized as contributing to cognitive growth and it is possible that these competencies will be stimulated by children working together in a collaborative manner so encouraging active discussion within the group.

COLLABORATIVE TALK

Teachers need to be aware of the range of styles of talk, from consensus and disputational to exploratory talk, and provide opportunities for individual children to voice their opinions amongst group members. Tolmie and Howe (1992) suggested that conceptual differences amongst peers may be 'one such trigger for developing discussion' thereby suggesting it is the participants and the task under discussion which are of particular significance in collaborative working (cf. Rogoff above). Tolmie and Howe consider that providing opportunities for discussion of participants' conflicting views resulted in differing *styles of dialogue* being generated and in consequence had an effect on the learning that took place. Studies from research (Mercer, Phillips and Somekh 1991; Wegerif 1994) developed this argument that the collaborative nature of exploratory talk enables pupils to make use of *linguistic expressions* not required in non-collaborative approaches: justifications, clarifications, reasoning and concessions, all of which are of great value to the learning process. This idea was also explored by Edwards (1990), who considered that the collaborative nature of exploratory talk would assist in the construction of *shared ideas* and meanings within the group rather than just for the individual in that group.

The significance educators place on collaborative discussion aiding understanding is recognised by Edwards and Westgate (1994). They support Phillips' (1990) affirmation that pupil–pupil exploratory talk is less threatening and hence more beneficial for low achievers than attempting to discuss with a teacher, who is perceived to hold 'unchallengeable knowledge'.

Text	Comments
Girl 1: If we did . . . there is this crayon right.	*Confidence to express ideas*
You couldn't just use this for day and use a different colour for night because it would not be a fair test.	*Exploratory talk; Understands fair testing*
Boy 1: No, you could use, I think, either red or white for day and definitely yellow for night.	*Disputes*
Girl 1: I only think the rest of the yellow shows up better than just plain yellow.	*Holds onto views/ argues point*
Boy 1: We could test white and red and yellow.	*Compromises*
Further discussion ensues:	
Girl 1: If we choose red, as we probably will, in daytime, to make it a better fair test, if we do red as well at night and then do yellow at day and yellow at night then it will be a fair test.	*Exploratory talk, makes use of group's ideas*
Discussion on the distance to use to test identification:	
Girl 1: We could try and camouflage it as well and see if it is good in camouflage.	*Introduces new idea*
Boy 2: What about green, we couldn't camouflage yellow or red or blue, to be a fair test it would have to be with just one colour.	*Takes up notion; adds own idea*
Girl 2: Black?	
Boy 2: Black and green.	
Girl 2: You said just one colour didn't you?	*Questions*
Boy 1: It would have to be black, green or brown.	*Justifies*
Girl 2: We could sort of like camouflage it with, camouflage all of them with one colour and then camouflage them with another colour.	*Consensual approach*
Girl 1: Yes	*Supports*
Boy 2: Like the army uses, it doesn't use all one colour.	*Supports*
Girl 2: Like brown or green.	
Girl 1: Brown and green, you get some brown leaves and some green grass.	*Concludes and adds to plan*

Sutherland and Boyes (1993) emphasise that access of opportunity is significant whether because of a pupil's physical needs or because of difficulties with literacy, an approach stressed in National Curriculum documents. The positive skills and attributes of children with special educational needs should be encouraged and developed. Providing opportunities for collaborative talk in scientific investigation embodies, therefore, an important principle of differentiation: that it should enhance children's strengths rather than confirm their weaknesses.

An example of how collaborative discussion between pupils of varying ability can assist learning can be seen in the extract (shown on p. 161).[3] The extract provides evidence of the role that discussion plays in collaborative group work. It enabled the participants to voice their ideas, question and build upon their colleagues' suggestions. The final outcome was a sensible yet imaginative plan for investigating a scientific concept. The roles played by both girls is significant. They were able to play key parts in the planning. This raises the question of whether a written plan produced by each individual would have resulted in the same outcome, even if some initial discussion had taken place.

RECORDING SCIENTIFIC OUTCOMES? OR RECORDING LEARNING PROGRESS?

The pressure on the teacher to provide evidence of achievement in the form of a written record of a child's achievement may, however, result in organising lessons so that children provide differentiated outcomes in *writing* as a common consequence to a science activity. The written outcome is then often presumed to indicate the child's perceived skill in a particular scientific activity. Such evidence does not reflect the aims of mixed ability grouping. It may be that the conventions of scientific enquiry, which include the careful and accurate recording of results, can become conflated with an educational objective, that children provide a written record of the work they have done. It may be helpful to distinguish between considering, firstly, what alternative acceptable means of the demonstration and evidence of learning teachers can include in their planning and, secondly, and not necessarily the same process, how children should keep a record of their scientific results. For example, the latter might be accomplished by producing a group record, the results of which are contributed by the whole group but presented using information technology and, if required, reproducing the record by photocopy as an individual record in children's workbooks, or displays.

Language in the form of pupil-to-pupil talk is a common element to be found in all models of primary science pedagogy. Its significance in generating cognitive development is widely acknowledged by educators, and an examination of its processes and practices within the field of primary science should be of value when considering the planning and implementation procedures of science. Working from theoretical explanations about the centrality of language and talk in learning (Vygotsky 1962; Bruner 1986; Fisher 1992), Edwards (1990) argues that the advancement of understanding is a *communicative* accomplishment that is strengthened by encouraging classroom discussion amongst pupils in their working groups. This assertion, relevant to all children, has particular force in relation to those children whose special needs are specifically concerned with their difficulties with literacy. Edwards acknowledges that Vygotsky's proposal that 'conceptual thought is derived from dialogue' formed the basis of his beliefs. He concedes, however, that a child also enhances his or her thinking through argumentation with others. Vygotsky's theories therefore give teaching (whether by an adult or another learner) a role in the development of understanding. Vygotsky argued that 'the child's *potential* for learning is revealed, and indeed is often *realised*, in interactions with more knowledgeable others.' (1962: 86). Vygotsky imagined the gap in understanding that exists between what a person is able to do alone, and what he or she can achieve given help from someone more knowledgeable or skilled than him or herself, as a zone of proximal development. The 'expert', perceiving aspects of salience, structure and organisation to the learning that will not be easily available to the less experienced learner, can provide the dialogic conditions in which these aspects can be perceived, articulated, and eventually internalised by the less experienced learner. Thus, in science, it is through the dialogue, the talking with a more experienced learner, that a child may develop her or his conceptual understanding of scientific concepts. The language of the appropriate ways of thinking about science, made manifest and articulated in the discussion between learners, becomes 'inner speech' for the less experienced learner, and thus becomes part of that learner's understanding of the task, and of how to think scientifically.

Howe, Tolmie and Rogers (1992) likewise emphasise this perspective. A research study indicated that there was substantial evidence that groups which allowed for the interaction of participants with differing scientific views had a beneficial effect on the participants' understanding of scientific concepts. They added that children can gain from interactions when their views are different, regardless of whether their understanding is more or less equal to their peers. Rogoff also found that some, but not all, research supports the proposition that working with a partner equal in skill, or even less advanced, can still yield progress. She suggests that the crucial factor may not be the learning status of the participants but may relate to 'the extent to which the partners share in problem solving and manage to establish a common ground for their investigations, from which they may proceed regardless of asymmetries in their status, expertise, or particular viewpoints' (Rogoff 1990). Similar conclusions were reached by Linn and Songer (1991) when studying adolescents' cognitive and conceptual changes.

There can be little doubt that the development of discourse is believed to be integral to cognitive growth, and thus teachers would be advised to exploit its potential in as many different ways as they can. In particular, teachers need to give attention to the fact that cognitive growth may well be stimulated by children working and discussing in groups. It is important to identify the range of styles of talking and learning to be found in groups of children working together, and to establish opportunities for children to voice their differences of opinions among group members.

Verbal interactions taking place between pupils during their science investigations can be of significance in developing the understanding of more able learners as well as assisting the less able learner to move, with help, through the zone of proximal development to a higher level of individualised understanding. The need to work with a less experienced learner creates opportunities for the more able learner to present, and, in so doing, to reformulate and/or clarify their own understanding.

Furthermore, Edwards (1990), Reay (1991) and Tolmie and Howe (1992) all suggest that where groups hold differing opinions, this tends to aid scientific understanding, while concordance can curtail progress. However, the dilemma for teachers is that while some children enjoy challenge and argument, others do not.[4] It was noted that one teacher in the second survey referred to grouping children who 'work well together'. This was glossed on the questionnaire as 'capable of working well together and co-operating'. Management of groups on this principle may sometimes be at variance with children's needs for challenge in order to develop their scientific understanding. Moreover, as the value and significance of 'argumentation' is linked to social and cultural contexts, it is likely to be favoured or at least experienced as a comfortable activity by certain social groupings but not others. This may reinforce other dissonances between community and school which lead to low achievement for certain social groups. The dilemma suggests that much more work may need to be done in helping children work together effectively, and deal with differences of opinion, using techniques such as that used by Linn and Songer (1991). The resolution of the dilemma will also relate to issues such as the expectations of the teacher, and the ethos of the classroom and the school; for example, the level of competitiveness among pupils and the valuing of difference as the place where learning occurs, as opposed to a narrowing view of correctness as the only goal of learning.

NOTES

1 Special educational needs is used in this chapter to refer to all children identified, by whatever means, as having a special educational need relative to the educational needs of the other children in their classroom and school. The definition would therefore include all children on the SEN Register, who are placed on the various Stages of Assessment under the Code of Practice Guidelines.

2 Participants from an English LEA who attended one or other of two 20-day DFE science courses for primary teachers were invited to complete questionnaires on their decisions about grouping children for science.

3 Four Year 5 pupils were engaged in planning a scientific investigation based on colour identification at low light levels. An adult was present during the discussion. Two of the pupils (both girls) were identified by the class teacher as having special educational needs associated with their spelling and reading competencies. They received extra help with these problems, though not during science activities.

4 Although this strategy might not benefit everyone to the same degree, extensive research has indicated that girls prefer a consensus style of discourse as opposed to an argumentative style favoured by males. (Maltz and Borker, 1982; Johnson and Johnson, 1985; Randall, 1987; Assessment of Performance Unit (APU), 1988; Slavin, 1990; Reay, 1991; Murphy, 1991).

REFERENCES

Assessment of Performance Unit (1988) *Science at Age 11*, London: HMSO

Association for Science Education (1994) 'News from the Primary Science Committee', *Education in Science*, 14 November

Bennett, N. (1987) 'Co-operative learning, children do it in groups or do they?', *Education and Child Psychology*, 4 (3): 7–18

Bennett, N. and Cass, A. (1988) 'The effects of group composition on group interactive processes and pupil understanding', *British Educational Research Journal*, 15 (1): 19–32

Bennett, N. and Dunn, E. (1990) *Talking and Learning in Groups: Leverhulme Primary Project*, London: Macmillan Educational

Black, P. (1991) Paper presented to the British Educational Research Association (BERA), Policy Task Group Seminar, University of Bristol

Bruner, J. S. (1986) *Actual Minds, Possible Worlds*, London: Harvard University Press

Department of Education and Science (DES) (1994) *Revision of the Science National Curriculum: Draft Order*, London: HMSO

Edwards, A. D. and Westgate, D. P. G. (1994) *Investigating Classroom Talk*, 2nd edn, London: The Falmer Press

Edwards, D. (1990) 'Classroom discourse and classroom knowledge', in Rogers, C. and Kutnik, P. *The Social Psychology of the Primary School*, London: Routledge

Fisher, E. (1992) 'Distinctive features of pupil–pupil classroom talk and their relationship to learning: how discursive exploration might be encouraged', *Centre for Language and Communications (CLAC) Occasional papers in communication*. June, 33, Milton Keynes: Open University, School of Education

Gipps, C., Gross, H. and Goldstein, H. (1987) *Warnock's Eighteen Percent: Children with Special Needs in Primary Schools*, Lewes: Falmer

Griffin, P. (1990) 'Science for All', *Questions*, March: 13

Gross, J. (1993) *Special Educational Needs in the Primary School*, Buckingham: Open University Press

Howe, C. (1992) 'Learning about physics through peer interaction', Paper presented to the Psychology Section of the British Association for the Advancement of Science: Southampton

Howe, C., Tolmie, A. and Rogers, C. (1990) 'Physics in the primary school: peer interaction and the understanding of floating and sinking', *European Journal of Psychology of Education*, V (4): 459–475.

Howe, C., Tolmie, A. and Rogers, C. (1992) 'The acquisition of conceptual knowledge in science by primary school children: Group interaction and the understanding of motion down an incline', *British Journal of Developmental Psychology*, 10: 113–130

Johnson, D. W. and Johnson, R. T. (1985) *Learning Together and Alone*, Englewood Cliffs NJ: Prentice-Hall

Linn, M. and Songer, N. (1991) 'Cognitive and conceptual change across adolescence', *American Journal of Education*, 99, (4): 379–417.

Maltz, D. and Borker, R. (1982) 'A cultural approach to male–female miscommunication', in Gumperz, J. (ed.) *Language and Social Identity*, Cambridge: University Press

Mercer, N., Phillips, T. and Somekh, B. (1991) 'Spoken language and new technology (SLANT)', *Journal of Computer Assisted Learning*, 2 (1): 1–8

Murphy, P. (1991) 'Assessment and gender', *Cambridge Journal of Education* 21, (2): 203–219

Murphy, P., Scanlon, E., Hodgson, B. and Whitelegg, E. (1994) *Developing Investigative Learning in Science – The Role of Collaboration*, paper presented to the ECUNET European Conference on Curriculum, School of Education University of Twent, Ensched, The Netherlands, Milton Keynes: Open University.

National Curriculum Council (1989a) *Science Non Statutory Guidance*, York: NCC

National Curriculum Council (1989b) *Curriculum Guidance 2: A Curriculum for All*, York: NCC

National Curriculum Council (1992) *Curriculum Guidance 10: Teaching science to pupils with special educational needs*, York: NCC

National Curriculum Council (1993) *Teaching Science at Key Stages 1 and 2*, York: NCC

Phillips, T. (1990) 'Structuring contexts for exploratory talk', in *Talking and Listening*, Lexington Spa: Scholastic

Reay, D. (1991) 'Intersections of gender, race and class in the primary school', *British Journal of Sociology of Education*, 12: 163–182

Rogoff, B. (1990) *Apprenticeship in Thinking:Cognitive Development in a Social Context*, Oxford: Oxford University Press.

Slavin, R. (1990) 'Co-operative learning', in Rogers, C. and Kutnik, P. *The Social Psychology of the Primary School*, London: Routledge.

Sutherland, J. and Boyes, D. (1993) 'Science for all pupils', in Sherrington, R. (ed.) *Science Teachers' Handbook (Primary)*, Hatfield: The Association for Science Education

Thorne, B. (1986) 'Girls and boys together ... but mostly apart: gender arrangements in elementary schools', in W. Hartup and Z. Rubin *Relationships and Developments*, Hillside, NJ: Lawrence Erlbaum

Tolmie A. and Howe, C. (1992) 'Relationships between task design, dialogue and learning in science group work', paper presented to the BPS

Developmental Section Annual Conference, Edinburgh

Vygotsky, L. S. (1962) *Thought and Language*, Cambridge, Mass.: The MIT Press

Wegerif, R. (1994) 'Educational software design features influencing the quality of children's talk', in *Centre for imformation Technology in Education (CITE) Report No. 192*, Milton Keynes: Open University

Whitelegg, E., Murphy, P., Scanlon, E. and Hodgson, B. (1992) 'Investigating collaboration in primary science classrooms: a gender perspective', *CALRG Technical Report 125*, Milton Keynes: Open University

Chapter 10

An ear to the ground
Learning through talking

Jennifer Reynolds

My love affair with talk began, I am reliably informed, at the age of nine months and throughout my life talk has taught me almost everything I know. Without talk I would not hold political views, question nature and science, hold a sense of empathy with my family's history, understand the history of Britain and the world and express my opinions on an inexhaustible fund of subjects from fashion to educational theory. I would, without talk, be lost in my classroom and most importantly, lose my sense of humour.

One of my saddest discoveries upon looking back at the role of talk in my learning is that although talk was bountiful and largely instrumental in my learning of social conduct at home as a child and at polytechnic in my training as a teacher, at least ten years of my life were devoid of talk at a time when it could have been invaluably utilised. My vacant ten years were my schooldays. I am not decrying the education I received; I am just highlighting the education and knowledge I could have acquired if my teachers had seen talk as a valuable way of learning. So it is with strong convictions about the use of talk in education that I approach my job as a class teacher. This chapter illustrates a number of ways in which I have used speaking and listening in the classroom to attempt to fulfil the diversity of my pupils' needs and abilities of acquiring and retaining knowledge and skills.

For me, differentiation is about learning – my own as well as the children's. Four activities outline my progression, as a class teacher of children in Years 5 and 6, towards identifying learning and planning for differentiation. Each activity gave me a slightly modified focus and as the work went on, I found myself not only planning for individual learning opportunities by using talk, but using children's talk to assess the learning of skills, the acquisition of knowledge and the application of knowledge. As I realised the enormous consequences of using talk in the classroom, I found myself evaluating the ways in which I could best provide the children with opportunities to develop their talk. I also began to plan ways in which I could record and recognise individual needs and achievements. I found myself in an interlocked system of planning, recording, evaluating and assessing, and using the evaluation to plan for further activities with individual children in mind, but with access for all the class to the concepts on offer. I also came to recognise the close interlinking between talk, reading, writing and learning in several curriculum areas.

The first activity involved the children working in groups, recording and transcribing their storytelling. This provided them with an opportunity to use their own language in spoken and written form to develop individual story writing techniques whilst also developing punctuation and spelling. The second activity combined storytelling with a study of local history which later progressed to drama and improvisation. The third activity I describe is the use of recorded role play in an historical context with the children working as partners rather than in groups; this provided me with evidence useful for planning for individual needs and assessment of knowledge gained.

The fourth activity illustrates the extent to which all the previous work had helped me to evaluate my classroom practice and develop other ways of using speaking and listening to aid individual learning. I discovered that it had allowed the children to share new knowledge, to 'own' their knowledge and had provided me with information about gaps in the knowledge of individual children. The activity involved tape-recorded exploratory group talk, the planning stages of a presentation and the presentation itself.

Although the main focus of the activities was humanities based, I believe that the use of speaking and listening as a vehicle for learning can help the teacher cater for individual needs in all areas of the curriculum. I have found that when children talk to each other, the knowledge gained and shared forms a firm foundation for future individual learning. Talking in group activities also provided children with the opportunity to think aloud and to establish their ownership of the newly acquired knowledge. So by planning for talk, the teacher is automatically planning for the sharing of individual knowledge and for the re-drafting and evaluation of children's ideas.

There are important implications for using talk for assessment purposes; children often know more than their written secretarial or transcription skills may reveal. Tape-recorded children's talk provides evidence of learning – or indeed lack of it. Teachers can only know what children have learned if they are able to communicate their knowledge adequately in the selected medium. A request to write down newly acquired knowledge may not always be appropriate to a child, firstly because its functions are limited if the audience for writing is almost always the teacher and, secondly, if the audience for the writing is another child, talk is usually the preferred and reasonable method of communication; why write something if you can tell it? From the teacher's point of view, allowing children to present knowledge in talk often reveals their real abilities and achievements. It is important, however, to offer varied groupings and contexts through which this is done.

STORYTELLING

The main aim of this activity was to encourage the children to use the tape recorders profitably and not allow them to inhibit their talk, discussion and telling of the story. It was also an individual learning process for each child as not only were they developing their skills of communication, they also used their memories, their vocabulary and their written language. The whole task took place during two group sessions, leading on to two further individual sessions.

I began by telling the whole class a story about a crocodile and a monkey in India. Following my telling of the story, the children worked in mixed ability groups of five to re-tell the story using the tape recorder. Previously when I have used this type of taped storytelling, I have allowed the children to switch the tape recorder on and off. But, as I wanted to record as much talk as possible and gain true impressions of how we tell stories, I asked the children to keep the tape running. This meant that all talk aside from the storytelling would also be included in the eventual transcript of the tape and would provide the children with a vivid contrast between the language used during storytelling and the language used for story writing.

After the separate groups had made their story tapes, the whole class listened to each one in turn. We agreed that although the stories were interrupted by shouts, laughs and self-corrections, each group had kept to the main storyline and had maintained characterisation. It was decided that if we had never heard the story before, we would have understood and enjoyed each group's version. The children were fascinated by how much each group's story was slightly different and yet these differences did not essentially change the story as a whole.

To enable the children to study in more detail the language they had used, we set about transcribing the tapes, again in the same mixed ability groups. Remaining in the groups ensured that almost every utterance recorded on the tape was transcribed because each child wanted to be included as much as possible. I explained that every noise and conversation aside from the actual storytelling had to be included in the transcript. Each group had worked on their transcript on a huge piece of paper and used coloured felt tip pens to draw attention to vocal expression by writing a description of how the storyteller was using their voice, for example: 'In a nasty voice'. They also included pauses and silences, coughs, laughs and whispers.

When each group had completed their transcript I read them to the whole class. I did not use expression or character voices, which resulted in barely understandable versions of the story. As a whole class we had a very interesting discussion about why the transcripts when read aloud failed to provide us with coherent versions of the story. It was surprising just how many children had an excellent sense of the differences between storytelling and story writing. They were able clearly to point out to me that if you were writing a story you would have to supplement voice expression with written information for the reader, sound effects would have to be replaced by descriptions, and pauses and silences by punctuation. I was astonished by the huge amount of written language work that was emerging from an activity that I had anticipated as being wholly vocal.

The discussion with the class led my planning for the next session of the activity. As individuals, each child spent time with their group's transcript and re-drafted it into a better written version of the story. This activity meant that the children were adding descriptions, information, and punctuation to the original transcripts. One of the reading activities in the class is group reading, carried out in language groups based on children's abilities to read and discuss the novels, plays, poetry and non-fiction books which we use as group readers. As I needed to spend time with each child as they read and re-drafted their first attempts at the written story, instead of reading the usual group reading books, each group read each other's written stories. Since the re-drafting process of each child's story involved their whole language group, this provided a lot of language work in the area of punctuation, spelling and descriptive writing. My role was no more time consuming than the usual group reading session and this arrangement gave me the chance to work with each child individually. By involving the whole language group, the children were learning and re-inforcing new skills together.

The task provided me with such a wealth of language-based work that I was reluctant to bring it to an end; I had to end it following the children's second draft of the story, however, or else run the risk of losing their motivation and enthusiasm for the task. The success of this work meant that I decided to integrate the skills which the children had learned into other areas of the curriculum.

BURWELL HOUSE – A LOCAL STUDY

I had recently taken about half the class on a residential visit to Burwell House in Cambridgeshire where we had studied the local history. A member of the residential staff told us a story of a local fire disaster and of a pictorial gravestone which stands in memory of the 79 villagers who died in the fire of 1727. As the story of the fire had survived largely due to the oral tradition, I decided to base our future study of the event on storytelling and drama.

Upon our return to the classroom, I told the story to the whole class. My aims were to make the story as real as possible for those children who had not had first hand experience of Burwell or seen the gravestone, and to maintain the interest of those children who had already heard the story. After I had told the story we talked about the attitudes of the Burwell villagers and the clergy in 1727 and also other aspects of fire safety, education, technology and entertainment. The children had lots to say during the discussion and I felt they were forming a good foundation for future research into life in 1727.

In a similar way to the storytelling of the previous activity, I asked three groups of six or seven to tell their version of the story into tape recorders. Another group taped their 'confessions' of starting the fire and a fifth group wrote the story in pairs to help us compare the written versions with the taped versions. The storytelling groups were fascinating to watch. As I did not want to interfere with the group discussions, I had plenty of time to observe. I recorded any child who did not participate in the group discussion or who seemed to be uncooperative, although listening to the tapes themselves provided evidence of this. The three groups told their versions of the story and set about the task in extremely different ways:

Group A was possibly the most friendship-based group and their telling of the story was loud and enthusiastic. Their tape contained giggles, self-corrections, shouts about facts and repetitions of parts of the story. Listening to their story was like eavesdropping on a group of friends re-living a film which they had watched previously.

Group B planned their telling of the story before they began recording and gave each other roles although I had told the story as a complete narrative and had not taken on any roles. I had attempted to give an historical account of the events and yet this group's version of the story took the shape of a radio play and was entertainingly performed.

Group C structured their telling of the story in such a way that prevented me from hearing any asides to the storytelling. They systematically turned the tape off whilst they discussed the story and they recorded what they thought were perfect narrations of each part. The children took it in turns to act as narrator and rarely slipped into the roles of other characters. Their version took the form of a news report.

We listened to each tape as a class, discussing the ways in which each group had changed the story and added non-factual information to their version. Following our class discussion the groups used their tapes in a variety of ways. As Group A's tape was such a relaxed and lively version of the story, I asked them to transcribe it in order to highlight how, although their story was perfectly understandable to listen to, a written version would have to take a completely different approach. Group B's tape was already an excellent attempt at a play and so I asked them to use the tape as a first draft from which to write a play as opposed to a transcript. Group C's taped version of the story was so structured that I asked them to use it as a story plan for a written version. To carry out this task they needed to switch the tape on and off and listen to each little bit of narrative, then decide as a group how they would elaborate on what had been spoken, and write it.

Whilst the groups who had tape-recorded their stories first set about writing them, the groups who had begun with the written story started to record their reading aloud of the joint stories. Obviously each group needed a different amount of time to complete their activity and so over the period of a week the children worked on their activities at various times. Throughout this week the activity took on a drama emphasis, which seemed to be a natural development from our work with the tapes. I wanted to provide myself with evidence that the children had all gained some knowledge of the facts of the story and had developed a sense of empathy with the villagers of Burwell.

I asked the children, as a class, to decide on the characters needed to present a play about the Burwell fire. Having settled on the characters required and the children who would be playing which roles, the children split into groups at different positions in the hall. All the children took part – thirty-two in all. I had never used improvisation to this extent and with so many characters I did not know what to expect. I explained to the children that as they were familiar with the story I would start to narrate it and as they felt it appropriate for their character to join in, they were just to do so.

I have to admit to being extremely surprised when the children began acting and telling the story in roles after I had only just set the scene. The children took on roles of villagers talking about the boredom that they felt as a result of living in Burwell in 1727. Those children who were pretending to be puppeteers visiting Burwell tried to speak 'olde English' and danced around the room trying to interest and excite the villagers. The clergy of the village had confrontational scenes with the villagers about the puppet show and when they banned its showing, the villagers talked angrily amongst themselves. The boy playing the opportunist farmer who allowed the puppeteers to hold their show in his barn was rubbing his hands together as he gleefully took a penny from each member of the audience queuing up outside his barn.

The children who tried to sneak into the barn were caught and sent away and the fire was clearly started by the child smoking a pipe whilst she was observing the puppet show from a secret spot in the barn roof.

Following the fire the children took on the roles of villagers who were looking for a scapegoat, some accused the farmer for nailing shut the barn door to prevent gatecrashers; some accused the clergy of starting the fire and others feared that God was punishing them. All became clear when the girl who had 'started' the fire confessed on her death bed in order to go to heaven.

The class activity during this improvisation workshop illustrated to me just how much historical knowledge had been gained and how historical skills had been developed, mainly those of empathy and cause and effect. The facts of the Burwell Fire had been acquired, initially from myself or during the visit to Burwell House, reconstructed and owned during the work with the tape recorders and used during the improvisation. The drama was a successful summary of the kinds of knowledge that the children had accumulated throughout this activity. It seems clear to me that if the children had not claimed, understood and owned the historical facts, they would not have been able to use their knowledge so effectively.

My work with the children on the Burwell Fire story proved to me just how important the use of speaking and listening was, especially for the children who had difficulties with their written work. But the only evidence of individual learning that I had was the success of the improvisation. As I was keen to investigate the possibilities of using talk to provide evidence of learning, I began to plan smaller group activities around tape recorders and use them for assessment purposes.

THE VICTORIANS: INDIVIDUAL AND PAIRED ASSESSMENT OF LEARNING

The following section explains how, for a later history topic, I planned for individual assessment and learning through group and partner work, focusing on four children whom I considered to have 'special needs':

Karl was having difficulties with written work and not providing me with evidence of his learning either from written tasks or from presentations.

David was having difficulty with 'owning' knowledge and only re-hashed information rather than remembering and re-using it.

Ambika was achieving an excellent standard of written work with facts of historical events, but showing no real sense of empathy.

Catherine was achieving an excellent standard of work and needed to be stretched.

These four children, along with the rest of the class, had been studying the Victorians for a few weeks. I asked David and Karl to talk to each other about the pictures I had given them of a chimney sweep and poor Victorian families. I wanted them to tape their discussion as they pretended they were some of the people in these pictures talking about their lives. The boys' first taped conversation showed evidence of their knowledge but they rarely slipped into role; they just talked about the pictures, asking each other closed questions:

D: If you're too scared to go up the chimney, the boss'll get a stick 'n' poke you up the feet.

K: (in role) Do you fink the children should go up the chimney?

D: I think the children were very worried about the job (pause) and scared.

K: (in role/strange voice) Why did they send their children up the chimney?

D: The parents sent their children up the chimney to get some money for the poor family.

K: They got very bad diseases.

The boys' questions and answers provided me with evidence of their learning. They were aware of the conditions of Victorian child labourers, were able to discuss the economic implications and showed evidence of empathy with poor people. They also revealed gaps in their knowledge such as the link between slums and diseases and health problems as a result of climbing chimneys.

In a second attempt to provide myself with evidence of Karl's and David's knowledge of the Victorians, I followed up more topic work with a similar exercise. I gave them a photograph of a Victorian politician and a newspaper reporter and asked them to take turns to be each character. The results were highly rewarding. They not only spoke in 'upper class' accents, they also showed a clear understanding of some of the kinds of views held by politicians in the Victorian times about child labour. I decided to try this type of activity with the boys once more and this time I told David that he was the wealthy man in the photograph and I told Karl that he was going to interview him. David had no option but to play along and in so doing he illustrated his understanding of class, jobs, child workers; he also displayed judgement and empathy. With this third activity I found the evidence of David's learning that I was looking for. By listening to the taped conversation I was able to plan future activities which would allow me to focus on the gaps in the boys' knowledge. The tape gave Karl a chance to express his opinions without them becoming entangled in his fears and frustrations with writing.

I gave Catherine and Ambika a similar activity using a picture of a poor Victorian man standing in the doorway of his terraced house, and asked them to carry out an interview with the man. Catherine decided to take on the role of the man and Ambika the role of the interviewer:

A: What do you feel like livin' in this street?
C: (cough, cough/husky voice) This street is dirty, smelly, stinky (cough, cough)
A: What does your house look like?
C: (cough, cough) We ain't got no heatin'. The windows are smashed in an' there's stains everywhere.
A: Have you got any children?
C: Yeh I have six.
A: Do they go to school?
C: No they all 'ave to work (pause) I can't bring enough money.
A: What does your wife do?
C: Noffing 'cos she's ill.
A: What does she normally do?
C: She normally works in the sweat shop.
A: Can you or your family read or write?
C: No 'cos we never went to school.
A: What do you do in your spare time?
C: Sleep (pause) that reminds me, I'm meant to be sleeping now. GO AWAY.

This excellent role play provided me with much evidence of the girls' learning. They obviously had remembered and were able to talk about a variety of facts about Victorian life in the slums. The activity clearly encouraged Catherine to use her newly acquired knowledge but Ambika was still displaying a detached empathy, although indirectly she was asking Catherine to empathise in an extremely active manner. I gave the girls no choice about which of them would act in the next activity, asking them both to talk in role about issues around child chimney sweeps. Catherine decided to be a politician and Ambika a sweep master. This time Ambika fully took on the role and used her knowledge of the Victorians to make a lively taped debate:

I think [strong London accent] . . . I think that it in't 'xactly right BUT who's gonna clean my chimneys if they don't?

and later on during the tape following Catherine's suggestion that she cleaned them herself:

But I know what it's like [protesting loudly]. I don't wanna clean chimneys I sweeped 'em when I was little!

The activity allowed Ambika to play with her knowledge and not just present it in a written form. Catherine took to this task straight away, using her knowledge and discussing facts; it gave her the opportunity to challenge and reconstruct the new knowledge which she had acquired. She told me after this activity that it must have been hard to be a sweep master since you would know the sort of pain that you would be inflicting on children because you would have done it yourself when you were a child. I am certain that Ambika put this idea into Catherine's head during their taped role play.

EXPLAINING THE EARTH'S TILT: LOOKING FOR THE EVIDENCE OF LEARNING AND PLANNING FOR INDIVIDUAL NEEDS

The previous activity had allowed me to recognise individual learning but I had carried out this activity very close to the end of our topic work and so it was more useful to me as a final assessment than as an aid to future planning. The following activity gave me the opportunity to build upon individual knowledge and plan a section of the topic work around the needs of individual children. As part of our topic on Earth and Weather, we were going to study the tilt of the earth and how the seasons happen as a result of it. This aspect of geography can be particularly difficult to demonstrate and explain. It is also difficult for the children to provide evidence of their understanding in written form as much of the work uses diagrams to develop the relevant concepts.

I decided to begin this activity with child-based research which I hoped would provide me with a foundation to plan for future individual learning. I held a very short class discussion about the world, just to remind them that the world is a sphere, how night and day come about and what the seasons are. I then told the children that, in groups, I wanted them to find out why certain parts of the world had seasons and present their information to the rest of the class. I put the children into mixed ability groups of seven or eight, expecting that they would split themselves into sub-groups to work on their presentations.

I set up tape recorders around the room and left out a range of topic books, encyclopaedias and geography books. I had chosen the books carefully to ensure that they varied in the ways that they presented information and that they had a range of pictorial and written texts. I asked the children to tape their discussions and the exploratory talk of each sub-group told me a lot about how individual children acquire knowledge. When listening to the recording of the group discussions I became aware of the fact that the greatest resource in the classroom was not my pile of carefully selected books or the availability of the library, but was in fact the children themselves. They were learning, and sharing their learning, loudly and enthusiastically. Children were asking to use globes, maps and torches; they were making posters and writing short plays set in Britain and Australia.

What I found interesting about this activity was that the factual research took up a very short time. The majority of the children's time was spent planning how they were going to share their newly acquired knowledge and in doing so the individuals in each group who had difficulty in reading the texts, were learning from their peers and using talk to establish and share their knowledge. The following transcript is of four very different children halfway through the stages of their planning, and is an example of the kinds of talk that were going on all over the classroom:

L: You can copy the same information but you have to say it in your own words.

E: So . . . er . . . when Great Britain is leaning away from the sun it is daytime . . .?. . . night time . . .?

R: Nooo . . . it's winter.

J: Hey, I know, you can be the weather reporter in Australia and I can be the weather reporter in England.

L: Are we doing the temperature as well?

R: Can you do an Australian accent?

E: G'day . . . ha. .ha. .ha. . . .

L: While you're doing the weather report for Britain, we can watch and pretend we're children watching.

J: Yeh and we say 'NOT MORE RAIN!'

The language used by the children is obviously their own and they are using their discussion to build on the knowledge they have acquired. The exploratory talk was illustrative of how the children were gaining their knowledge; the presentations showed me which facts had been retained and shared.

Group One decided to do just what a teacher is tempted to do – they lectured about the earth's tilt:

E: [to the rest of the group] Right then class, sit down. I'm going to talk to you about the earth's tilt . . .

E goes on to talk about the equator and the tilt towards the sun at different times of the year. The whole group planned a demonstration using a yellow sponge ball to represent the sun and a small ball with stickers on to represent the earth. They followed their demonstration with their weather reports. Their presentation allowed me to give them the correct terminology for 'above the equator' and 'below the equator' but they had taught themselves the basic facts of how the seasons come about.

The other groups provided me with tapes and presentations which were just as informative. One group showed a clear lack of understanding which came about largely because of poor group co-operation and also because they had repeated large chunks of information from text books without telling it in their own words. I later asked this group to design posters to explain the earth's tilt so as to limit them to pictorial representation and prevent them from copying information without really understanding what it means.

Throughout all of these activities, I was planning for individual learning and the development of individual skills. I was not intentionally attempting to satisfy the 'Range of Key Skills' of Speaking and Listening as defined in the National Curriculum for English. But upon reflection, I realised that they had been covered to a great extent and at an individual level for every child in the class. Throughout each task the children were exploring, developing and explaining ideas. They were sharing their ideas, insights and opinions, reading aloud, telling and enacting stories and presenting their work to an audience.

They also went far beyond the requirements of the National Curriculum in that they provided each other with a respectful, sympathetic and interested audience. Their work had a purpose and was seen in most cases as fun; the children were using talk to help structure their own learning and establish new knowledge in their mind and, most importantly, they were teaching each other to organise their thoughts. By sharing their new ideas the children were highlighting to me the gaps in their knowledge and enabling me to cater for their individual needs and assess the acquisition of their knowledge. Without a purpose, Speaking and Listening as defined by the National Curriculum, would be pointless. Talk is a valuable tool for individual learning and the skills of Speaking and Listening can only develop if children are given the opportunities to use them individually and collaboratively. The children were also covering geography and history study units although ultimately it was not only historical or geographical knowledge that I hoped to have led the children to, but the knowledge that they themselves can be in control of their learning and share their knowledge with others.

CONCLUSION

Throughout this chapter I have been illustrating a number of ways in which I have used talk as a vehicle for learning and a means of providing evidence of learning for individual children in my class. The skills and key aims for each activity were different, and indeed were different for each child involved, but in catering for individual learning I found I could use a common task. The storytelling activity had implications for literacy skills and involved a range of language work all of which was based on individual or group needs but the task also provided me with evidence of content learning, memory skills, use of language and the development of collaborative skills.

The Burwell House activity focused upon historical knowledge but allowed each individual child the opportunity to empathise with the topic in a way I feel many history topic books fail to allow for. The activity brought history to life and stimulated the children's interest and discussions. Upon realising the potential for individual assessments flowing from this activity, I discovered the importance of talk for children with a range of 'special needs' and began to plan for individual learning in a much more detailed way than previously. I believe now that it is impossible to separate planning, assessment and evaluation when catering for individual needs and feel strongly that the use of talk in the classroom makes the teacher's task less arduous as the children can scaffold their own learning and so guide future planning.

Chapter 11

'Snjezana i Sedam Patuljaka'

Developing language through writing bilingual texts

Ian Eyres

In working with young writers I am keen to encourage the development of each author's individual voice. All children have their own experiences and all have their own way of expressing those experiences. In addition, at any given point in their writing development each will have acquired skills in the various aspects of the writing process to differing degrees. Thus one child may be most proficient in questions of textual organisation while another may use a wide-ranging vocabulary and another may excel at spelling. Children make advances in different areas at different times and it cannot be taken for granted that any individual's level of attainment (as judged against National Curriculum or other norms) in one area will imply a similar level of attainment in other areas. It has for some years been my conviction that children have the best opportunity to use all their skills to the best of their ability in a regime which emphasises the supreme importance of the meanings which they are attempting to convey and develop, and where formal skills and strategies are seen as the servants of meaning.

In the workshop approach which I take to teaching writing, the first element of differentiation is choice. Children have complete freedom over what they write. Looking at things negatively, we can say that this removes any risk of demotivating learners by asking them to deal with subjects they are not really interested in. More positively, my experience is that children are happiest writing about the subjects which they know most about and are therefore able to write fully developed texts about these subjects, especially when given the opportunity to discuss and answer questions on their ideas with adults and peers.

Once a writer has generated sufficient text for it to be the subject of a conference (a one-to-one discussion with the teacher, which follows a predictable pattern through which children are able to rehearse their own ideas and problems), individual attention can then be given on a regular basis. In such a context it is, of course, impossible to fail to meet required standards. So far as a writer is concerned I am predominantly interested in knowing about the subject in hand. As well as being concerned with the child's particular subject or story, however, I will be actively giving the kind of support which enables the development of all aspects of the current text as fully as possible. This should mean that the final draft will include all the things the author intended to say and should say those things as clearly as possible. As I have already noted, this clarity will in part be due to the efficient use of spelling, hand-writing and grammatical conventions. These elements will have been refined through a process of revision which involves, in addition to conferences with the teacher, conferences with peers and the sharing of work in progress with larger groups and the whole class. (It is worth saying that the desired clarity is also achieved through the clear thinking which results when unshaped ideas are questioned and challenged and that in this way writing supports learning in a wider sense.) Within this framework, redrafting is something which is seen by young writers as an essential part of the process of writing, and children will commonly make additions and deletions to their texts and often feel the need to make a fresh start.

One further element of differentiation in this approach comes from the differing levels of support given to each child. Within a pattern of work-ing which involves the class in writing for 30–40 minutes on four or five days a week one child might regularly be taking part in a brief confer-ence every day, while I might see another only once a week. It is not necessarily the case that less confident writers receive more of my time, though such children will probably enjoy a number of periods of more intensive attention in the course of a year. Often I will spend more time with a child who is just making a significant advance, in order to affirm the new learning and to encourage its application. Additionally, bilingual children can usually expect some regular support from a bilingual assis-tant, who will be able to discuss children's ideas in their mother tongue.

Although I developed this approach based on the work of Donald Graves (Graves 1983), as a teacher of monolingual classes, l have found the respect for what each individual brings to the task of writing to be, if anything, even more relevant when working with children whose first language is not English. The chance to bring into the classroom personal and cultural experiences which, all too often, have little or no place in an overcrowded curriculum is particularly valuable. So too are oppor-tunities to rehearse ideas for writing through talk. With children whose English is at an early stage of development, these discussions may take place with peers or bilingual assistants, in the writer's first language. Such discussions can be shown to have a positive effect on the quality of the resulting English text (Eyres 1995). In the main, however, my experience has been in working with children whose English has reached a stage where they are able to operate with a degree of success in one-to-one discussions with me.

My experience, then, had not fully prepared me for the work I was to do with three Bosnian girls (Selma, Semra and Medina) in the upper junior classes of Fawcett Primary School in Cambridge. When I was assigned to the school it had been receiving Bosnian children, from a nearby hostel, for the best part of a year. Most stayed for a matter of weeks before moving to settle more permanently in some other part of the country. In this short time the school endeavoured to make the children feel as comfortable as possible with the routines and conventions of an English school and to give them at least a grounding in the kind of English that would help them settle into their next school. These aims (rightly in my opinion) took precedence over any requirement to introduce the children to the details of the National Curriculum. Much of their time when they first came to the school was spent on practical activities during which they were able to converse with other children, learning support assistants and teachers. Both my own background and the rationale of Section 11 funding[1] led me, however, to seek ways of developing the girls' English through the medium of the conventional curriculum. I should like to describe one of the paths the girls took towards a confident command of English. The work outlined took place on two afternoons a week over the course of about a term. Naturally there were many other contributory factors, including the experience of activities which were designed to encourage purposeful talk within the context of the mainstream curriculum and the support of a very co-operative class and of two unusually thoughtful and sympathetic teachers (Ann Rowbottom and Caroline Ribton) who work closely together, team-teaching the two upper junior classes.

When I first met the girls they had been in school for a few weeks. They spoke very little English and I had no idea of how much schooling they had received in Bosnia. 1 soon realised that my elaborate routine for getting older children started on their own writing would have been useless with these particular girls, since they apparently understood little of what 1 was saying. Furthermore, I had no evidence that they were in fact able to write at all and I did not want to run the risk of setting them up to fail. With very young children I start by giving them lots of interesting pens and types of paper and telling them that they are welcome to write. I decided to take this kind of approach with these pupils, loaded a 'Writer' program onto the class computer and managed to convey to the girls that they should write together on it. After the first few lines I was able to tell them that I was happy for them to write in their own language. After a hesitant start they worked with increasing speed and enthusiasm, discussing their writing as they went. Using the computer was obviously an exciting novelty to them, but my impression was that they were most excited at the thought of writing something in Bosnian.[2] They wrote for the whole afternoon and were obviously

please giv me paper, molim vas da mi date papir
where is toy come frome.
odakle dolazite.
i em selma
ja sam, selma
i em semra
ja sam semra
ja se zovem medina imam brata
i sestru i mamu itatu
ja sam jucer isla na izlet.
lojepo sam se provela.
selma.
ja sam jucer isla na more.
lojepo mi je bilo.
nisam se kupala.
zato sto je bilo hladno.
kupila sam skoljke.
na kupila sam jednu malu kesu.
isla sam na cirkuze.
na cirkuze sam se lijepo provela.
igrala sam se i vozala.
krenula sam u centar.
vozili smo se 2 sata.
semra
selma je sljedeca.
danas je bilo lijepo vrijeme
igrala sam se sa prijateljicama.
jucer sam isla na more.
isli smo u kraljevsku vikendicu.

Text 1

very satisfied with what they had produced. I was pleased with the way
they had worked and told them so. I was less certain as to how I should
respond to the text itself (Text .1), when I worked again with the girls
the following day.

Again I went back to my way of working with very young children
as I support their emergent writing. Early writing may consist of nothing
more than some apparently unconventional marks. Closer examination,
especially in the context of children's previous work, usually reveals a
number of features which are demonstrably part of their developing

system of writing. If I analyse my behaviour when responding to such writing, two strategies emerge: 'make an assessment of what the child is currently capable of' and 'find something to respond to'.

What did this text then reveal about the girl's capabilities? Firstly it showed that they were capable of producing a text together and were quite proficient (if at this stage a little slow) users of the computer. Secondly it showed that they were capable of producing a much more interesting and developed text in Bosnian than they were in English. Although I couldn't understand a word it seemed obvious that *danas je bilo lijepo vrijeme iqrala sam se sa prijateljicama* was a more sophisticated example of language in use than *please giv me paper*. The work was apparently organised in sentences (though they either did not know about capital letters or – more likely – did not know about the shift key) and the few English words at the beginning suggested a willingness to take risks with spelling and a budding awareness of the idiosyncrasies of English orthography (*frome*, for example, indicates an awareness that words often end in an apparently unjustified 'e', – as in the word 'give', which the girls spell *giv*!). I formed the impression that their literacy skills were probably not very different from those I would expect in English children of a similar age. At this stage I made no attempt to assess their work individually since, although different sections of the work are signed by each of them, they were clearly talking and supporting each other throughout. Besides, I simply wasn't capable, without bilingual support, of discerning significant differences between the different sections. One important assessment I did make was that this had been a very successful session. The girls had talked a great deal about their text as they composed it and had written a lot. That seemed a good enough start.

Finding something to respond to was not as difficult as I had feared. I was, of course, able to be enthusiastic about the length of their piece and it was a straightforward job to spot their names. I also guessed that *brata i sestru i mamu* referred to Medina's brother, sister and mother and that *cirkuzu* was the circus. (This all involved a bit of miming!) As a rule I find that children respond well when teachers take an interest in what they are saying in their writing. I felt now that these three girls were particularly pleased that someone was willing to try to understand *their* language, instead of making them struggle with English the whole time. The following week I managed to ask the girls if they would write something about the weekend. They chose to split into a pair (Selma and Semra) and an individual (Medina) and the beginning of Selma and Semra's text is reproduced as Text 2.

This time I was able to understand a few more words than the previous week and to engage in something approaching a conversation involving the circus and playing badminton and football in the park. Toward the

---

Selma and Semra

na vikendu proveli smo se lijepo.
igrali smo se dobro.
isli smo na cirkuze.
mnogo smo ucili.
igrali smo i bagminton u parku.
lijepo smo se zabavljali.
Igrali smo i fidbala sa odraslima

Text 2

end of the afternoon I asked if any of them would like to write something in English. Note that I did not ask for a translation. I felt sure that
although there would be some parts which they would be able to trans-
late efficiently, there were bound to be other parts which were more
difficult and would cause frustration and possibly a sense of failure. I
also feared that if they got into the habit of writing with the intention
of later translating their work into English this would lower the status
of their Bosnian texts and probably lead to a restriction of the content
to matter which could be easily translated. This would, of course, defeat
one of the main purposes of asking them to write in Bosnian in the first
place. Selma offered the English text printed here as Text 3.

Diary pieces such as this gave the girls good opportunities for talking
about their everyday experiences, and our conversations became easier
and wider-ranging. One day the subject of stories came up and I learnt
that the story of *Snow White* was one that the girls had learnt in Bosnia.
I suggested that they write the whole story out, in Bosnian, with a view
to making a book for younger children to read. They took to this idea
with great enthusiasm and set to work. It was at about this time that
Medina moved, with her family, to another part of the country, leaving
Selma and Semra to work as a pair. The writing of the Bosnian draft

---

At the weekend
On weekend we are play badminton.
We are play dolls and football.
We are going in the circus and plays be byutyful.

Text 3

(*Snjezana i Sedam Patuljaka*) took several weeks, during which time the girls explained to me, as best they could, the episodes they were developing. I was not in the least worried about the fact that in my capacity as teacher of English I was giving them substantial blocks of time in which to write and speak in their own language. The process of writing the story gave them opportunities to use linguistic skills which they would have been unable to exercise in English (so the activity was giving them the chance to produce the best composition they were capable of) and gave us lots to talk about (in English) every week. Of course, I had no way of making judgements about the technical merits of what they were writing (though I did voice my doubts about their view that all dialogue should be written in capitals), but it seemed clear to me that what they had written made sense. When they reached the end of the draft I could do no more than ask them to read it through very carefully to see if there was anything they wanted to change. In the event they didn't choose to change very much, which may have meant that they had got it right first time or it may have been because when children write collaboratively they are constantly checking each other's contributions. The third possibility, that they simply didn't care (or know) about spelling and other conventions, did not seem congruent with the care which they had obviously put into the detail of the story.

The girls printed out a copy of the text while I made a simple 20-page book out of folded paper. I then gave them a pair of scissors and some glue and asked them to cut the text into a number of 'pages' for a picture book. They decided that the story divided well into twelve episodes and did the necessary cutting and sticking. The next stage was to work on the English version.

Just as with their early diary pieces, I did not ask for a translation. They did, however, seek to convey as much of the original text as they could. Some of the first draft of this version was written without support, while other parts are the result of quite lengthy discussions during which they generally managed to make me understand what they were trying to say and, generally, I was able to find some suitable words. Text 4 is the original draft of the first two pages.

Obviously the next stage involved editing, but again I could not use the procedure I would have used with monolingual children of the same age, which would have been to make them read the text through in the first instance to see if it made sense, especially since, by the phrase 'Does it make sense?' we generally also mean 'Do the patterns of the language correspond to your (native speaker's) intuition as to what are conventional structures?' The girls were simply not capable of the kind of immediate response to words and phrases expected of a native speaker. Instead, I asked them to focus on particular points. My first idea, running it through a spell checker, turned out not to be a great success (or any

---

SNJEZANA I SEDAM PATULJAKA.

1

Jednom davno u prijeljepom zamku ziveli su kralj i kraljica.
Ocekivali su rodjenje djeteta.

Before the king and queen lived in a palace ans thw queen was pregnant.

2

Iznenada umre kraljica i kralj ostane ozaloscenj.
Prije mnogo godina kralj se ozeni po drugi put zenom lijepom, ali okrut-
nom. Kraljica je imala svoje carobno ogledalce i sto ga je uvijek pitala
[TKO JE NAJ LIJEPSI U OVOJ KRALJEVINI].

Queen day and king kray and kray. After mach year king marid dyadar
wumen beauutyifal wumen but she is bead. Queen heav hers mirror and
what is ol ways ask mirror whu is beautyifal wumen in the this cantry.

Text 4

other kind of success!). Even after we had got round the problem of the
machine's querying every single Bosnian word, the computer was simply
not clever enough to understand the girls' intentions when their spelling
differed from the conventional by more than a letter or two. It was too
much to ask it to see *kray* as a representation of the word 'cry', for
example, or *dyadar* as 'the other'. It strengthened my belief that dictionaries and spell checkers are for people who can spell. On the other hand,
the search/replace facility was more useful, as it allowed an examination of the use of certain words.

As a rule, 1 avoid the formal teaching of points of grammar and
vocabulary, believing that when learners reach the point where they
are communicating fluently and confidently they become more adept
at mirroring the formal patterns of the speech they hear. The exercise
of editing their text did, however, offer the girls a meaningful context
in which to explore some of these patterns, so I took the time to discuss
some of them. Two recurrent problems concerned the words 'much',
'many' and 'very' and the use of both definite and indefinite articles,
words which simply don't exist in Bosnian. After separate explanations
of each of these, Selma and Semra searched through and attempted to
render at least some of these forms conventional. They found the job
difficult, but they were not completely without success. The changes to
page 5 of the story (Text 5) are fairly typical.

> The Dworfs were much skered becoos chimney was smoking. When
> dworfs camin in the hause theey saw soom girl how sleeping on the
> theem beds. Dworfs was sker. Quyklle woke up and dworfs asked Snow
> White what was her name and Snow White answered Snow White and
> Snow White. Snow White asked dwrfs how was theem names amd dworfs
> answered.

Text 5

I am certainly under no illusion that the girls would immediately
become more efficient users of (for example) definite and indefinite articles after undertaking this exercise, but it may be that it raised their
awareness of the matter and made them more ready to listen and look
out for examples of their usage. In case the last sentence seems to be a
justification of any kind of abstract, decontextualised grammar exercise,
I should stress that for the girls the activity was purposeful and practical as part of the process of editing their text in preparation for
publication. If they learnt anything about English usage it was, in their
eyes, a by-product. In addition to these guided activities the girls did
make a few alterations for the sake of sense (e.g. in Text 5 *Quyklle woke
up* becomes *She is Quyklle woke up*). Once they had done their best to
edit the work, the girls had taken the text as far as they could, so I
offered to give it a final edit, as is my usual practice with any piece of
writing. With this particular piece I tried especially to change the
wording as little as possible, so that while the text became easily compre-
hensible to the rest of the class, it remained recognisable to its authors.
I went through the edited text with the authors before typing up and
printing off a final version which was pasted into a hardback book which
we had made together. The girls then worked together for several afternoons on the illustrations. They also produced an accompanying audio
tape, which was completed on the afternoon before Selma left the school
to move to another part of the city.

Ann, Caroline and I agreed that the project had been a great success.
The book had provided a focus for my work with the girls and had
given them an absorbing long-term project. They had obviously enjoyed
the work and the opportunities it gave them to talk and write both in
Bosnian and in English. The final product was professional enough to
make an impression on the other children in the classes and to raise the
profile of the Bosnians in the school. Most importantly, over the period
of the project Selma and Semra's English had developed by leaps and
bounds. Evidence of this is to be found in their increasingly choosing

to begin their written work in English, rather than producing an English version of a Bosnian first draft. To what, then, was their success due?

In my view, the most important feature of the project was that it matched well the girls' interests, abilities and current levels of attainment. In doing this it also showed that for the work children are doing to be appropriate to their needs it is not necessary to provide them with differentiated tasks or materials. In fact, during the project period I worked with a much larger group of children writing stories, and it would have been quite feasible to have accommodated the three Bosnians within this group, ostensibly working on the same task, though with each pair approaching the work in its own individual way. I think there is a case for saying that this kind of approach offers a greater degree of differentiation than one which presents a task in two or three different formats, thereby lumping children into a limited number of broad categories. I am not unaware of the dangers of activities which are differentiated by outcome. The differences of outcome can all too easily be due to differing but unmistakable degrees of failure. This approach can work well only if all the children concerned are sufficiently supported and challenged to do the very best they are capable of. Even in activities involving the whole class it is possible, given proper planning, to ensure an appropriate level of teacher contact for each young writer. In this particular case it was easy to offer support when needed, with the need to communicate offering both support to the endeavour and a considerable challenge. The lack of any bilingual support, which had worried me at the outset, turned out, in fact, to be an advantage.

As well as my support and the support of Anne and Caroline, the girls had the support of each other. In an activity whose goal is full and clear communication the need constantly to share one's proposals with a collaborator who is both co-creator and first audience is a consistent spur to accuracy and completeness. The wider collaborative ethos in the class was a help too. In a context where children value each other's work, individual writers have the security to try out new ideas and take greater risks. The sharing of ideas and mutual support which exists in collaborative classrooms thrives on the variety of interpretations which children put on a task and on the variety of skills and experiences which each child brings to it.

The acquisition of literacy and the acquisition of a second language are both highly complex processes and it is reasonable to expect that learners will show greater skill in some elements than in others. It was obvious in the present case that Selma and Semra's proficiency in many of the skills of writing far exceeded their command of English (not to mention the various levels of attainment within these two broad areas). The open-ended nature of bilingual story writing meant that they were able to exercise all of their skills, including those rooted in their first language, at the highest possible level, and through working at this level develop them further. A further significant factor was the part played by choice. The girls had chosen the subject of their book and they had complete control over all the elements of the process of writing it. Ultimately they had the choice of whether to write or not. This meant not only that they had a personal commitment to the work, but also that they would develop the text in the way best suited to their learning needs.

The whole process of writing the book was founded on the need to communicate. The girls had to communicate clearly with each other, in Bosnian, as they negotiated what to write. Later they had to find ways of communicating their ideas to me, in English, while the final text needed to convey the story clearly in both languages. Everything the girls were doing had a genuine purpose.

All this, then, contributed to a rate of development in English and literacy which was so remarkable that it hardly seemed possible. Even if l had perhaps underestimated their knowledge of English in September (it was quite possible that they were at the 'listening' phase, which beginner bilinguals often go through before they are willing to chance using the English they have absorbed during this period) their achievements remain impressive. So, one might conclude, these were very bright children who were bound to do well, however they were taught. l would take a different view, however, believing that bright children, just like any other group of children, will not achieve their full potential unless the work they are asked to do allows them to exercise their existing skills and knowledge whilst challenging them to work in unfamiliar territory. The creation of *Snjezana/Snow White* enabled Selma and Semra to show just how accomplished they had become as users of language and of English. It also enabled them to achieve the kind of learning that is every child's right.

NOTES

1. My post is part funded by the Home Office, under Section 11 of the Local Government Act of 1966. Current Section 11 regulations promote the view that the role of the support teacher is to work in partnership with mainstream teachers to develop practice which will enable developing bilingual pupils to learn English through the medium of the (sometimes modified) mainstream curriculum.

2,. The children call the language they speak 'Bosnian'. Five years ago it would have been called Serbo-Croat, whilst in published works use of the term 'Croatian' is now becoming common. Their mother tongue is a significant part of the children's personal and national identity and for this reason, both in school and in this chapter, l follow their lead in using the term 'Bosnian'.

Part IV

Issues of assessment

Introduction to Part IV

This section takes a 'sideways look' at assessment. It is not so much concerned with 'how to do assessment' – teachers are very practised at that – but with 'why', 'what', 'when', 'how', 'where' and 'for whom'. The emphasis, time and effort spent on key stage testing has tended to shift attention away from more important questions about assessment. However, the National Curriculum claims to help teachers to:

(a) assess what each pupil knows, understands and can do;
(b) use their assessments and the programmes of study to identify the learning needs of individual pupils;
(c) plan programmes of work which take account of their pupils' attainments and allow them to work at different levels;
(d) ensure that all pupils achieve their maximum potential.

(NCC 1990)

But will it?

In both ordinary and special schools good practice is most likely to be advanced when all members of staff are committed to the same aims: providing a broad, balanced, relevant and differentiated curriculum, and raising standards for each of the pupils they teach.

(NCC 1989)

If only it were that easy – or that unproblematic!

The anodyne – and ambiguous – language of National Curriculum documents could seduce teachers into accepting differentiation as a term which does not need investigation. The invocation of 'good practice' suggests that with a nudge and a wink 'we' can all agree on just what it means and implies. As the contributions to this book demonstrate, it just isn't that easy, nor that unproblematic. 'Allowing children to work at different levels', and making assessments of 'the learning needs of individual pupils' could mean either providing an open curriculum with opportunities for active involvement in their own learning, or it might mean worksheets graded for different levels of literacy and decontextualised exercises to 'assess' learning. It could mean offering a robust, but supportive curriculum which is varied enough to provide for a range of ways in to learning or, on the other hand, 'levelling down' by not moving beyond what is contained in the National Curriculum levels of attainment. No document can be expected fully to capture the breadth and richness of learning which is possible with a fully diverse curriculum, and the terminology can be used to serve sometimes quite opposing views of educational value. Mary Jane Drummond makes explicit the unstable nature of the terminology of assessment:

> Understanding learning ... necessarily involves, for adult teachers, understanding children.... Ways of understanding children vary from place to place, from time to time from culture to culture.... As we set about assessing our pupils, we do have, deep in our mind's eye, some dearly held belief about what we are looking for.
>
> (Drummond, 1993)

These 'dearly held beliefs' realise themselves in the practices and principles which inform curriculum planning and the theoretical positions which underlie decisions about what are important educational values to any group. These theories will, in turn, inform the planning, execution and evaluation of teaching and learning. In terms of differentiation, the assessment of learning – and the relationship between assessment and planning – are important in considering how best to offer a curriculum which will offer diverse experiences for a diversity of learners.

The critical questions which need to be asked include *What is assessment for?* and *Who is it meant to inform?* Taking a critical and analytical view of curriculum and assessment decisions need not imply that careful and thoughtful assessments will not be carried out. Assessments in various forms are made by teachers every day, probably every minute. These kinds of professionally embedded assessments are most likely to be diagnostic and formative, evaluating the processes of learning and the teacher's own practice and so helping to develop plans for future learning. However, these are not the forms of assessment which have been seen as important in the National Curriculum. As a means of creating 'accountability' the formal assessment tasks at the end of each of the key stages, even with their most recent revisions, are intended to be summative and used judgementally, rather than developmentally. There is nothing wrong with the idea that any profession should be able to account for the decisions it makes in carrying out its professional responsibilities; what is questionable is the reliability of the kinds of measures used as a focus for raising issues of accountability.

One of the most effective and useful ways of accounting for what teachers do is in the careful recording of children's achievements and the regular and explicit reporting of these to colleagues, the children themselves, and to parents and carers. Much time has been spent on developing formats for such reporting; after trial and error many teachers have found that continuing records, supported by samples of children's work, most authentically help describe what children can do and how they are making progress. One carefully tested example is *The Primary Learning Record* (Hester *et al.*, 1993). In the introduction (p. 1), Hilary Hester explains the learning continuum which forms the basis of this cross-curricular record:

> This continuum describes five dimensions common to children's learning that need to be observed and recorded:
>
> - children's developing confidence and independence
> - their growing experience as learners
> - the strategies they use and develop in their learning
> - their knowledge and understanding of the subject
> - their capacity for reflecting on their learning
>
> An analysis of children's development along these dimensions yields a broad picture of their progress, and one which can be used across the curriculum.

The explanation continues:

> It is important for continuity and progression in children's learning that detailed, informative records about a child's progress and development are passed on to the next teacher.... Records that consist only of ticks and numbered boxes cannot give the in-depth information needed for further planning. What is needed is qualitative record-keeping that provides in-depth information on children's progress and development as well as summarising achievements in the National Curriculum.

What is made clear here is that 'summarising achievement' is another – and more reliable – way of assessing children's learning. Part IV begins with a thorough and thoughtful examination of the complex nature of assessment. In his chapter, 'Assessment and Diversity', Ian Frowe points out that any process of assessment or evaluation presupposes certain standards or criteria. However, simply sorting out criteria is not sufficient for adequate assessment; there are not only variations in the kinds of criteria which might be selected, but any selection of criteria will reflect the values held by those selecting them, also, there are likely to be differences in the ways in which any set of criteria might be applied. Ian Frowe carefully leads towards the view that assessment is an 'activity whose legitimation and nature must be determined by a prior examination of the process of education itself'. Our view of assessment will depend on how we view education itself. This is a fundamentally critical point; whatever might be asserted about the supposed objectivity of assessment procedures they nevertheless reflect the values held to be important by those who create and manage them. Ian Frowe warns against the dangers of settling for assessment objectives simply because they can be easily counted or because the administration of the assessments is more economical of time and money.

In this analysis, Ian Frowe makes it clear that teachers have 'a responsibility to question proposed changes and a right to be consulted'; they also have a responsibility to take a critical attitude towards educational initiatives and to guard against practices which will serve the interests neither of pupils, teachers nor society. This must apply to differentiation and assessment of learning as much as to the fundamental principles on which any view of education is built. Such a critical view will help in devising means of assessment which will be firmly interrelated to the whole process of planning and providing for learning. Assessment which involves the learners themselves, which can be made in a range of different circumstances and which reflects the widest educational aims, is that which is most likely to answer to diversity. Finally, Ian Frowe offers a critique of 'the over-determination of the content and method' of education and urges continuing debate about assessment.

The view of differentiation taken by contributors to this book is one which is predicated on diversity, which urges a view of the individual set within a frame of the communality of learning. Teachers who want to provide a variety of ways in and out of learning have to be prepared to break down some of the barriers between areas of the curriculum or processes of learning. This might mean putting more emphasis on negotiations with learners themselves in designing and carrying out activities; it also implies much more recognition of the value of greater pupil involvement.

The importance of active involvement in learning led Tatiana Wilson, the writer of the second chapter in this Part to use a range of learning experiences as means of assessing learning – none of which involved the usual formal measures of written accounts or records. In her chapter, 'Teaching the art of detection: differentiated approaches to learning and assessment or how to give all the clues without spelling out the answers', she describes how she was able to assess her Year 5 and 6 children's learning in a range of areas – historical concepts, technology, drawing, and talk – as well as involving the children themselves in negotiating and assessing their own learning. In explaining her view of the value of differentiation through the range of tasks on offer, Tatiana Wilson points out that if children are offered a variety of activities using a wide range of resources, then the assessments, too, must be as diverse as possible. Any record keeping structure will have its limitations, and she echoes Ian Frowe's view that teachers need to be alert when making assessments so that they do not go for 'over-determination of content and method'. In suggesting different ways of assessing and recording children's achievements, Tatiana Wilson offers a clear view of managing learning opportunities so that both the children and the teacher get the most out of the activities. Evaluation of learning involves teachers looking at their own practice, too, and Tatiana Wilson explains: 'From the experience I have also been able to identify many personal learning points that have influenced my classroom practice.' Her account of classroom practice gives an insight into the spiral of planning, carrying out, assessing and evaluating activities so as to plan in a more informed way for future work.

The third chapter in this part makes tongue-in-cheek reference to some of the clichés which inform the worst of educational rhetoric about raising standards. In 'Back to basics: planning for and assessing the progress of children with a range of learning difficulties', Peter Fifield's account deals with the diagnostic uses of assessment, and his development of a vocabulary through which to describe the progress of pupils who are struggling with learning, achieving at levels much below their chronological ages – for many reasons. Although these children are 12 years old, and so beyond the primary age-range, the lessons he and they learned have much to offer to teachers of younger children. The mix of ability in the class is broad, but their confidence is commonly fragile and this chapter is an example of how a set of common experiences can provide the chance for small shifts and bolder experiments. Peter Fifield gives a detailed description of each pupil's reading and writing fluency and experience and follows their progress through the small but successful steps of a poetry project which offered activities which the pupils saw as low-risk but which allowed a high yield in terms of increased confidence and achievement. The 'short sharp shock of success' which Peter Fifield wanted – and got – for this class serves as an example of how diagnostic assessments can inform teacher planning for differentiation by careful classroom management and staged and thoughtful presentation of experiences, chosen and designed for individuals within a deliberately collaborative and communal setting. Formative and summative assessments covered both the intangible areas of confidence and experience, for example, as outlined in *The Primary Learning Record*, as well as demonstrating the genuine improvements in literacy which can result from purposeful work. In this classroom the need to take account of a range of individual qualities as well as aiming to help all the pupils make progress towards confident literacy was achieved without letting the need for assessments restrict learning; rather the opposite – Peter Fifield used assessment tailored for the specific context of his classroom as a basis for pushing at the leading edges of the children's potential for learning.

Chapter 12

Assessment and diversity

Ian Frowe

Of the many changes which have occurred in education over the last ten years the raised profile of assessment and testing is one of the most obvious and dramatic. Education is not an isolated case, for the growth in a demand that various 'services' be subjected to a thorough going appraisal of their 'effectiveness', 'efficiency', 'quality' and 'value for money' has been ubiquitous. In the days before the implementation of a compulsory curriculum within the state sector, the amount of testing or assessment undertaken by schools was largely a matter resting within the discretion of particular establishments, perhaps further informed by the wishes of the local education authority. Most schools assessed basic literacy and numeracy using the well-known tests available but beyond this there was little uniformity in content, type or regularity of procedure. The weekly spelling test was probably the highest common factor to be found.

The curriculum – certainly in the primary sector where the determining influence of public examinations had largely diminished – varied considerably across the country and although there was some common ground, schools were allowed to tailor their teaching along individual lines. The effect of this was that in many primary schools subjects which are now compulsory were absent or of a radically different nature; for generations of primary school children 'science' *was* tadpoles, frogs, leaves and trees. Similarly, the effect of a statutory curriculum may well have removed, or significantly decreased, the presence of activities which previously enjoyed a place in the school day.

In a situation of such variability any attempt to undertake a systematic and extensive assessment of children's abilities in different areas of the curriculum was clearly going to be fraught with problems. It is obviously unfair, and to some extent pointless, to try and gauge a child's understanding or knowledge of a subject of which they have little or no experience. The introduction of a common curriculum changed the position completely. Now that all children in state schools were legally required to follow the same courses of study in the same subjects, be

assessed by the same national tests at the same stages of their schooling, it would be far easier to measure the progress being achieved,
identify schools who were not up to standard and provide parents
with 'objective' evidence as to the effectiveness of the education their
children were receiving. In the early days it was intended that children
be assessed in all ten National Curriculum subjects against a ten-point
scale covering the period of compulsory schooling from 5 to 16. The
relative paucity of knowledge of those with direct teaching experience
on the curriculum working parties combined with a selective deafness,
enabled this *ignis fatuus* to present itself as a practical proposition for a
considerable period. The inevitable, although protracted, re-entry to the
real world of schools, children, teachers and the fixed period of the
earth's rotation led to a considerable slimming down of this ambition
with assessment being confined to the three core subjects of mathematics,
science and English. Although there is now some light on the horizon,
the pressure on teachers to assess their pupils against a plethora of attainment targets left little time, and no doubt little inclination, for any serious
reflection upon the underlying issues presupposed by the exercise of
assessment procedures. At a time when the screw is being released to
some extent, an examination of such questions is apposite. The main
purpose of this chapter is to explore some of these underlying questions
and indicate how assessment is related to fundamental concerns
regarding the value and nature of education. The discussion begins with
an examination of the notion of 'criteria', then considers the relationship
between assessment and different conceptions of education and finally
deals with some of the problems which can arise when assessment is
conceived of in a narrow fashion.

ASSESSMENT AND CRITERIA

Assessment is something of which we all have a vast wealth of experience. Everyday we assess numerous aspects of our life from the quality
of books we read to the effectiveness of soap powders. Often we carry
out these assessments in an almost automatic fashion; we cannot help
but engage in the process of evaluation, for many of the choices and
decisions we routinely make are based on such a process. We do not
normally carry on our everyday existence in a completely random,
arbitrary fashion but exercise judgement in order to weigh up various
alternatives and produce informed, discriminating choices. If someone
decides to change their car they do not normally open the local paper
on the appropriate page, close their eyes and stick a pin at random into
the paper, the car thus 'selected' constituting their 'choice'. Rather, they
select a car on the basis of a consideration of various factors which will
narrow down the range of possible alternatives. They may want a vehicle

within a certain price band, that is economical, easy to service, environ-
mentally friendly, etc. On the other hand, someone else may desire a
car which is powerful, expensive to maintain and conveys the appropriate image. Clearly the choices made by two such individuals will be
very different because their selection has been informed by different
considerations. Neither will have chosen randomly but they have chosen
differently because they have employed different *criteria*.

This example illustrates a necessary feature of any process of assessment or evaluation: it presupposes the existence of standards or criteria.
This presupposition is a logical presupposition; without criteria no
assessment is possible. In the two cases above different sets of criteria
were employed so different assessments were made. Without some
criteria, however, no assessment at all could have been made.

What exactly are we doing when we assess something? Essentially
we are engaged in a process of *comparison*: we're comparing something
with something else. In the case of the car above we are comparing
different cars with a set of criteria – cost, reliability, ease of maintenance,
power, etc. – and judging how individual models match up to these
criteria. Based on how they do (or do not) match up, a decision can be
reached which represents an informed choice, a choice achieved through
a process of comparative assessment or evaluation.

In the example above and in numerous others, the criteria employed
are personal. By 'personal' I mean that the criteria used are such that
individuals are free to decide for themselves which criteria they will
employ. Many of our choices in life are based on personal criteria –
clothes, home decoration, holidays, food; in these areas of life people
are, given some obvious caveats, free to exercise choice with regard
only to those criteria they wish to employ. Of course, fashion, custom,
tradition or coercive laws may hinder or restrict such choices producing
a uniformity. Restrictions of these kinds may be freely entered into,
perhaps through religious beliefs, or externally imposed, perhaps
through political force. In societies where diversity is valued, the ability
to exercise particularistic judgements through personal deliberation
rooted in individual criteria is seen as highly desirable. Liberal societies,
in contrast to the authoritarian, are characterised by a concern that, wher-
ever possible, individuals should be free to exercise their own judgement
when making decisions about how to live their lives.

There are, however, limits to the areas of life where the criteria used
to assess or evaluate something can be personal. Criteria may be
'publicly' determined not only through the influence of religious, political or social forces but also because a consensus as to the relevant criteria
to be used may arise from a consideration of the nature of that which
is to be assessed. In certain cases there is little or no room for personal
criteria to operate. Whereas in the case of, say, home furnishings there

are no publicly established criteria such that an individual's choice could be shown to be 'wrong', 'incorrect' or 'inferior' if the individual concerned thought otherwise, in some areas judgements can be made which have a far more objective basis. In these instances it is just not an option to employ radically different criteria without lapsing into incoherence or irrationality.

Opticians use a variety of tests in order to assess a person's eyesight. By comparing an individual's responses to an established set of criteria it is possible to judge their eyesight as average, below or above average. The criteria used are 'public' criteria in the sense that there exists a widespread consensus as to their appropriateness in the assessment of visual ability. If I were to claim that my eyesight was excellent despite the fact that I continually scored below average in the tests, then unless I could provide some convincing reason to the effect that established methods of testing eyesight were radically flawed or that 'excellence' in eyesight needed to be understood in a completely different way, my claim would be rightly rejected as mistaken. Similarly if I rested my claim on the belief that the criteria for assessing eyesight involved the colour of your eyes, whether you had children or not, or what political party you voted for, these also would be dismissed as 'criteria' inappropriate for the assessment of eyesight. In a case such as this I am simply not free to formulate my own criteria and expect to have them considered as equally valid as that which is publicly accepted.

The strictly personal and the publicly agreed represent the poles of a continuum, the former characterising areas of choice where individual fiat may legitimately hold sway and the latter those areas where it may not. In between, as we might expect, the position becomes more complex, interesting and contested. Here there are real disagreements and debates regarding the criteria by which various things are to be assessed or evaluated. Obvious examples of areas where rival or competing criteria exist would be art, morality, politics and religion. Disputes and disagreements arise for a variety of reasons but one central cause is that the criteria by which works of art, actions, laws or beliefs are evaluated are heterogeneous not homogeneous. The criteria used are not idiosyncratic but neither are they objective in the strong sense that the criteria for testing eyesight could claim. They are public in the sense that a significant number of people may hold them and may be more or less coherent such that not anything can be a possible standard for evaluation or assessment. Amongst these diverse sets of criteria there will clearly be areas of common ground but also, in many cases, profound polarity and exclusion. Consequently, the same object, action or belief may be assessed in very different ways by groups who bring particular sets of criteria to bear upon it. (The now almost *de rigueur* public dissent amongst the judges for literary or artistic awards illustrates the difficulties that supposedly informed persons run up against in their assessment of various works.) This issue will be further examined below but first I want to introduce a consideration which follows from the need for criteria.

I want to move the discussion to a more clearly educational context. The first part of this chapter attempted to show, amongst other points, that any process of assessment logically presupposes the existence of criteria. If appropriate criteria do exist then a second question arises: 'Is it possible to determine whether the criteria have been met?' (This is clearly subsequent upon a positive answer to the prior enquiry as to the existence of any criteria.)

In many cases appropriate criteria do exist and it is a fairly straight-forward matter to decide whether they are met. For example, if a requirement for receiving a swimming certificate was the ability to tread water for one minute, then i) there exist criteria to assess this and ii) it is fairly easy to tell if the criteria have been met. The criteria are public criteria; it is not possible to invoke just *any* criteria to assess this, for example knowledge of Olympic gold medalists, and because we are concerned with overt behaviour, it is relatively simple to decide whether the observed performance meets the criteria. In instances such as this we are not concerned with assessing anything which might be termed 'understanding' or 'knowledge' (above a minimal understanding of knowing 'what to do'); successful performance is both the necessary and sufficient condition.

Next, take the case where we are asked to assess, say, whether a child can draw a square or not. Here there are public criteria regarding what a square is; it is not an option to have personal criteria involving such things as 'has five sides', or 'contains no right angles'. The second question – 'Is it possible to determine whether the criteria have been met?' – may not, however, be quite as easy to answer as in the example above. We are presented with a figure which we can compare with the established criteria in order to see whether it meets them. The problem now is that it is conceivable that given the same figure, two people may disagree as to whether what is presented actually counts as a square, for example the lines are not straight enough or the angles are not recognisable as right angles, etc. The disagreement is not about what a square *is* – the criteria themselves are not in dispute – but if this figure *satisfies* the criteria. The example may seem trivial but the underlying point is not; people may agree about the criteria for assessing something but still disagree about whether what is presented fulfils those agreed criteria.

Children's writing has been the subject of much debate in recent years and highlights many of the problems encountered in assessment. Imagine we were asked to assess a piece of writing produced by a child of 9 or 10 years. Are there any criteria by which we can assess this? Clearly there are – spelling, vocabulary, neatness, originality, self-expression, paragraphing, coherence, honesty, vitality, handwriting, length, interest, imagination, style . . . Given a piece of writing there is no shortage of criteria by means of which it may be assessed. The first problem that arises is over which criteria to employ; should all the above be used, in which case should they all have equal weighting or should some be seen as more important than others? Should some be ignored? In a case such as this, disagreement may result not at the secondary level of whether the criteria have been met, although this can also occur, but at the more basic one of which criteria should be used.

It is clearly open for people to disagree about which criteria should be used and/or to rank criteria differently in order of importance. One person may believe that what is important at this stage of a child's education is proficiency in the technical aspects of writing – spelling, handwriting, sentence construction, punctuation, etc. – and assess highly a piece which exhibits these qualities. Conversely another may feel that what is important is imagination, originality, interest, vitality, etc. and rate these as more important than the technical skills. Many may see both elements as of value but there will be a significant number whose opinions pull heavily in one direction rather than the other. (Incidentally to assess a piece of writing against both sets of criteria equally is not a solution to this problem but simply to adopt one position which sees the two sets of criteria as of equal value – others will not see them as of equal value.) The technical aspects of writing are generally more easily assessed because the criteria governing punctuation, spelling, etc. are public, whereas notions such as interest, imagination, etc. are more difficult to tie down; what one person finds interesting and imaginative another may not.

The situation is complex. We have a range of criteria by means of which we may assess something (in the case above, a piece of writing), some of the criteria are public whereas others are more subjective. There may be disagreement about i) which criteria are to be used; ii) what importance is to be attached to these criteria, that is, how are they to be ranked; iii) how these criteria are to be interpreted; and iv) whether the criteria used have been satisfied.

Education, no less than art, morality or politics, is an activity about which there exists a wide range of views regarding the practices, values and purposes which should inform its operation. As there exist, for example, rival notions as to what the purpose(s) or goal(s) of education should be, any attempt to gauge the 'success' or 'failure' of an education system will be contingent upon which purposes or goals are selected. If there were one universally accepted goal for education, for example, to fit people for employment, then the success or failure of the system might be measured in a fairly crude fashion simply by ascertaining what percentage of school leavers gained jobs on completing their education. However, even if this goal were accepted there would still be room for disagreement about *how* best to prepare people for employment; what type of education should they receive – a narrow vocational approach or a more liberal, wider ranging one? What, precisely, does it mean to 'fit people for employment'? Once one recognises the diversity of goals or ends that have been proposed for education – autonomy, self-realisation, happiness, employability, knowledge acquisition, liberation, the needs of society, authenticity, good citizens, to mention but a few – then the position is far from straightforward.

The implications of this for any process of assessment are fundamental. If we ask why different criteria are employed, or why criteria are ranked in different ways, or why criteria are interpreted in different ways, then the answers to these questions cannot be supplied simply by a closer examination of the process of assessment itself. The process of assessment cannot tell us which criteria to use or what value to attach to certain criteria or how we should interpret criteria. Neither can it tell us *what* we should assess or *why* we should assess. The answers to these questions can only be found at a deeper level of inquiry where we reflect upon the underlying goals, principles and values of education. On this view, assessment cannot be conceived of as a uniform, 'bolt-on' accessory to the educational enterprise but rather an activity whose legitimation and nature must be determined by a prior examination of the process of education itself. How we view assessment is dependent on how we view education and as there is no one view of education there cannot be only one view of assessment.

Consider the question 'Why assess this?' If we assess something it is presumably because we think it is important. There are numerous things which we never assess although it would be quite easy to do so, for example we do not assess children's ability to spit, eat large quantities of food or their knowledge of swear words. Only under radically altered circumstances might proficiency in such areas take on an urgency lacking at present. It would be absurd to say, 'I think it is important to assess children's progress in x but I don't attach any value to x', (unless the 'importance' was of a prudential nature rather than an educational one). What we choose to assess is not a neutral procedure but reflects certain values which we hold and consider to be important. Asked to justify our decision to assess x, y or z the expectation will be that we provide a rationale which goes beyond a simple rejoinder to the effect that x, y and z are easy to assess therefore I assess them or, in a different vein, that I have been told to assess them. What ought to be forthcoming is a justification which seeks to situate their importance in a wider and deeper analysis of the nature of education, perhaps relating the process of education itself to moral, social, religious or political concerns. In the case, for example, of assessing children's reading, the justification for this would include the central place occupied by the ability to read in educational advancement, its utility and the pleasure to be gained from it, and the serious disadvantages which will attend those who fail to acquire this ability in terms of their future life choices. We may also point to the need for a democratic society to have an educated citizenry and, although not all ideas, opinions and beliefs are transmitted through the written word, to be barred from this source is highly debilitating. Thus the ability to read links to several of the proposed ends for education such as autonomy, employability or knowledge acquisition. However, whilst there is widespread agreement on the desirability of reading ability and, hence the need that it be regularly assessed, this is not the case in other areas.

ASSESSMENT AND CONCEPTIONS OF EDUCATION

The longstanding debate between so-called 'progressive' or 'child-centred' theorists and their 'traditionalist' or 'subject-centred' counterparts provides a clear example of the relationship between assessment and fundamental conceptions of education. Briefly, the progressive view emphasises the cultivation of particular attitudes and dispositions within the pupil whilst allowing the content and methods of learning to be flexible and arising through negotiation between pupil and teacher. What is learnt is considered of less importance than how it is learnt – the spirit within which learning occurs. There is a distinction made between learning conceived of as the accumulation of various pieces of knowledge and 'real' learning where what is learnt has personal significance for the learner via its origination in his or her individual concerns and commitments. Depth of understanding and knowledge are more important than breadth. Co-operation is rated above competition and the ends of education are characterised in terms of independence in thought and action and a questioning attitude to life.

The traditionalist view emphasises the need for all children to acquire particular abilities, skills and knowledge through a curriculum whose content is open to little or no negotiation and draws heavily on the established subject disciplines. There is an assumption that children, being 'children', lack the experience, rationality and foresight of adults and thus are ill-equipped to play any significant role in determining the course of their own education. The individual concerns of children are largely irrelevant in the process of their education. There is the belief that children should be introduced to a wide range of disciplines with their learning being strongly teacher-directed. Competition is often used as a motivating force and the ends of education cashed out in terms of the production of knowledgeable, useful members of society who, whilst possessing critical faculties, are largely respectful and supportive of established institutions and values.

It needs to be borne in mind that both these philosophies of education see the education they provide as in the best interest of the children who undergo it and society at large. It is immediately apparent that these two positions have different priorities and purposes, which stem from deep-seated differences regarding such things as the nature of learning and knowledge, the nature of children and what they can contribute to their education, the role of the teacher, the relationship between education and the state and what qualities of personality should be fostered and valued. Given these differences of orientation, what will be the function and character of assessment within each?

Within the traditional approach, assessment has always been a high priority. The requirement that all children acquire proficiency in a set of predetermined curriculum goals entails regular monitoring of progress to ensure that this is occurring. As content is drawn from established disciplines and the emphasis is on knowledge acquisition, traditional views can justify the use of uniform, public examinations in order to assess pupils' progress. 'Success' is primarily to be understood as achievement in public examinations where knowledge of a wide range of subjects is tested.

The progressive position is different. The acquisition of specific content is seen as of less importance than the 'spirit' in which learning takes place and whether what is learnt has personal significance for the learner – and is 'real learning'. From this view, learning is essentially individualistic; each child will learn what he or she chooses to learn in consultation with the teacher. As depth of learning is considered more important than breadth, there will be no compulsion to make sure that pupils acquire knowledge over a wide range of subjects, rather the emphasis will be on allowing individuals to pursue those aspects in which they find meaning and value. The nature of assessment in this conception of education is going to be far removed from that found in the traditional version.

Assessment will need to be more individual, tailored to the specific learning which a child has undertaken. The use of public examinations which assume a common curriculum content and wish to measure knowledge acquisition over a wide range of subjects will be seen as inappropriate. Indeed the very notion of 'success' will be understood in a different way with less concentration on academic achievement in public examinations and more on the development of attitudes and dispositions towards learning and life in general. This position is explored by Michael Bonnett in his book *Children's Thinking* (Bonnett

1994). Bonnett argues strongly against the idea of a curriculum governed by a set of pre-specified learning objectives against which all children will be assessed. He writes:

> close pre-specification of learning objectives on anything but an individual basis is likely to be highly detrimental to the learners who are at the centre of the exercise. Such pre-specification ignores the myriad routes it is often possible to take through our complex web of interrelated concepts, and infringes the freedom of individual children in negotiation with informed teachers to follow those paths which have most personal meaning.
>
> (Bonnett 1994: 87)

The objection here is not simply about the nature or content of a set of pre-specified ends such that we may agree on the desirability of a set of ends but disagree about what they should be, but to the idea of pre-specified ends in general, irrespective of what they might be. Writing from a stance firmly within the child-centred tradition, Bonnett sees learning as individualistic and taking its cue from those interests and concerns which have personal significance for the pupil, consequently the educative process is always 'open' in the sense that its course cannot be mapped out in advance and then imposed on all children. Indeed, what characterises a process as educative is not the reaching of some pre-specified goal but the spirit in which one embarks on a journey whose destination is unknown.

One implication of this position for assessment is that the process may only occur retrospectively: we cannot decide in advance of any experiences what to assess because we do not know what experiences the child will have. Similarly, the choice of what to assess from a set of experiences, considered retrospectively, will need to reflect in part the importance attached to those experiences *by the child* not just the teacher. What emerges from this account of education is the implausibility of seeing assessment as any sort of universal, 'bolt-on' auxiliary whose nature and purpose can be determined independently of our deeper reflections regarding the enterprise as a whole.

The relative merits of the traditional and progressive approaches – and both have their strengths and weaknesses – is beside the present point; what they illustrate is that whichever position you adopt will influence how you see assessment. The values and principles of each supply the criteria which enable the process to take place, but as these values and principles are different, so too will be the criteria they produce. Having said that the merits of these positions are beside the point, any attempt to evaluate the methods of assessment each advocates will *of necessity* have to engage with the philosophical theories and beliefs which underpin the practices.

ASSESSMENT AND PRACTICE

There is a danger, long acknowledged although often ignored, concerning the relationship between assessment and the process of education where assessment gains the upper hand and rather than being subservient to the activity of education, effectively shapes and controls that activity. As Barrow remarks, 'the nature of education can and should dictate the methods of assessment, rather than the science of assessment be allowed to dictate the nature of educational experience' (Barrow 1984: 235).

The use of the phrase 'science of assessment' is contentious: it is far from evident that the process of assessment always meets the conditions which would be required for it to claim to be 'scientific'. True, in certain areas of assessment we may be able to claim some degree of objectivity, but this will be those cases where the criteria are agreed and it is fairly easy to decide whether or not they have been satisfied. The belief that assessment can always claim to be 'scientific', ignores its limitations and suggests an authority which, outside a narrow area, is spurious. Consider the manner in which the assessment of 'intelligence' portrayed itself during this century as a 'scientific' undertaking. The elaborate use of mathematical processes – formulae, graphs, statistics – and scientific testing methods was intended to persuade that what was being measured was a quality or capacity whose precise value could be accurately quantified. Even if we accept that the tests measured some- thing, to identify that 'something' with 'intelligence' is to engage in a procrustean exercise. A narrow, degenerate conception of 'intelligence' was presented as *the* definitive account of what intelligence was, an account legitimised by the 'scientific' nature of its divination. When one also reflects upon the decisions regarding the appropriate course of a child's education which were made on the basis of such tests, the age at which the tests were often carried out and the scarcely veiled ideo- logical motivation which ignored serious deficiencies within the entire project, then the dangers of claiming a 'scientific' basis for some kinds of assessments is clear. The desire to quantify abilities or capacities is strong but the perceived authority of numbers over words can be misplaced, misleading and mistaken.

Barrow's main point, however, is well made; some things are much easier to assess than others, be they pieces of knowledge or abilities, and the danger is that priority may be given to such things simply because they are easily assessable. It is straightforward to judge whether someone can run 100m. in under 15 seconds or knows the names of Henry VIII's six wives. At a higher level, although there is more room for manoeuvre, it is still possible with a fair degree of confidence to assess whether a person can throw a coil pot or knows the causes of the

French Revolution. Whilst such knowledge and abilities may well constitute an important aspect of gaining an education, there are many other
elements whose importance may be equal or greater but far more difficult to assess. In a system which is assessment-driven the temptation to
ignore that which is difficult to assess and to concentrate on that which
is relatively simple can be difficult to resist.

If assessment is motivated by the need to select pupils or provide
'hard' evidence for parents (often in a quantified form) then the temptation to concentrate on those aspects which are relatively easy to assess
because they are largely objectively assessable, is clear. In such a situation simple 'paper and pencil' tests may suffice and given the demands
for published school results, league tables and performance related pay,
the pressure to mould one's teaching to fit the tests may appear simple
prudence. This amounts to nothing less than a distortion of the educational enterprise, for rather than deciding what, how and why we are
to assess through a prior reflection upon our underlying values and
principles, the need to assess and assess in a particular way takes centre
stage and determines the nature of education itself. The more specific
the to-be-assessed learning outcomes, the greater the pressure to gear
the process of education to service these objectives. The whole activity
becomes assessment-driven with a shift toward those abilities or pieces
of learning which best fit the needs of assessment.

Why should such a move be resisted? One argument would be that
the imposition of a uniform set of assessment procedures measuring
pupil progress against a list of pre-specified objectives will, of necessity,
reflect a particular selection of those things which it is thought all children should know. This choice will not be neutral but will reflect the
values of those who have drawn it up; it will stress the importance
of certain values whilst ignoring or marginalising others. The danger is
that the imposed values may well be chosen not on educational grounds,
but on a far more pragmatic basis reflecting the interests of particular
sections of society. Groups who can wield influence and power and have
access to extensive resources, can effectively present their own position
in ways not open to those who lack equivalent means. (It should be
noted that there is no necessary connection between the ability to ensure
a particular set of values are seen as dominant and the extent to which
such views are widely held. An illustration of this phenomenon might
be the way in which the ethos of the National Health Service has been
altered by the importation of commercial values and practices when it
is far from apparent that this view attracts widespread public support.)

If the pre-specified objectives are largely framed in terms of the
acquisition of propositional knowledge, that is, knowledge capable of
being expressed in propositional form, then whilst this is an important
type of knowledge, it is not inclusive of all kinds of knowledge. Much

of the knowledge we acquire is essentially non-propositional in character: it cannot be adequately expressed in a set of propositions. This non-propositional knowledge is gained through experience, through spending time engaging in particular activities whether practical or intellectual. There are ways of thinking, acting and judging which cannot be set out in a sort of 'how to do it' manual consisting of a set of propositions. If, for example, becoming a good teacher required only propositional knowledge, then once conversant with the 'manual' anyone who adhered to the propositions contained in it, would be a good teacher. However, this is not how things work in practice – despite the obvious wish in some quarters that they did. Whilst this 'expertise' or 'professional' knowledge may well be assessable in some ways it clearly cannot be assessed under any system which is exclusively concerned to assess only propositional knowledge.

By allowing assessment to govern educational practices and accepting a concomitant siting of educational importance upon a set of (easily) measured proficiencies, we are liable to lose sight of the more fundamental qualities which supply the process with purpose and value. Often these qualities, which we may see as constituitive of education, are assessable only in the most informal, impressionist fashion and yet they underpin most of what teachers do. They may be aspects of the intellect – rigour, imagination, impartiality, love of a subject – or more general personality traits – modesty, tolerance, truthfulness, generosity, a sense of justice and morality, etc. Such qualities exhibit an 'indetermination'; we could never produce a list of objectives in order to assess compassion or imagination. These attributes develop slowly; we may never know whether efforts to promote such qualities have been successful, but this fact should not divert us from a belief that the promotion of such qualities is at the centre of education. Their resistance to simple assessment or quantification may well lead to their being relegated to the lower divisions, there to languish whilst the 'real' business of education steams ahead. Just as the fact that something is measurable does not mean it is of any significance or interest, so the fact that something may be extremely difficult to measure does not mean that it may not be of the greatest significance and interest.

Despite the efforts in recent years to 'de-professionalise' teaching many practitioners still consider themselves to be members of a profession rather than simply paid employees. One of the characteristics of a profession is that its members have the right and duty to speak out on issues of a broad and general kind which affect their work. Judges and doctors see their role as not exclusively confined to the administering of punishments or potions to the wayward or sick, but also to comment on the state of the law or medicine in general. They have a responsibility to question proposed changes and a right to be consulted. Teachers, in so far as they see themselves as professionals, similarly take on this wider public role to comment on, and be involved in, the formulation of educational policy. Their duty to the educational well-being of the pupils they teach requires a vigilant and critical attitude towards all educational initiatives lest practices may appear whose purposes run counter to the interests of both teachers and learners. Given the central role which assessment plays in the education system it is incumbent upon teachers to seek out and scrutinise the underlying assumptions and values which inform various conceptions of assessment and decide to what degree they benefit or harm the process of education.

CONCLUSION

The discussion above has attempted to show that the process of assessment is a complex business. The complexity arises not from problems regarding the validity, reliability or statistical analysis of assessment procedures – although these aspects represent another area of complexity – but at a more fundamental level which involves the values we hold and the way we view the educational enterprise as a whole. Whilst in certain areas a fairly widespread consensus exists regarding the desirability that children acquire basic abilities and knowledge, for example numeracy and literacy, outside of this rather narrow common ground there are real differences of opinion regarding how the education of children should proceed and, consequently, what role the process of assessment should play in that education.

It is sometimes claimed that politics should be kept out of education. However, a moment's thought reveals the absurdity of this position. All political theories make educational demands. In order to answer the question 'What should be the aims of education?', the prior inquiry 'What kind of society do we want?' presents itself. This latter question is a political question for it asks us to consider how we are to live together. Whatever our reply to this (and there are many possible replies, some of which are incompatible) it will influence the sort of education system we wish to see, for we will want a system which reflects the values of our vision of society and which prepares young people to become members of that society. Any society which contains a diversity of social visions will therefore contain a diversity of views as to the nature and aims of education and, as I have tried to show above, these competing views will produce differing accounts of assessment. (A parallel argument to this one based on the interconnection between politics and education could also be made out for religious or cultural visions.)

At a time when the bureaucratisation of education seems to be in abeyance and there are inklings of a recognition that the over-determination of content and method may not be the *summum bonum* once imagined, combined with a renewed interest in the place of values in education, a more informed and eclectic debate on the nature and function of assessment may be forthcoming.

REFERENCES

Barrow, R. (1984) *Giving Teaching Back To Teachers* Brighton, Wheatsheaf.
Bonnett, M. (1994) *Children's Thinking*, London, Cassell

Chapter 13

Teaching the art of detection

Differentiated approaches to learning and assessment, or how to give, all the clues without spelling out the answers[1]

Tatiana Wilson

The assessment of learning depends on the opportunities which have been offered for learning. This chapter emphasises the importance of giving children the chance to be actively involved in their own learning, and how it can be practically provided for. I hope to demonstrate the benefits of such an approach when teaching children with a wide variety of needs and abilities, through an account of a project undertaken by my school with Zoe Brooks from the Vauxhall Saint Peter's Heritage Centre in London.

I work in an inner city junior school. We have 25 languages represented in a roll of about 150 children. Seventy per cent of our roll are eligible for free school dinners. We are also special in the respect that we have an Autistic Unit in our school with which we actively try to integrate according to each child's individual needs. Our Borough is unusual in that it does not have a local history museum, so when I first heard about Zoe's work at the Vauxhall Heritage Centre I was keen to establish links. What she proposed was to work with individual schools putting together travelling exhibitions about the local area and its history.

Two Year 5/6 classes, including my own, agreed to work with Zoe on a project about Victorian Vauxhall. From the outset the focus was the exhibition. It was to be an exhibition that other schools in the area would be able to use for themselves. The children were given an audience and a purpose for their work along with real deadlines. These were all important factors which contributed to the project's success. They also placed assessment in a purposeful framework.

USING ARTEFACTS

We told the children that they were 'history detectives'. They had to look for evidence and clues about the past and to question the reliability of their sources. This was first put to them when they were asked to try and identify a collection of mysterious objects that had been found

nearby. They included a milk cooler, an inkwell, a bell, some frag-
ments of pottery with writing on them, bits of clay pipe and a sweet
wrapper.

The children first had to work out if any of the artefacts were unlikely
to be Victorian. The sweet wrapper was eliminated as it looked too new
and was thought to be litter from the present – which indeed it was. In
groups they then had to try and work out what the objects were and
what they told us about everyday Victorian life. For example, the milk
cooler told us that the Victorians did not have electricity or fridges, that
they did not have refuse collection like ours and that they buried what
they could not recycle (the milk cooler had been found buried at the
end of a garden). This also meant that the Victorians had to shop more
frequently and preserve food in different ways. The children then represented their findings in spider charts (Illustration 1).

This activity was a wonderful starting point to our work as the skills
involved mainly included speaking and listening to other people's
ideas about the artefacts. The artefacts themselves were there and could
be touched. It opened up historical research as something anyone can

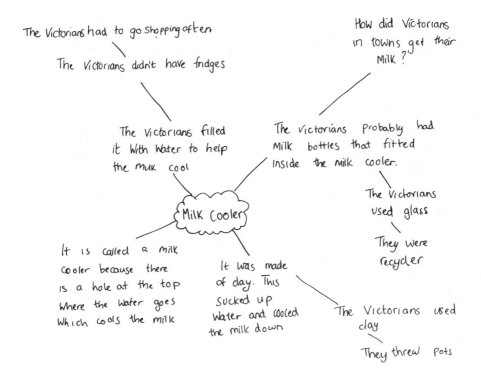

Illustration 1

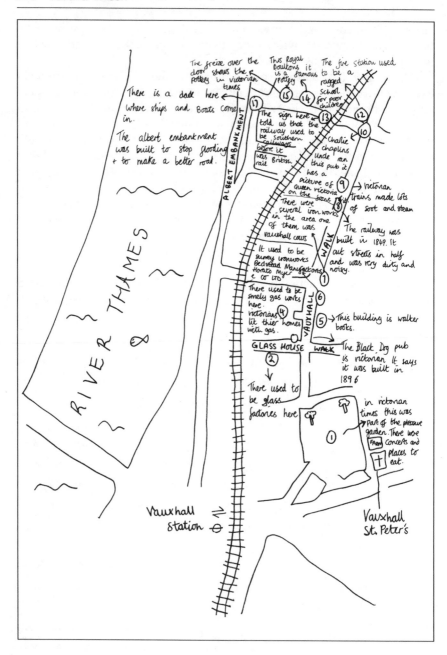

The freize over the door shows the pottery in victorian times

This Royal Doultons it is a famous pottery

The fire station used to be a ragged school for poor children

There is a dock here where ships and Boats come in.

The albert embankment was built to stop flooding + to make a better road.

ALBERT EMBANKMENT

The sign here told us that the railway used to be southern railways before it was British rail

Charlie chaplins Uncle ran this pub it has a picture of Queen victoria on the front

→ victorian trains made lots of soot and steam

There were several iron works in the area one of them was vauxhall cars

The railway was built in 1849. It cut streets in half and was very dirty and noisy.

It used to be surrey ironworks Bedstead Manufactores Horace Myer & co LTD

WALK

There used to be smely gas works here. victorian lit thier homes with gas.

VAUXHALL

→ This building is walter books.

GLASS HOUSE

WALK

The Black Dog pub is victorian It says it was built in 1896

There used to be glass factories here

in victorian times this was part of the pleasure garden. There were concerts and places to eat.

Vauxhall Station

Vauxhall St. Peter's

RIVER THAMES

Illustration 2

do, even if reading and writing are not their strengths, and gave us valuable opportunities for assessing their abilities to make deductions from non-literary historical sources.

The spider charts also helped the children to order their conclusions about the artefacts in a clear and concise way and to distinguish between what they could tell by looking at the artefact, for example the milk cooler was made of clay – the Victorians threw pots, and what they could further deduce from the artefactual evidence, for example the Victorians probably had milk bottles that fitted inside the cooler. The children's imaginations were immediately captured and this resulted in several excavations of the school garden and surrounding plots of land. As a class we categorised these findings of pottery, glass, stones and bones.

USING THE LOCAL ENVIRONMENT

The children participated in an historical walk. This took a specific route that Zoe had planned as being most instructive. Every fifty yards the children were confronted with a different Victorian phenomenon, for example, a ragged-school site, building inscriptions, old railway plaques, a dock, street names, public houses, factories and Victorian industries. The walk worked very well as the children enjoyed immediate success as they were able to see for themselves concrete evidence of a Victorian presence in Vauxhall and to recognise this, albeit with support, despite newer buildings and changing building uses in the area.

When we returned to class the children worked together in groups producing annotated route maps of their walk. To help them to do this they had a street map of the locality, the results of the work-sheets that they had taken with them and photographs of the things we saw on the walk. Having done the walk together they were able to make good representations of what they had seen; they could also name familiar features on their maps and comment on past and present building and land use (see Illustration 2).

USING THE LOCAL COMMUNITY

We also visited St Peter's Church where the Vauxhall Heritage Centre is based. Here again the children were detectives, finding out about Victorian Christian religion. We listened to the acoustics of the church and discussed its internal architecture. We looked at the baptistry, statues, pews, doorway, inscriptions and other main Victorian features which gave us clues to the past. Being in a church that still had a congregation as well as several other roles also gave the children a better understanding of how the function of many churches has changed in contemporary society. One of the children in the group worshipped at the church and he was able to explain how the services were conducted now and this gave his peers a useful comparison with Victorian Christian worship. For a few children this was a highlight as they had never set foot inside a church before. This hands-on approach and the worksheet that went with the activity enabled the children to glean a strong picture of what the church and its services may have been like.

USING PEOPLE

An unexpected discovery was that one of the class actually worshipped at the church. Using his expertise was also very beneficial as he was able to bring another dimension to class discussions that would otherwise not have been there – his own experience and perceptions. Seeing a peer as a resource was a really positive experience for everyone; it added a further dimension to the range of historical resources the children tapped in to, from artefacts, maps, real places to people and later on to photographs and archive material.

WIDENING THE PROJECT'S FOCUS

After these four common experiences – looking at the artefacts, the walk, drawing annotated maps and comparing maps over time, as well as the visit to St Peter's Church – the children then split into groups to collect and analyse further data for the exhibition. Having given the children the same initial stimuli and core of experiences they had a common starting point to help them in this further research. In a similar way to the previous work they had done, these new research groups had an emphasis on detecting as well as reporting back important findings to their peers and collating their findings for the exhibition.

USING PHOTOGRAPHIC EVIDENCE

One group of children looked at photographic evidence of the River Thames before the Albert Embankment was built and discussed what they could detect from the images. From these the children then had to select the pictures which they felt would be most beneficial for others to see in the exhibition. The children managed to draw a lot of information from the photographs and were able to comment on their relative usefulness to the exhibition. Recording the things that were said was a useful form of assessment as it highlighted the processes that the children went through together before making their decisions. The children selected five photographic images that they felt captured life on the Thames before the Albert Embankment was built. They then explained their final choices orally to their peers who were in turn able to see the evidence for themselves. It was only after this that they were asked to write about one of the photographs that they had chosen and the evidence that it had provided. By this point the children were clear in their own minds about what the photographs showed and they were therefore able confidently to draw their conclusions.

Interestingly, though, when they came to put their work together for the exhibition, their writing was not included as they felt that it would stop other children from being detectives themselves and would therefore be less interesting to the 'reader'. Clearly the children were developing quite a sophisticated understanding of the thinking that needs to go on behind the planning of a successful exhibition. They were able to appreciate the activities that they found the most interesting and to conclude that a good exhibition, in their opinion, was one which gave all the clues without necessarily spelling out all the answers for the reader.

The photographic work led on to research into the life of Henry Doulton, his pottery and the Lambeth School of Art. These had previously been touched on by everyone on our historic walk when we passed the Royal Doulton building and admired its carvings and decorative exterior. The children were able to get their information from a variety of sources including Royal Doulton itself and this work complemented what had gone on before.

USING PRINTED MATTER

Another group of children used a variety of printed sources to detect the devastating effect of disease, especially cholera, in Victorian times and then tied this work into Henry Doulton's role in creating a sewerage system that literally saved lives. Other children studied plans of a local ragged school (now a fire station) and then researched into what life might have been like for the children in the school. They were able to use their own school experiences and relate these to the pupils in Victorian times. As a result they were able to empathise with them and try to express what it must have been like to have attended a ragged school. The group working on this also started to talk about the fairness of the ragged school system and its pros and cons. The children were at the beginnings of political debate and it was interesting to hear them start discussing these issues together.

PRESENTING THE FINDINGS

The exhibition was a highlight of our school year. The children worked hard designing invitations, planning and organising refreshments for our visitors. Using other children in the school, they practised guiding people through the exhibition and explaining their contributions to it. The launch was a great success. The children felt very proud that their hard work had amounted to something so splendid and permanent. The exhibition was featured in the local press and our visitors and parents enjoyed celebrating the children's success and seeing an exhibition of work that could be used and built on by other schools in the area. Although the volume of work was immense for a term's topic, it was the best historical experience I have been able to give the children I teach. From the experience I have been able to identify many personal learning points that have influenced my classroom practice. Probably the most important thing I have realised is that in order to draw out the best work from my class it is vital that certain conditions exist within the scheme of work I offer them.

CLASSROOM DETECTIVES

Firstly, the emphasis must be on children discovering things for themselves; that is why the concept of being detectives is such a strong one. If this is the focus then the activities teachers provide will encourage children to make the things they learn their own. We must let children experience the satisfaction of knowing that they have found out something for themselves. We must enable them to have the confidence to express why they have drawn the conclusions that they have. In doing so we will make what they have been taught relevant to their personal experiences. If this is true then it follows that the activities we give children to do *must give all the clues without necessarily spelling out all the answers.*

ISSUES OF RESOURCING

In their work with the Vauxhall Heritage Centre the children were exposed to a variety of sources of information. They looked at artefacts, used the local environment, wrote letters, considered maps, photographs and printed material, as well as using other people and their peers to help grasp as full an understanding of the topic as possible. Similarly, when we approach our topic work we must consider how we can provide a variety of sources of information. Not only does this give us more scope in the types of activities we are able to plan for our pupils, it also gives our children better access to the information we are trying to impart. Some of the best ideas I have come across are the simplest:

- Making audio tapes to accompany information texts to support less fluent readers. This opens up new avenues for investigation for many children.

- Having interactive displays and 'discovery tables' for children to use collaboratively. This gives children the opportunity for hands-on experience.
- Using television documentaries and dramas helps to fuel children's imagination.
- Using people as a resource whom they can write to, interview and interact with, can broaden their understanding and make learning more personal.
- Using the local environment to its full potential helps children to see the relevance of what they are learning.

This list is by no means complete. It emphasises that as teachers we do not see ourselves as the primary resource but as one of many sources of information. In doing so we enable ourselves to become more creative and open-minded as we plan our schemes of work.

PLANNING ACTIVITIES

If we do offer our children a wide variety of sources of information then in turn it becomes easier to offer them a greater variety in the types of activities we expose them to. In doing this we make greater opportunities for them to demonstrate, and for us to assess, their skills, insights and understanding. In this project the children learned by interacting with each other, by looking for and recording clues from the local environment. They used map skills to compare key features over time. They constructed spider charts to demonstrate their understanding. They used worksheets to guide them around the church and print to aid their research. They wrote biographies of key figures in the period and justified decisions about what they were going to include in the exhibition. They compared 'then' and 'now' and discussed the virtues and downfalls of both. They passed on their expertise to others both in class and through their exhibition. In other words, they were given a large variety of activities which supported their learning in different ways and meant that they all had the opportunity to succeed.

Many of the activities used a visual approach, looking at the artefacts, mapping our walk and examining photographic evidence; these activities particularly supported those less fluent in English in the class as well as those who had difficulty with writing and/or reading. The activities allowed children to work at different levels. The more able were give opportunities to demonstrate their abilities in the way they presented and extended their work; they showed that they could link together the different facets of their studies. The less able showed their understanding within the context of each activity both orally and in their own records; many other children fell within both ends of the spectrum.

In different contexts, other learning approaches can also be used to enhance children's understanding and success, for example using drama, music, practical activities, oral sources and print. It is, therefore, our responsibility as classroom teachers to approach how we tackle the curriculum in as creative a way as possible. This is not to say that we should abandon traditional teaching styles altogether, far from it. Instead we should consciously be looking for ways in which we maximise the success of our pupils. By broadening the types of stimuli that they encounter and the activities that they are asked to do, we can only improve the quality of their learning and in turn this must have knock-on effects on the standard of work they produce.

ASSESSING WORK

If we offer children a variety of activities using a wide range of resources it follows that when we assess their work we must try to have as holistic a view as possible. Within any record-keeping structure there are limitations. We need to be aware of these and try to see beyond them in order to glean the most information we can about our children's successes. This is particularly true for younger children, those less fluent in English and for children with special educational needs. As a junior school teacher I have learned much from reflecting on the good practice of other colleagues and applying it myself. In particular I have found that assessing the children in terms of what they have said has given me more information than I would have gained from solely marking a piece of written work. The depth of insight the children demonstrate would be difficult to capture if I always insisted on written evidence of learning.

Flexibly differentiated activities allow us to move the emphasis on learning and assessment away from outcomes alone and to pay more attention to the processes children are involved in. The range of assessment opportunities in the project I have described allowed children with diverse abilities, strengths and experiences to do themselves justice as active and successful learners. The approach used allowed for cross-curricular work. As well as covering many of the historical skills required in the National Curriculum, we also covered much geography, speaking and listening, writing, information reading, and technology in designing the display. This allowed not only for assessments of a range of facts, concepts and learning strategies, but also of some of the dimensions of learning which relate to all areas, for example developing children's confidence and independence and their capacity for reflecting on their learning.

CONCLUSION

Approaching topic work in a way that maximises the strengths of all pupils has four main ingredients:

- **Resources**: these should be varied and include as many different forms as possible.
- **Activities**: these should be varied in approach and demand different types of skills to allow for different children's abilities.
- **Assessment**: this should strive to be holistic and consider the processes that children have been involved with as well as the outcomes.
- **Purpose**: finally, children need to feel that their studies have a point. They need an outside audience to celebrate their success with them. This is crucial – it is the engine that drives the rest and a source of motivation for everyone.

NOTE

1. I would like to thank Zoe Brooks and Clare MacDonald for their involvement in the project, the Sir John Cass's Foundation and the Walcot Educational Foundation for their funding, and Anthony Wilson for reading my drafts and supporting me.

Chapter 14

Back to basics

Planning for and assessing the progress of children with a range of learning difficulties

Peter Fifield

If children are to gain full entitlement to the National Curriculum, then their level of fluency and their confidence in literacy can be critical. The class whose work is described here is a Year 7 class in an urban special school catering for pupils with a wide range of learning needs. Most children in the class have some particular medical condition that has slowed their learning, others have quite unusual or complex emotional difficulties that affect their learning. None is a really confident reader or writer, but they represent a wide range of fluency and experience. As a staff we wanted to improve the children's literacy achievements. The pupils, too, wanted to see more progress; many expressed a wish to improve their reading and writing. These children have had six years of schooling and although most are still willing learners, they all find literacy a struggle. The effects of this struggle, combined with their other special needs meant that many had just run out of steam. We needed to get back to the basic entitlement for learning which each had a right to expect. What they needed was a 'short sharp shock' of success to boost their confidence and competence and raise their self-esteem.

This was the position at the beginning of the second term of Year 7:

Peter, for example, had his self-confidence and self-esteem knocked, when, at the onset of adolescence, he was diagnosed diabetic. This meant coming to terms with managing blood tests, self-injections, and dietary needs. He was only beginning as a reader at the end of Key Stage 2 and the diagnosis of his illness had put his confidence and his learning back even further.

Similarly **Steve** has only recently been diagnosed as suffering from an unusual form of epilepsy. He had been described as 'a problem' in his primary school, behaving oddly and often in an anti-social way. He has missed regular periods of schooling due to ill health and so his progress in learning has suffered. Steve has a grasp of the basic techniques of reading and writing but is unpractised and was becoming unwilling to use them.

Three other children whose progress has been seriously affected by their medical conditions are Jane, Melanie and Naomi. **Jane** has suffered from a life threatening condition that hospitalised her for lengthy periods of her primary schooling. Despite this, she is a confident reader and enjoys writing but finds both activities tiring. She needs opportunities to convince herself that she is making progress. **Melanie** is still a seriously ill child, suffering from epilepsy and the effects of medication. When the work began she had almost given up trying as she was so used to failing. **Naomi** also has a complex medical history. She is a fluent reader and writer and in contrast to Melanie is probably the keenest in the group. However, her perceptual difficulties are so acute that the casual observer would often have problems deciphering her meaning.

Simon has impaired hearing that has slowed his literacy development. He had reached Year 7 and was still finding reading and writing a struggle – a struggle he was not keen to engage in. Motivating Simon was an important target to aim for.

The same could be said of **Alan** and **Sean** both of whom have histories of emotional difficulties and failure in mainstream schools. They, like Simon, have become disenchanted with academic life and find making an effort increasingly difficult .

Roger has muscular dystrophy and his learning has been hindered. The condition in itself has not caused the learning delay but his anxieties over his illness mean that he needs a thorough input of psychotherapy. The effects of his emotional and physical condition, combined with the time taken during the school day for his therapy, have slowed Roger's learning. He is a keen learner but needs the support of an adult in order to achieve.

David is another boy who shows anti-social behaviours. He is diagnosed as having Asperger's syndrome. David has a lively imagination and enjoys playing word games and making pun jokes. This is all too often at the expense of his class mates which can lead to social difficulties.

The learning histories of these children are diverse and complicated, producing a wide range of difficulties and needs. There were some common experiences, however; they had all known failure and the frustration of lack of progress in literacy. It was important to find a manageable way to meet individual needs and allow all to experience success. At the same time, their individual experiences and difficulties meant that they often found it hard to work together, so that as well as individual success they needed to experience the pleasure which can be gained from working collaboratively. When this work started, I was teaching this group for English and Religious Education – a total of five 45-minute sessions per week. Ideally the aim was to seek cross-curricular links to consolidate achievements. Since the first aim was to promote success in literacy I needed to develop a series of activities which would lead to individual success in reading and writing, offer opportunities for pair or group work, span both English and RE – and, most importantly, be enjoyable!

STARTING WITH ASSESSMENT

Before planning for this, however, I felt that I needed more information. That these children had learning problems surrounding reading and writing was evident, but I was unsure of the next step to take. The priority was to discover as much as possible about what each individual could already do in terms of literacy. I had recently attended a half-day conference about literacy and had picked up a format for describing children's reading and writing fluency and experience.[1] By looking carefully at work that they had previously produced, I was able to detect where the gaps in their achievements were and to take them into account in my planning.

First I selected particular pieces of their writing to examine in detail, trying to determine how developed each child was in terms of shaping their writing to take account of the needs of the reader and success with organisation and technical conventions. Looking carefully at samples of their writing, and using the format I had picked up, I was able to see that Melanie and Sean could still be described as beginners in writing; while they understood that writing was meant to communicate meaning, they needed help with tackling the demands of more extended writing. They could construct simple sentences, labels, captions, lists and greetings, and they knew about direction and orientation of their writing, but needed substantial help with the technical conventions of spelling and punctuation. They were quite keen to write at times, although Sean was more prepared to experiment with some individual words and phrases than Melanie. Naomi, Peter and Roger could be described as gaining in fluency as writers; they did show enthusiasm for writing most of the time and demonstrated rather more confidence than Melanie and Sean. They could write some texts independently and use brainstorming techniques to help them plan their work or to note specific vocabulary, themes or ideas. Their narratives were quite clearly structured and they could write accounts of experience in chronological order. All three showed some readiness to vary their chosen vocabulary and experiment with newly discovered words, drawing on phonic awareness and some rules for spelling.

Alan, David, Simon and Steve could be described as fluent but less experienced writers, and Jane as a moderately experienced and fluent writer. While they could write extensively at times and were becoming more selective about detail and content, with the exception of Jane, they still needed help in deciding how to improve their writing and needed greater experience in the techniques of drafting. They were learning to collaborate over writing and use a thesaurus and dictionary and were becoming more discriminating and bold in the use of punctuation and different genres of writing. Jane's work consistently showed that she could write for a range of readers and purposes.

In terms of reading, the range was broadly the same although most were a little more confident at reading than writing. Melanie was the most unsure and dependent on adult help in reading, although she showed awareness that print is meant to communicate meaning. Most of them needed greater or lesser degrees of help with unfamiliar texts and several of them could not draw on the full range of phonic, sight, shape and pictorial cues to help them read aloud. Few of them showed confidence or enthusiasm for routine classroom reading tasks which might be associated with the general demands of curriculum reading and most of them had difficulties with getting information from texts. Jane and Alan were the most assured about reading and the only two who could properly be described as 'independent' readers.

This full picture of their fluency and confidence in literacy was invaluable in being able to plan for differentiation. Although the learning problems were varied, there were certain similarities between the children's abilities and so I could begin thinking about how they might be grouped or paired for learning as well deciding on the strategies, resources and support they needed. I had also been able to see a significant gap – the experience of reading, reflecting on and evaluating their own work successfully. I needed to allow opportunities for this in my planning.

PLANNING FOR POETRY

I chose to use poetry as the basis for the scheme of work because it seemed to me to offer some clear advantages for non-confident readers and writers to achieve success:

- The pupils would already have had some experience of poems, raps and rhymes that they could draw on.
- There is a rich vein of published, accessible poetry available.
- There are plenty of examples of impressive poems that are also short.
- It is possible to find and use formats for poems that produce quick, entertaining and rewarding results.

I looked on this as a six-week project and began by using a planning grid to see how I could provide for diversity (see Figure 1).

The right hand column was the most important and it was here that I was able to outline my aims and the learning outcomes that I expected. I wanted the pupils to begin to appreciate the ways text can be arranged on the page to do different things. I also wanted them to have a range of phonic, aural and oral experiences: rhyming poems, rhythm and cadence, narrative poems, group poetry and performance, shape poems, acrostics. By planning for a variety of lively, imaginative and enjoyable experiences I would hopefully build confidence in many literacy skills – graphophonic cueing, repetition and patterns in texts, grammatical conventions and spelling.

I wanted the pupils to select from their own poems for their folders and also to choose from published poetry – as well as their own – for a class anthology. An important aspect of their choice would be their comments on why they liked particular work. The school was also holding a Spring Festival at the end of term and this allowed for a built-in opportunity for public performance of a poem relating to Easter, linked to the theme that we were covering that term for RE.

I began the project by getting 'back to basics'. I wanted them to start from what was familiar as a way of establishing confidence and a sense that they were 'experts' in one genre of poetry. This meant looking at those poems that they had known for many years – nursery rhymes. We began by them re-telling ones they remembered. Interestingly, they were pleased to demonstrate their knowledge and they didn't find it embarrassing or immature. We went on to discuss why nursery rhymes have been popular for so long. They were often silly or nonsense but because they *did* rhyme they were fun and enjoyable to say out loud. We looked at some collections of nursery rhymes and how they were illustrated. The pupils' first task was to design a page for a nursery rhyme book as a part of their anthology. This was intended to achieve stress-free success for all the pupils. Melanie and Peter wanted to use the nursery rhyme books as a model and this gave them a firm basis for success. Others needed help with spellings and some scribing, but Alan, David and Jane were able to get on with little intervention. All achieved a successful outcome. David's attempt shows his humour in his illustration of a very worried Humpty Dumpty toppling over (Figure 2).

I ended this first session by introducing them to Roger McGough's poem 'Shark' (McGough 1988). I read it through and then we took it in turns to read it to each other, putting in the correct emphasis. This is a short but easy-to-follow poem and the continual repetition meant that the least confident readers were able to attempt it. Reading aloud to the class was a real achievement for many of the group. Most were usually self-conscious about performance and needed plenty of encouragement, but on this occasion all were keen to have a go. Another short, sharp, success!

Subject	Week 1	Week 2	Week 3	Week 4	Week 5	Week 6	Learning Outcomes
E	Introduction to poetry:- Nursery Rhymes Shark Poem.	Group work on 'Don't Put Mustard....' in, on, under, near, over prompts. Pied Piper poem.	Animal Shape poems – individual work.	In the Dark Dark wood.... Individual/paired work	Class writing of Easter poem Selection of poems for Class anthology Self evaluation	Easter poem practice and performance at the Easter Festival	THEME: POETRY • Experience of : rhyming poems, rhythm, cadence, Narrative poems, Group poetry and performance, Shape poems, Acrostics, repetition and pattern
N							
G							
L	Don't Put Mustard.... paired work for class poem	The Car Trip performance poem. –tape recorded	Improvised why poems – individual performance	Alphabet poems and name poems. use of dictionaries	Easter poem redrafting reading aloud practice.		• self assessment • collaboration – group/ paired.
I							
S	Work on class poem and reading aloud.	Why? poem – tape recorded	Class Why? poem				• Confidence building.
H							

Figure 1

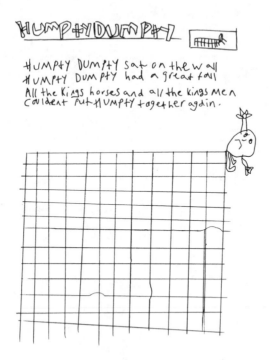

Figure 2

Building on this initial success the pupils needed to be moved on to creating their own poems. I wanted to get them thinking about the sounds of words and to look for similar sounding words. In the previous term the pupils had been compiling lists of 'words to work on'. Each of them had a book where they were encouraged to find similar sounding or shaped words, for example 'str ...' words and 'thr ...' words, so they had some experience of concentrating on the sound of words. I decided to use the first line of Michael Rosen's poem 'Don't put mustard in the custard ...' (Rosen and Blake 1985) as a stimulus. The pupils worked in pairs to produce lines for a class poem which was written up on a flip chart.

Some found this initial step into independent writing daunting, but they were able to produce some writing together and see the immediate result written up on the chart and read out:

Naomi: Don't put the jelly in my welly,
            Don't put the jam in with the spam
            Don't put the snowflakes in my cornflakes
Simon: Don't put a fox in a letter box

	Don't put the snake in the lake
Roger:	Don't put the pea in your tea
	Don't put the rake in the lake
	Don't put the tele in your belly
Melanie:	Don't put the ice cream where I dream
	Don't put the cake in the lake

We were all pleased with the results. When read aloud they sounded both rhythmic and amusing. I particularly liked Naomi's rhyme of 'snow-flakes' with 'cornflakes' and I was especially pleased with Melanie's 'ice cream where I dream'. Melanie in particular found this task demanding but already her confidence was growing.

Not all the class were present for this lesson, and as it had proved successful and enjoyable, I thought that we could extend the activity. I noticed that nearly all the pupils had used the model line 'in the . . .' and wanted to see if they could think of alternatives. The previous session had shown that certain individuals had found the writing physically demanding and so it was important to find a strategy to help them so as not to stifle their enthusiasm. In groups of three and four they were given cards with a simple noun written on each to get them to start thinking of rhymes (pen, train, fruit, meat, bread, rat, dog). They were also given cards with prepositions (over the, near the, under the, in the, on the), to help vary their sentences. There were blank cards for the groups to write down their rhyming words. Using cards rather than pages of books or files helped them to compose lines because they could move the cards around to decide which combinations sounded best. This technique was successful and each group was able to produce a five-line poem. Some groups felt confident to use all their own nouns but found the preposition cards useful as prompts:

Alan's group:	Don't put cheese near the bees
	Don't put the coot in the fruit
	Don't put the pears under the stairs
	Don't put ink over the mink
	Don't put meat on your feet.
Sean's group:	Don't put the newt in the Brut
	Don't jog with your dog
	Don't put your lynx in the sinks
	Don't let Ken get the pen
	Don't put the colour pink in the ink.

These poems showed that the children had not only used the model but had made it their own by adapting the original format for their purposes. Each group had the opportunity to read out their poem or to have it read aloud. This proved to be another enjoyable activity that produced pleasing results for each child. As a way of capturing that success for them, I asked each of them to copy the group poem neatly into their personal anthology folder. We ended the lesson by listening to how other poets had used repetitive rhyme and rhythm to produce an effect. I had decided that I would read a variety of poems to them as often as possible so as to provide some examples of how poems sound when read aloud. This was also an opportunity to introduce them to the idea of a narrative poem by reading them an extract from Robert Browning's *Pied Piper of Hamelin* (in White 1960). Again most of the children were familiar with this story and so found the poem easy to follow and enjoyable.

Now that the ice had been broken by them reading their rhymes to each other, I was keen for the pupils to repeat the experience of getting satisfaction from reading poetry aloud in class. Michael Rosen's 'The Car Trip' seemed an ideal starting point; there are four clear voices in this poem – a narrator, two children, and the Mother. I read out the poem first and was surprised and delighted that Sean and Simon (not confident readers), were very keen to take part – and that they did it well. Alan was persuaded to be the narrator which helped boost his self-confidence and David proved to be an excellent Mother. We swapped the roles around and the group really got into the swing of this activity. We had tape-recorded their readings so that they could enjoy hearing what they had achieved. In the discussion about the poem afterwards Peter showed that he had begun to notice how different poems can do different things and to develop a way of talking about texts when he commented, 'This is more like a story.'

In the next session we tried another collaborative effort we based on the format of Michael Rosen's 'Why?' (Rosen 1981). This is another accessible poem that is both repetitive and familiar for the reader; Michael Rosen is particularly good at capturing the cadences of ordinary speech and making it into memorable poetry. We read 'Why?' through in different ways. The class joined in to chorus 'Why?' after one child read the linking lines. Pairs of volunteers wanted to read the poem together. Those pupils who had real difficulties with reading such as Melanie and Peter were keen to take part. This was also taped and played back.

As mentioned earlier, David likes playing with words and enjoys cracking jokes. He volunteered to improvise some lines. We began with, 'I'm staying at home tomorrow' and the class asked 'Why?'. David then tried to keep going as long as he could. This was a demanding task but he did really well, thinking very quickly to develop and tell a story about how he was going to the doctor's. Sean and Paul also tried to keep going and this proved a challenging but very amusing task. Melanie had also gained enough confidence to try; she managed three sentences (a real achievement for her) by using real events and her own experience:

I'm staying at home tomorrow.
Why?
Because I've got to go to the hospital.
Why?
Because I hadn't slept well.
Why?
Because I had fits.

This raises one of the important spin-offs of using poetry like Michael Rosen's which so evocatively echoes children's own lives. Melanie often expresses her anxiety about her nightly fits through anger; even this very brief example is a real break-through in emotional terms for her. However, she found it very taxing to think of anything which was not rooted very firmly within her own experience; imaginative thoughts do not come readily to her.

This proved to be such a popular poem that the class decided to write their own 'Why?' poem with me scribing on the flip chart. Each child took a turn to answer and had to think quickly:

I'm not coming to school tomorrow.
Why?
Because I'm going to the Doctor's.
Why?
Because my foot hurts.
Why?
Because I dropped a brick on it.
Why?
Because I was cementing a wall.
Why?
Because it was falling down.
Why?
Because it wasn't put up properly.
Why?
Because I couldn't be bothered.
Why?
Because I was too tired from school.
Why?
Because I was working too hard.
Oh, okay.

IDENTIFYING SUCCESS

One of learning outcomes included in my planning, was to move on from the awareness of sound and rhythm prompted by poetry to look at how poems can be arranged differently on the page. I was interested in using shape poems and began with a frog as a model poem shape which I had drawn on the board. We talked about how animals move and what they look like and each member of the group then had to decide on an animal that they could build into a poem.

All the pupils were able to produce a finished poem. Most were simple, but impressive and when read aloud sounded very good:

> *Peter's cheetah:* fast
> big teeth
> sharp claw
> big body
> powerful.
> *Steve's shark:* Big sharp teeth
> with long smooth body
> and powerful gills
> and tail flicking through the water.

There were some lovely illustrations too, like David's Pig and Sean's Mouse (Figures 3 and 4).

Success like this had to be acknowledged so I suggested that the pupils might like to take their work to some of the teachers and other adults to show and receive well-deserved praise.

Another poem format that all the pupils were familiar with was 'A room bewitched'. Variations to this poem appear in many collections

Figure 3

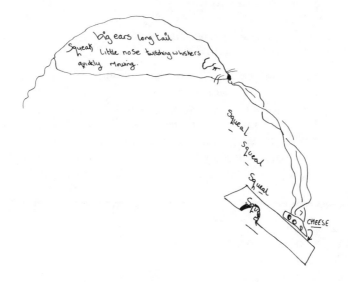

Figure 4

with different titles. The one I used listed the author as 'unknown' (Woodward 1984). The poem begins:

In the dark, dark wood, there was
a dark, dark house . . .

I wanted to get the pupils to think up their own variations on this theme, starting with alternative words to 'dark'. They came up with 'old', 'new', 'bright', 'hot', 'cold' which they then worked on individually. There were opportunities here for humour, imagination and tension and these were combined to produce pleasing results again. Sean's attempt shows a maturing sense of humour. He and Simon found this particularly funny:

In the old, old garden there was,
an old, old shed
and in the old, old shed was
an old, old cupboard
and in the old, old cupboard there was
an old, old box
and in the old, old box was
an old, old match box
and in the old, old match box was . . .
some old, old matches!

Steve wrote a very similar poem to Sean's but ended:

in the old old tin there was
some old, old beans
Among the old, old beans there was . . .
a diamond.

Which was an interesting and surprising ending.

Although this was a simple poem form some of the pupils did find the narrative drive difficult as well as following the 'rules' of how the poem was laid out. Nevertheless, all of them again succeeded in producing a finished poem, that was easily read and readily shared.

The final poem types that I wanted to use were a simple alphabet poem and acrostic. The idea was to get the children thinking of words beginning with certain letters to make a coherent verse. The pattern was very simple:

I love *a*pples
but I loathe *b*ananas
I love *c*abbages
but I loathe *d*ogs

. . . and so on through the alphabet.

The pupils had dictionaries to help them find words that sounded right or pleasing. This task meant that they had to concentrate on getting their alphabet right, they had to find suitable nouns from the dictionary, they had to use plurals and they had to ensure the poem made sense. The more fluent readers and writers produced some satisfying poems independently, but others experienced some difficulties. Naomi, for example, had no problem with the alphabet but found it difficult to find suitable words, and so she chose 'I love scarce but I loathe term'. She needed specific help to think about nouns rather than just any word. Melanie again found it difficult to get beyond the literal – she had to find words that she *did* in fact like or loathe and therefore refused to include any more imaginative ideas. Some were able to develop this task by spelling out their names in the nouns that they like or loathe.

One gap that I had identified in the pupils' literacy profiles was the experience of self-evaluation. There needed to be an opportunity for the pupils to think about their own poems and why they particularly liked them. I went through each child's anthology folder, and discussed their work with them. Sean was most pleased with his 'Old, old matchbox' poem 'because it's funny and was all my own idea'. Simon thought the poem he liked best was 'Don't put the jelly in the telly' because 'I made it myself and I like the way it sounds.' Alan was pleased with his poem about not putting the cheese near the bees because he thought it was funny. Naomi liked her rabbit shape poem because 'It looks nice'. Melanie was more suspicious of my intentions; she liked the 'Dark,

dark, wood' poem, because, 'I just liked it that's all. It sounds good. Why do you want to know?'

The pupils' rather hesitant replies seem to me to reflect their inexperience of being asked to make their own judgements about the value or interest of their efforts. I was struck, however, by frequent mention of 'it was my own idea' or 'I did it myself'. This tiny flicker of pride of ownership is a signal to me that this group deserves more experience of independence and success. It is all too easy to assume that children who are somehow delayed in learning will need work which is safe, repetitive and 'skills-based'. It seemed to me that their language experience of phonics, sight vocabulary, aural cues and word patterns was ably extended in a very short space of time, through these very enjoyable, but, for many of them, challenging writing activities. The open-endedness also meant that each of them, no matter what their level of fluency and experience, could push up to the edges of their competence.

For the Easter festival we chose some poems from John Foster's anthology (Foster 1989) that Jane, Sean and Paul were keen to read out. However, very gratifyingly, all of the group participated in performing for the school some of their own poetry including a group 'Easter' poem which needed collaboration and group work; it was the first time Alan had ever felt able to take part in a public activity (he found even reading aloud in the classroom a great trial) and the congratulations of staff, parents and other children have made this whole activity an important milestone for many of the pupils. This testing performance in front of parents and visitors proved a suitable conclusion to the project.

WHAT HAD BEEN ACHIEVED?

Peter still has a great many problems with his reading, but this poetry project really made him enthusiastic and eager to write. He is very good at art and, as well as some satisfying poetry, produced excellent illustrations which were then included in the class anthology. He is also beginning to see the links between different forms of writing, describing how some poems tell stories.

Prior to this project, Steve was usually reluctant to write and needed a great deal of support to produce more than a minimum. The fact that extensive pieces of writing were not required was quite a relief to him. He was able to contribute well to paired, group and class collaborations and to begin to identify elements of his work which he could be proud of.

Jane is a much more experienced writer than many of the others in the group, but her condition means that she finds the task of writing a strenuous experience. She was able to achieve success at her own level by writing deliberately short pieces, which nevertheless carried complex messages, and thus develop her confidence, whilst also flexing her intellectual muscles.

Melanie is used to failing. She often gives up before attempting new or demanding work. She benefited from the structured approach that the simple poem formats offered. She found getting her ideas together difficult but she did enjoy the performance poetry and insisted that she was taped reading one of the parts in 'The Car Journey'. She knew that she would find this difficult but was very eager to have a go. She also took home Michael Rosen poetry books to read to her mother and became very enthusiastic about them. This has been an important step in building her confidence in literacy.

Naomi also very much enjoyed the narrative poems. She still has problems getting her ideas out in a straightforward and intelligible way and the same structured formats helped her to achieve clear, coherent poems that she was pleased to read out.

Simon was able to develop his technical skills. He demonstrated a good ear for rhyme and rhythm and was a 'star performer' on the tape and at the Easter festival. These were considerable steps forward for his confidence.

Both Alan and Sean are emotionally vulnerable pupils. Their need for positive success was probably the most urgent. The poetry project gave them this opportunity and both enjoyed not only the making of the poems, but also reading publicly in class. This is a significant step forward particularly for Alan who is intensely shy. They also achieved a boost to their confidence and self-esteem through the praise from other adults in the school for their impressive achievements. When he read his poems aloud, Sean said, 'I didn't think I'd be able to read this but I can. I think I'm really getting better at my reading.' This is, for him, a really assertive remark, and one that he can only move forward from.

Roger had come to rely on a great deal of adult support in order to achieve. He gradually developed more independence as the poetry project went on. He had been able to use the visual models of clear formats, and came to 'tune in' to the different rhymes and rhythms he encountered, and although he still needed adult help for the technicalities of writing, he was always bursting with ideas.

One of the long-term targets for David is to improve his social skills. His literacy abilities are more developed than most in the class, but he does not find it easy to co-operate with others. He did enjoy playing games with rhymes and words and was able to chant the latest rap record from the charts, for example. This poetry project therefore had lots of ingredients in it that appealed to him. The collaborative writing and performing of the poems were two areas that helped David's social interactions. He was able to respond with the group in a very positive way as well as showing his ability for rhyme and rhythm.

All the pupils have gained and moved on over these few weeks. They have had experience of different activities in reading, writing, speaking and listening and all have achieved success. The impact on the group has been extremely important. It has boosted their self-esteem and confidence and convinced these young learners, who find learning hard, that they can enjoy themselves as well as achieve success. The poems provided them with challenges that they could confidently meet. One of the great advantages of a project using poetry is that it is a 'low-risk, high-yield' activity. While offering open-ended opportunities for all of the pupils to take their ideas as far as possible, it also offers important 'safety' structures for those who have learned to fail, or who find even very ordinary everyday tasks almost more than they can bear to think about.

In terms of assessment, as well as its diagnostic uses at the beginning of the project, I have been able to make a range of formative observations about the pupils' reading, writing and oracy. As far as their reading is concerned, I have had much more fruitful opportunities to gauge their understanding of what they read from the previous, rather stilted sessions of pupils reading aloud to me. They all read with expression and varied intonation according to whether they wanted to create atmosphere or evoke humour. The successes of paired and group reading mean that I shall build these into our reading curriculum from now on. As a whole, the group has tackled a range of much more challenging texts than I might have thought possible. Most importantly, they have begun to see some of the satisfaction to be gained from understanding – and expressing – the meaning of written text. In writing, I have been able to identify a range of markers of progress: increased abilities in awareness of audience; in accuracy linked to redrafting for final publication; in the organisation of their work; in presentation, handwriting, spelling, punctuation, syntax. As far as speaking and listening are concerned, each individual pupil has had a chance to experience a range of 'performance' opportunities with familiar and unfamiliar audiences. They have been put in the position of explaining their ideas to each other, negotiating and sharing in groups and pairs. They have had to pay close attention not only to *what* they and others say, but to *how* it is said. And finally, they are beginning to get used to the idea of using talk to reflect on their own learning and achievements. Importantly, I have been able to assess the 'intangible' elements which are so fundamental to successful learning: confidence, new experiences to build on, successful collaboration, more harmonious social relationships. I am sure that a set of language exercises designed to improve the children's literacy skills would not have reached either the literacy or social/emotional achievements these children have enjoyed.

We began this project with a sense that this group of learners needed to get back to the basic entitlement for learning. The approach of getting 'back to basics' by building on what they knew as familiar and could identify as relevant to them proved exactly the right vehicle for the 'short sharp shock' of success. Not only was this project an excellent vehicle for catering for difference and diversity in any classroom, it provided us all with some valuable hours of purposeful fun!

NOTES

1. The format has a Writing Progression Framework and a Reading Progression Framework inspired by the Reading Scales found in *The Primary Language Record*. (Barrs *et al.*, 1988).

REFERENCES

Barrs, M., Ellis, S., Hester, H. and Thomas, A. (1988) *The Primary Language Record: a handbook for teachers*, London: ILEA/CLPE

Foster, J. (1989) *Let's Celebrate*, Oxford: Oxford University Press

McGough, R. (1988) *An Imaginary Menagerie*, London: Puffin Books

Rosen, M. and Blake, Q., (1985) *Don't put Mustard in the Custard*, London: André Deutsch

Rosen, M. (1988) *The Hypnotiser*, London: André Deutsch

Rosen, M. (1981) *Wouldn't You Like to Know*, Bungay: Puffin Books

White, E. (1960) *Poetry for Today*, London: Odhams Press

Woodward, Z. and I. (1984) *Witches Brew*, London: Beaver Books

Conclusion
Constructing a policy for differentiation

The surest way to identify a school's policy about any area of the curriculum is to see what goes on in the classroom and school. Policy documents in different forms – from those with glossy covers to drafts in process of review – may line headteachers' bookshelves but there can often be a gap between what a document says and what is done. The crucial element of any useful or workable policy is that it will capture a set of live and active practices. It will not be a set of pious platitudes or abstract statements (often unattainable) repeating the word 'should' with frightening frequency! Shared understandings are essential for any school to provide the most satisfying learning environment and experiences, and this is the strength of any thought-out, discussed, negotiated and agreed set of principles; they are still alive even when captured on paper. The written document represents not a frozen once-for-all statement but a point in the history and development of shared ideas. It has to be tailor-made for the specific context of the school and capable of modification as the context changes. For these reasons, Part V will be concerned with examining how a policy-in-action for differentiation might be described, and how existing policy and practices in curriculum provision might be reviewed.

Because a policy needs to capture daily practice it ought to be a useful summary of what goes on and a document which can be continually updated in a planned process of school development and review. For that reason, the framework offered in this section is a series of questions and suggested strategies for review, ending with a summary including guide questions and prompts. This is not to suggest, however, that there ought never to be a 'finished' document. On the contrary, a policy document, at whatever stage of development, is important in order to summarise the principles which underlie the practices affecting the everyday lives of the pupils, their families and the local communities served by the school. The view of a policy outlined in this section represents a process of professional debate and negotiation as well as a document which offers a clear statement to parents, governors and others about the school's approach to diversity (the principles) and a practical reference for staff, helpers and visitors reflecting the implementation of practices for differentiation.

At the end of this part there is a summary framework for use in staff in-service sessions or in discussions about reviewing policy.

START BY TALKING

If a policy for differentiation is to mirror the needs and experience of pupils, teachers and the community which feeds the school, it is important to establish at the outset just what colleagues find most important about providing for diversity. Asking people to identify principles can sometimes be tricky, because it may seem that they are a million miles away from the hectic everyday reality of the school. Nevertheless, every classroom, and the school itself, will be a mirror of the implicit principles in operation – and it is worth getting them out in the open. It is important to include all the professional adults who work with the children, for example support workers and classroom assistants, since policy can only work to the benefit of children and staff if it is commonly owned and acted upon. To some extent, the work may have already been done if colleagues have jointly developed policies to describe the school's view of equal opportunities, special needs or assessment; many of the issues relating to differentiation are concerned with the individual's entitlement to access to the curriculum, and to teachers' ways of monitoring, assessing, describing and recording progress in achieving those educational goals. These may already be enshrined in statements about each child's entitlement being accorded equal value, regardless of differing abilities, aptitudes and interests. It may be, then, that there is no need for a separate policy on differentiation, but that discussion might focus on where issues of diversity and differentiation enter other areas of school policy and practice.

Then there is the matter of who might be responsible for discussions about differentiation – is it the school's Special Educational Needs Co-ordinator? Equal Opportunities Co-ordinator? Assessment Co-ordinator? Or the person who has responsibility for an overview of the curriculum? Whoever takes on, or is given, responsibility for reviewing policy, discussions and decisions will only be valuable if the process of policy development is built in to a whole-school plan of curriculum development and review. Policy development needs to be given status and the person responsible provided with planned support from the senior management members of the school as policy is established, monitored and revised.

Debates about differentiation strike at the centre of what a school is all about – to foster learning. The areas which will need examination in checking out provision for differentiation are broad; questions which a staff might ask themselves might include the following:

- How do we identify the needs of a diverse range of learners?
- How do we provide differentiated contexts for learning?
- How do we provide differentiated approaches to learning?
- How do we assess differentiated learning?

The rest of this section aims to put some flesh on the bones of these somewhat stark questions.

One way to open up ideas about how best to offer a differentiated curriculum to cater for diversity might be to use the cards from Chapter 1 or start by asking as a quick – if tough – 'opener' to discussion: *What is learning?* or *What helps children to learn?* and recording ideas so that they can be returned to later. Lists of ideas can readily be represented as 'statements of principle' – because that is what they will be! From there it is possible to move on to investigating what a school provides to support learning.

The following replies might be given to the first question:

- Putting existing experience or knowledge alongside new knowledge, experiences, facts. . . .
- Finding things out; making discoveries.
- Increasing awareness.
- Continually updating ideas.
- Reflecting on experience.
- Learning 'how' as well as 'what' and 'why'.
- Having curiosity and satisfying it.

And suggestions for the second might be as follows:

- Having chances to experiment
- Tackling challenges (with support).
- Gaining – or being given – confidence.
- Working with others.
- Experience – making mistakes and trying again.
- Imitation and observation.
- Making connections between ideas.
- Learning how to talk about learning . . . .

If ideas like these were to be presented as 'principles' about providing a differentiated curriculum they might be redrafted as:

Children will learn most effectively when we:

- recognise what they already know and build on it;
- acknowledge that learning isn't just fact-gathering, but to do with confidence, security, and a sense of being valued;

- create an environment where learners can take an active part in negotiating and organising their own learning;
- provide opportunities for collaboration, reflection and evaluation;
- offer models and examples of how to learn and how to talk about learning.
  . . .

Of course these are not exhaustive lists and should not be seen as representing what *ought* to be said. The most important aspect of any activity like this is that it opens up discussion – some of it quite challenging. This kind of discussion can then be followed by an 'audit' of provision for entitlement to a full curriculum for all. If learning is developed both from the individual's unique base of experience through collaborative interaction and agreement, what does this look like in classrooms which genuinely try to offer differentiation for diverse learners?

IDENTIFYING THE RANGE OF LEARNERS

Several of the contributors to this book have described their practices in discovering the experience and existing knowledge of children, and how this significantly informed their teaching. It is important to have a clear view of the range of learning styles, experiences and behaviours which children bring, since differentiation to ensure progression rests on being able to offer diversity in classroom approaches. Discussion of the range usually starts with identifying children whose lack of progress is worrying. The reasons might well vary, from social and emotional factors to being under-stimulated. Observation and identification are important, and for those children who come within the Code of Practice, steps towards providing statements of special educational need are firmly in place in most schools. As suggested in Part III, however, there may not be established practices for identifying those who are achieving very highly and a first step might be to attempt a definition of just what this might mean, before thinking of individual children and their exceptional abilities. One such definition might be:

> Very able children show outstanding potential or ability in a single area or in all areas. This ability might not be in traditional academic learning but could be in physical, creative, spatial, mechanical or technical aptitudes. The abilities may be so well developed that these children are operating significantly in advance of their peer group and will require provision of additional learning experiences which develop, enhance and extend the identified abilities.

Debating an example definition like this can be a useful way of opening up discussion without getting involved in the details of the performance of particular individuals in the school – such discussion would come later when everyone on the staff, including support teachers and class-room assistants, have had a chance to hammer out the issues. There is one problem about the definition above, however, which will soon be raised when colleagues get to grips with what 'very able' might mean, and that is the problem of the covertly able. It may be necessary to enter a discussion of how to identify such children through a more general description of the range of learners.

Since literacy is such an important aspect of learning and of the assess-ment of learning and is now part of the statutory requirements within each subject of the National Curriculum, one way to identify a range of learners might be to start by looking at reading and writing. What kinds of readers and writers inhabit our classrooms? The list of different readers (Figure 1) was compiled by a group of teachers who discovered as they put the list together that the range was very wide and varied indeed.[1] Their next step was to identify how they made provision for the range of readers and reading requirements across the subject range. As the introduction to Part II suggested, writing is used as the principal means of assessing progress in learning. Although it is not always a reli-able indicator of ability, nevertheless its central importance to the process of learning means that attention must be paid to those whose writing is a cause for concern. The same group of teachers put together a list of characteristics of children whom they would describe as 'struggling' with writing (Figure 2). Again, they found that the range was wide, including some children who might be seen as 'covertly able'. A similar activity could be done in any other area of the curriculum. How might the range of developing mathematicians be described? Or what would 'struggling' in science, art or physical education mean?

IDENTIFYING GOOD PRACTICE

Identifying some details of the range of learners and learning styles leads naturally towards questions of how their learning needs are catered for. Certainly, children learn in a variety of ways and a differentiated curriculum will need to take account of this. The next move after looking at the range of learners might be to identify the range of contexts and opportunities for learning which are already on offer and which seem to be working well.

The school environment

A quick audit of the school and the classroom as contexts for diversity might be a starting point. How 'hospitable to diversity' is the physical setting of the school? It does not take long to go round a school looking at the notices, for example, and asking if they are sufficiently accessible

Providing a reading curriculum which can allow for differentiated ways of getting meaning out of text involves providing for a range of readers. In any classroom we might expect to find readers who:

- return to the same book again and again – for support, enjoyment of the 'familiar', to read at different levels, etc.
- like to read to others
- prefer to read pictorial text
- always want to read whatever the teacher has just read to them
- always read with friends
- enjoy reading plays
- almost always read *either* fiction *or* fact
- can read detailed pictorial text with ease
- prefer an adult to read to them
- read to escape from everyday reality
- pretend to read – as rehearsal for reading verbal text; from fear; from idleness!
- are over-ambitious in their choices of books – sometimes because of genuine interest in a subject
- don't yet know how to choose successfully
- know when to leave a book which they don't like
- are series/serial readers
- love Enid Blyton
- read comic strips
- choose to read *TV Times/Radio Times*
- read interest magazines
- are avid readers
- like a 'slow' read
- see progress in reading as status
- read mostly poetry
- prefer to read extracts than whole texts
- are reluctant to read
- like the security of the reading scheme
- love reading although they find it difficult . . .

The challenge is – how to provide for all of these readers, and how to help them move on.

Figure 1 Differentiating reading . . . for different kinds of readers

Those who:

- 'can't think what to write' because they: are paralysed by fear of failure; have poor techniques; do not value their own experience; lack motivation . . .
- delay the act of writing by pencil sharpening, etc. . . .
- don't understand the task
- can't make the literacy link between what we say and what we write
- have had their progress delayed in some way; 'gaps' in schooling
- find classroom timings and timetabling constraining
- write technically correct but boring work
- are frustrated because they don't have the means, vocabulary, strategies, techniques . . . to write what they want to say
- show a mismatch between reading and transcription techniques (e.g. fluent readers, poor writers)
- find the classroom environment inhibiting
- have very low self-esteem
- are naturally slow at working
- find the physical effort too great at times
- have hearing loss/sight loss/difficulties with manual dexterity
- are too proud to ask for help
- do not yet speak English fluently
- produce so little that there is no evidence to use to help them
- have language or neurological disorders
- are stuck in a particular genre
- have so many ideas they find it hard to follow one through

What can be done to support them?

Figure 2 Writing – who are the strugglers?

to children and adults who read iconic or pictorial texts more readily than print – or the reverse. What about different languages – are the languages of the community represented properly in the school, not just with a token multilingual notice on the office door, but in languages reflecting the specific school context? Is there access for people whose mobility is hampered – do doors open wide enough and are there ramps for wheelchairs, for example? These aspects of differential provision may seem peripheral but they are, in fact, a reflection of the general approach to diversity which will operate in the provision of learning, too. More 'learning-focused' questions in terms of the school environment might be to do with the value given to children's contributions to the life of the school: How is children's work presented and displayed? Is there only 'the best' – or everyone's? And what about resources? How accessible is the library or resource centre and what provision has been made for differentiation here? Does it have books of maps and photographs, technical magazines and manuals ...? How does the school shape up as an environment for mathematics, geography, science, technology, music ...? Is children's work in maths, science, design and technology displayed as much and as frequently as art work and written work, for example?

The classroom environment

An audit of the classroom might start with the simple question 'What messages about diversity does my classroom give?' As Avril Dawson points out in Chapter 5, it's worth looking at the walls as a good indicator of attitudes; is the work or display material *all* teacher selected and mounted? What messages about, for example, gender might be signalled by the home corner and dressing up box? What images of boys/girls or different cultures are represented in the books and pictures? Is there a variety of materials to work with? Are there special areas for listening to tapes? Making things? Working on the computer? Reading quietly as well as with friends? Researching, trying out ideas, tackling problem-solving activities? The environment for learning is a powerful factor in making a classroom hospitable to diversity, and exchanges of ideas between colleagues after a classroom audit can be a useful way to focus discussions about differentiation.

Perhaps the most obvious area for discussion of good practice, however, comes in examining teaching methods and the management of learning. What strategies have been known to work in promoting particular concepts in ways which offer differentiated access to learning? Encouraging pupil activity is an important way of getting to grips with learning. Valerie Walkerdine presents some forceful work on the development of mathematical concepts through the translation of action into numbers (Walkerdine 1984: 146) as she describes a teacher moving blocks to help children shift from the understanding of iconic representations of numbers into symbols. Her work emphasises the importance of adult intervention or modelling, but Siobhan Barker, working with Year 1 and 2 children on number and recording number, found another way in which activity could prompt concept formation. The children were coming towards the idea of place value and beginning to take on new vocabularies, for example the word 'digit'. She writes:

> I had previously worked on multiplication with years 5 and 6 in dance, which they had enjoyed. It had aided their speed and

versatility with mental mathematics – when the rhythms were very fast they had to think fast to fit in with the music! So I decided to give it a try with these much younger children. First of all I introduced the idea of each child working in dance to create their own shape for 0, 1, 2, 3, etc. It was interesting to observe those who made the iconic shape of the number and those who invented different ways of depicting it. Even in these very early stages there was a clear pattern emerging; the children who were less experienced in mathematics, often the younger ones, were more inclined to make up the shape of the iconic representation of the number in their dance, as well as enjoying experimenting with movement. The more confidently numerate tended to make the shape of the symbol for the number. I have been intrigued by one child who has learned to hop and did everything by hopping (and continued to do so for some time!) All of the children practised counting to five and backwards creating shapes for the numbers in movement. The word 'digit' has been painlessly introduced and most of the children use it automatically now. The development from this has been for the children to work in pairs, and after practice with numbers up to nine (which the hopper hopped and gave evidence for the first time that he could count to nine!) I then introduced two-digit numbers and we have since gone on to adding and subtracting. This project, zany though it might be, did, however, give me a chance to assess the children's grasp of number concepts as well as observing how they could move purposefully in dance – and have fun! What I am certainly convinced of now is that some children learn best when they can place themselves in the learning and orientate themselves spatially and that you can use dance to teach almost everything – cogs, levers, the water cycle.

(Barker 1995)

The teacher intervention involved here, of course, was in the initial thinking and planning related to observations of a specific 'moment of learning'. It is often assumed intervention for learning is about teachers 'doing things' in the classroom. In fact, the most effective teacher interventions probably take place before teacher and children even reach the classroom.

Managing groups

Several of the chapters in this book describe careful and flexible planning for differentiation which equates with careful organisation for learning. Threaded throughout the contributions have been issues about grouping – how groups are constituted and how they are varied. In taking stock of good practice it might be worth asking colleagues how they make decisions about groupings. When this question was put to teachers on a course about oracy they explained:

We group children according to:

- friendship patterns
- expertise or aptitude
- mixed ability
- confidence in numeracy
- single sex
- ability relative to the task or subject
- home language
- mixed languages
- their own decisions
- the content of the activity[2]

Strategies to organise groups included using numbers; jigsawing and/or envoying;[3] setting up a talk table; partnerships for particular activities or for regular practices like reading and responding to each others' writing; mixing age groups and allowing the children to choose groups for themselves.

When a group of colleagues have begun to identify their own good practice in classroom management for learning, they can then get on to the kinds of issues reflected in questions such as these:

What is a friendship group? Does it change? What is my role?
Is a familiar grouping always productive? Can children get stuck in social roles or become 'stale'?
Does offering children choice of groupings mean they may be less challenged?
How important is variety? Should we offer different group experiences to encourage confident social grouping?
What about the isolated child? Or the child who prefers to work in isolation?
What are the gender implications?
What about children whose grasp of spoken English is insecure?
What are the issues of classroom control?

The last question is fundamental to productive group work, so a further question might need to be asked: How do we teach children to work in groups? The following answers might include:

- Negotiating ground rules for talk.
- Giving children written question prompts to guide discussion or to ensure turn-taking.
- Developing ways of time-keeping for fair chances to contribute.
- Using role play situations and simulations.

- Reviewing and evaluating with the children the ways in which they managed (or did not manage) to work together.

That set of questions might, in itself, offer a way of opening up discussion of differentiated classroom management.

The process of learning

If differentiation is to do with organising teaching and learning to accommodate and stimulate future learning, then much of the evidence of differentiation is seen in the process of teaching and learning. For certain activities, differentiation is unnecessary, although attention to diversity will be important; storytime is one familiar example of this. Much of the time, however, teachers consciously and automatically make decisions about how best to adapt the presentation of ideas to suit the range of learners. The commonly acknowledged areas for differentiation are explained below.

Input

What decisions are made about factual information, the concepts and the vocabulary which will be used to help learners grasp content and ideas? At this point it's useful to find out what the learners already know, in order to build on existing knowledge. How is this done? Acknowledgement of the diverse experiences brought to an activity (or series of activities) can signal the value given to home or cultural knowledge. At the same time, there is the chance to identify what new information or concepts individuals and the group as a whole might now be introduced to.

Tasks

This has often meant providing different tasks within an activity to cater for different levels of 'ability' (often judged on literacy). In its worst manifestation it is represented by three, or so, different worksheets: one with mostly pictures and few words; one with more words more densely packed and one picture; and a third with lots of words and no pictures. It is not difficult to imagine the messages this kind of practice gives to all the learners in the classroom. While recognising that such practices are implemented with the best intentions in the world to support children who experience difficulties, it is clear that some who have difficulties with literacy are perfectly capable of working at a high conceptual level on tasks involving practical application of ideas or talk. The challenge to the teacher is to find ways of framing tasks which can not only genuinely stretch all the learners, but which might provide for the variety of ways in to learning. This is likely, also, to involve an element of choice in order to encourage increasing independence in learning as well as providing for different paces of work. How are tasks differentiated? It might be useful to select one activity – possibly from the term's theme or agreed school scheme of work – and, with a colleague, list how tasks are – or might be – successfully differentiated without suggesting a 'sheep and goats' view of the children.

Resources

These might be part of the answer to the challenge. While it is important to identify a range of material resources which do not depend on developed literacy to be used or understood – for example tape recorders, videos, pictures, photographs, maps, diagrams, it is also important to acknowledge and use the range of human resources available in the classroom, school and home. What range of resources are – or might be – used for the activity above?

Support

This might use some of the human resources available, but it might also mean use of IT or other tools for learning. Perhaps the most critical element in considering this area of provision for diversity concerns teacher time. There is never enough time to give the individual support which a teacher almost inevitably and continuingly wants to offer. What methods are used for supporting learning? What strategies and activities have been identified to help in time management?

Outcome and response

Outcomes can be both tangible and intangible. Products like information sheets for younger children, newspapers, mathematics games or activities, maps, models, tape recordings, diagrams, and instructions provide opportunities for assessing children's capabilities across a range of areas and kinds of abilities. Intangible outcomes are equally open to observation and assessment – increased confidence, ability to carry out a particular operation or to present ideas orally, new-found enthusiasm or (a fundamental matter) the articulation of concepts which have been understood. What range of outcomes might be expected in the activity selected for discussion? The end points of learning are often used to determine how well children have achieved. This kind of summative assessment has its place, but if assessments are to inform future teaching and learning, then there may be a need for diversity of *kinds* of assessments and variation in *times* when those assessments are carried out. Response to the outcomes of learning, by teachers and children, make the process of learning explicit and acknowledge diverse abilities. Response also encourages learners themselves to evaluate their work and leads towards future progress. What kinds of responses are – or might be – made at the end of a learning process or activity?

Assessment and reporting progress

Teachers are continually making assessments and judgements – minute by minute, hour by hour, day by day – as they work alongside children. Those assessments are based on implicit criteria of what counts as success and will necessarily be adjustable to take into account all the learners in the classroom. That is a teacher's professional expertise. What seems to be important is to make these criteria explicit; in doing so, a teacher can check that s/he is using a differentiated range of types of assessment which will accurately describe the achievements of a diverse set of learners. This is particularly important when considering what SATs do *not* reflect in terms of achievement. If teacher assessments are to be seen as equivalent to SATs, then it is essential to be able to measure the kinds of progress which cannot adequately be tested in single one-off conditions.

Before establishing criteria it is important to know the following:

WHY assessments are being made:	for feedback to individual pupils?
	to give information for colleagues or parents?
	to identify problems?
	as part of evaluating your teaching?
WHAT is being assessed:	curriculum content?
	a grasp of processes or strategies for learning?
	attitudes or personal qualities?
WHEN might assessments be made:	as work is beginning?
	during an activity or series of activities? (formative)
	at the end? (summative)
HOW will assessment be carried out:	by observation?
	by questioning?
	by looking at outcomes?
	a combination of these or a different method?
WHO will carry out the assessments:	the teacher?
	the child?
	teacher and child together?
	someone else?

Having thought about some of these issues, a good way of reviewing policy about differentiated assessment would be to look at the kinds of assessments and forms of recording which are happening in the school now. It can sometimes be an eye-opener to have an open exchange about methods of recording and assessing progress in the full curriculum range.

THE WIDER CONTEXT

As has been reflected throughout this book, school, home and community work together to contribute to children's learning. There is a breadth of experience to be drawn on if children are to make the most of the learning opportunities on offer. When looking at the wider context and the links which can profitably be made to provide a differentiated set of learning experiences, a group of teachers might ask themselves the following questions:

How do we (or can we) involve parents and others in the curriculum?

Parents, governors and other adults are often involved in school activities, but these may be largely as 'an extra pair of hands' – for reading, games, art work, accompanying trips – rather than aiding curriculum learning. The issues of supporting the very able or welcoming the diversity of languages or cultures brought to the school could profitably be addressed here to see how adults other than teachers might be seen as extra resources for learning. Much enjoyable and open-ended work has been done, for example, by asking older people to talk about transport when they were young; by inviting parents to demonstrate the process of taking a technology (perhaps DIY) idea through from plans to execution; by working collaboratively with parents and children to build a wildlife or conservation area; by involving parents in storytelling or working with older children to make mathematics games for younger children.

But what about those parents or carers whose working patterns or circumstances do not allow them to come in to school when others can? It is well worth looking carefully at ways in which parents can be used as supportive resources in learning – watching and discussing television documentary programmes about wildlife, for example, with their children at home; gathering memories of their own early school experiences; putting together collections of photographs or other artefacts; working out calculations and joining in problem solving; looking at maps with their children – all of these can be done by most parents, even those whose own confidence with school-based learning may not be too secure.

And it's worth remembering the valuable input that siblings, grand-parents, aunts, uncles, cousins, neighbours ... can make.

How can we make our practices and principles about differentiation and diversity clear to parents, governors and others?

'Going public' is possibly the toughest test a policy – and those who make it – can undergo. At the same time, it is probably the most helpful way of clarifying the practice and principle inherent in the policy. Having to explain ideas to others is an effective way of coming to under-stand something. The way this is done will also indicate the school's view of diversity. Traditional relationships between schools and parents are often based on the idea that the teachers tell the parents what they want them to do to support what is going on in the classroom. Different contributors to this book, and much work in schools, support the value of establishing more equitable partnerships where, for example, parents might write (or at least be involved in the compilation of) the advice booklet about children's early introduction to numeracy or literacy or give advice about how best to build on children's existing practical or technical capabilities. Explanations of principles and practice are not likely to be authentic unless they are accompanied by demonstration of those principles and practices in action – within school and between school, homes and the community.

The curriculum which most successfully caters for diversity through differentiation has to accommodate two apparently contradictory requirements – of equity and of individual growth. On the one hand it has to reflect the broad aims of education which should be on offer to all children, whatever their abilities; on the other hand it has to allow for individual development, to cater for differences in abilities, aptitudes and needs. If it is to be effective, the curriculum must allow for – and build on – diversity. It is a tall order. This book ends with a suggested framework for discussions to aid that process. The contributors hope that their reflections and accounts of classroom practice will have fed into the continuing debate about curriculum entitlement for *all* our children.

NOTES

1. Figures 1 and 2 lists were compiled by a group of teachers in Suffolk working on an English GEST course, February, 1995.
2. Teachers following the Oracy Module of the Advanced Diploma in Language and Literature at Homerton College, Cambridge.
3. These are strategies for varying groupings, written up in several publica-tions by the National Oracy Project, for example the Teaching Talking and

Learning series, available through the National Association for Teachers of English, Birley School Annexe, Fox Lane Site, Frecheville, Sheffield S12 4WY.

REFERENCES

Barker, S. (1995) personal communication.
Walkerdine, V. (1984) 'Developmental psychology and the child-centred pedagogy: the insertion of Piaget into early childhood education', in Henriques, J., Hollway, W., Urwin, C., Venn, C. and Walkerdine, V. *Changing the Subject*, London, Methuen

Appendix: A framework for discussion

SECTION 1: AIMS OR RATIONALE.

This might start with a **statement of principle** about entitlement or access, for example:

> Pupils have equal value but differing abilities, aptitudes and interests. In this school we aim to provide a diverse and challenging curriculum in order to support and promote the learning of all pupils to the furthest extent of their capabilities. . . .

or

> Children will learn most effectively when we:
>
> - recognise what they already know and build on it;
> - acknowledge that learning isn't just fact-gathering, but to do with confidence, security, and a sense of being valued;
> - create an environment where learners can take an active part in negotiating and organising their own learning;
> - provide opportunities for collaboration, reflection and evaluation;
> - offer models and examples of how to learn and how to talk about learning.

or

> It is the business of our school to provide for individual learning within a communal setting since effective learning depends on interaction and agreement as well as personal intellectual progress. In doing this we need to:
>
> - identify the needs of a diverse range of learners;
> - provide differentiated contexts for learning;
> - provide differentiated approaches to learning;
> - assess differentiated learning.

These might be used as a prioritising exercise, or simply as starting points for discussion.

Alternatively you might use the cards which were developed for the investigation in Chapter 1

SECTION 2: IDENTIFYING THE RANGE OF LEARNERS

The best starting point is staff discussion. Starter questions might be:

What is learning? or What helps children to learn?

These can then lead to questions such as:

- What kinds of readers and writers inhabit our classrooms?
- How do we make provision for the range of readers and reading requirements across the subject range?
- How do we make provision for the range of writers and writing requirements across the subject range?
- How might the range of developing mathematicians in the classroom be described?

or

- What would we mean by describing children as 'struggling' in science, art or physical education?
- What do we mean by a 'very able' child?

The examples given as Figures 1 and 2 'Differentiating reading' and 'Writing – who are the strugglers?', as well as the sample definition of a very able child, might serve as useful starting points for discussion.

SECTION 3: THE ENVIRONMENT FOR DIVERSITY – DIFFERENTIATED CONTEXTS FOR LEARNING

What strategies have been known to work in promoting particular concepts in ways which offer differentiated access to learning?

As a means of recognising good practice, and identifying any 'gaps', it might be worth carrying out audits/surveys of the school and classroom as supportive environments for learning.

How 'hospitable to diversity' is the physical setting of the school?

What messages would a visitor get about the status or value given to the diverse school population?

Look, for example, at:

- Displays and notices – do they reflect a variety of languages or ways of reading?

- Access for people whose mobility is hampered – do doors open wide enough and are there ramps for wheelchairs, for example?
- How is children's work presented and displayed? Is there only 'the best' – or everyone's? What about resources? How accessible is the library or resource centre and what provision has been made for differentiation here?
- How does the school shape up as an environment for mathematics, geography, science, technology, music . . .? For example, is children's work in maths, science, design and technology displayed as much and as frequently as art and written work?

The classroom as a context for differentiation

What messages does the classroom give about the status or value given to the diversity of the pupils?

Look, for example, at:

- Special areas for activities – technical, practical, role play, listening, working on the computer, problem-solving, etc.
- Variety of materials
- Wall displays – whose choices? Maps, photographs, three-dimensional objects? Do the images reflect a variety of cultures? Positive images of boys and girls?

How do you provide for differentiated approaches to learning?

For example:

Is there a balance of experience between whole-class teaching, group work, paired work and individual work?

Notice the variation in groups which any one child is involved in during the day. Are the children working *in* groups or *as* groups? Does it matter?

Some further questions about group work:

- How are children taught to work in groups?
- What is a friendship group? Does it change?
- Is a familiar grouping always productive?
- Does offering children choice of groupings mean they may be less challenged?
- How important is variety?
- What about the isolated child? Or the child who prefers to work in isolation?

- What are the gender implications?
- What about children whose grasp of spoken English is insecure?
- What are the issues of classroom control?

Where does differentiation come into the process of learning?

It might be worth taking one activity which has been done recently and considering the different stages of the process:

Input

What decisions were made about factual information, the concepts and the vocabulary used to help learners grasp content and ideas? What strategies were used to discover what children already knew?

Tasks

How were tasks differentiated without suggesting a 'sheep and goats' view of the children? Could tasks be designed more effectively and equitably?

Resources

What range of resources – human and material – were used? What could be used to ensure variety for children to read pictures, maps, diagrams, and photographs, as well as more usual forms of text?

Support

What methods/people were used to support learning? Could there be better support arrangements? What strategies and activities help in time management?

Outcomes and response

What range of outcomes – tangible and intangible – came from the activity? What kinds of responses were offered at the end of the activity? What other responses could have been made?

Assessment

Why?   for feedback to individual pupils?
                    to give information for colleagues/parents?
                    to identify problems?
                    as part of evaluating my teaching?

What?	curriculum content?
	grasp of processes/strategies?
	attitudes or personal qualities?
When?	as work began?
	during the activity?(formative)
	at the end? (summative)
How?	by observation?
	by questioning?
	by looking at outcomes?
	a combination of these?
	a different method?
Who?	the teacher?
	the child?
	both together?
	someone else?

How were the types of assessments varied throughout the activity to reflect all styles of learning and aptitudes?

A good way of reviewing policy about differentiated assessment would be to look as a staff at the kinds of assessments and forms of recording which are happening in the school now.

What kinds of records are kept?

How is information passed on from one teacher to another, from one Key Stage to another, when the children go to another school?

SECTION 4: PUTTING DIFFERENTIATION INTO A WIDER CONTEXT

The school is part of a wider, diverse community and it is worth examining how links and partnerships can support and reflect that diversity. Some questions about parental partnerships might be:

What role do parents and other adults play in the classroom? In the school as a whole?

How do we (or can we) involve parents and others in the curriculum?

How can we make our practices and principles about differentiation and diversity clear to parents, governors and others?

Whenever you are developing policy you need to:

a) Decide who will be responsible for its establishment, implementation, evaluation and review, and

b) Fix a timetable for:

- continuing discussions – with observation tasks or audits to do in between
- drafting the policy
- implementation
- observation of how it is working
- evaluation of its operation
- review

Index